Romans 8

THE GOSPEL'S CROWNING GLORY

Bruce W. Newcomer, Thd.

Copyright © 2025 by Bruce W. Newcomer

Paperback ISBN: 979-8-9993560-1-7   All rights reserved.

All rights reserved. This book or any portion thereof may not be reproduced or used in any manner whatsoever without the express written permission of the publisher except for the use of brief quotations in a book review.

"Scripture quotations are from the ESV® Bible (The Holy Bible, English Standard Version®), © 2001 by Crossway, a publishing ministry of Good News Publishers. ESV Text Edition: 2025. The ESV text may not be quoted in any publication made available to the public by a Creative Commons license. The ESV may not be translated in whole or in part into any other language. Used by permission. All rights reserved."

Layout and cover design by Bruce W. Newcomer

Contact at: bigbendpublishing@gmail.com

Contents

Dedication	1
Preface	2
Introduction	5
1. No Condemnation	14
2. Freedom from the Law of Sin and Death	21
3. What the Law Could Not Do	28
4. Fullfillment of the Law's Righteous Requirements	36
5. Two Ways of Thinking	44
6. The Consequence of Mindset	51
7. Conflict with God	59
8. Inability to Please God	66
9. Indwelling Presence: Marked by the Spirit	74
10. Spirit-Life Amid Mortal Bodies	81
11. Resurrection Power: Life from the Spirit	88
12. Obligation Redefined: The Debt We No Longer Owe	97
13. Life Through the Spirit	104
14. Led by the Spirit: The Mark of God's Children	111

15.	Spirit of Adoption: Freedom from Fear	119
16.	Assurance from the Spirit: Children of God	126
17.	Heirs with Christ: Sharing in Glory and Suffering	133
18.	Present Sufferings Versus Future Glory	141
19.	Creation's Eager Expectation	148
20.	Creation Subjected in Hope	155
21.	Freedom from Decay	163
22.	The Groaning of Creation	171
23.	The Waiting of the Redeemed	177
24.	Hope that Saves	184
25.	Patience in Expectation	191
26.	The Helper in Our Weakness	199
27.	The Searcher of Hearts	206
28.	The Assurance of Divine Purpose	213
29.	The Pattern of Predestined Conformity	219
30.	The Chain of Salvation's Glory	226
31.	God is Our Invincible Ally	234
32.	The Supreme Proof of God's Love	242
33.	No Accusation Can Stand	250
34.	Christ Our Perfect Advocate	258
35.	The Unanswerable Question	266
36.	The Cost of Discipleship	274
37.	Super-Conquerors	282
38.	The Comprehensive ListSuper-Conquerors	289
39.	No Separation	296
40.	Conclusion	303

About the author 311

To the Marines who taught me that true strength comes not from self-reliance but from unshakeable dependence on God's grace.

To the seminary students who challenged me to make theology accessible without compromising its depth.

To the congregation members who allowed me to shepherd them through valleys of doubt into pastures of assurance.

To my beloved wife, Susie, whose courage through cancer proved that God's love sustains us through the deepest trials. Her faith strengthens me.

And to every believer who has ever wondered if God's love is strong enough to hold them;

May you discover in these pages what the apostle Paul declared with apostolic certainty: that neither death nor life, nor anything else in all creation, will be able to separate you from the love of God in Christ Jesus our Lord.

Preface

This book was born in battle.

Not literally, though I spent my share of time in those during my years as a United States Marine. Rather, it emerged from the spiritual battles where every believer eventually finds themselves: that dark place where circumstances scream God has abandoned us, where our failures mock our profession of faith, and where the enemy's accusations threaten to overwhelm our souls.

I discovered Romans 8 as a young Marine struggling to reconcile my faith with the realities of military service. Later, as a seminary student grappling with the intellectual challenges to Christianity, these thirty-nine verses anchored my theology. Throughout decades of pastoral ministry, watching saints face cancer, betrayal, persecution, and death, I witnessed Romans 8 transform despair into hope, fear into courage, and defeat into victory. Then, as a seminary professor, I've seen these truths liberate students from the crushing weight of performance-based religion and ground them in the unshakeable bedrock of God's sovereign grace.

Romans 8 stands as the gospel's crowning glory, Paul's most comprehensive presentation of what it means to be united to Christ. Here we discover we are not condemned criminals hoping to avoid punishment but beloved children crying

"Abba! Father!" We learn that our present sufferings, however intense, cannot compare with the glory that awaits us. We find that even when we don't know how to pray, the Spirit intercedes for us with groanings too deep for words. Most magnificent of all, we're assured that nothing, absolutely nothing, can separate us from the love of God in Christ Jesus our Lord.

I write from the Reformed tradition because it provides the most consistent interpretation of Paul's teaching. When the apostle traces salvation from God's eternal foreknowledge to our certain glorification, he's describing God's sovereign grace from beginning to end. When he asks who can bring charges against God's elect or separate us from Christ's love, he's building our assurance on divine faithfulness rather than human performance.

This isn't an academic commentary filled with Greek word studies and scholarly debates, though I've done my homework. It's a pastor's heart poured out on paper, shaped by decades of watching Romans 8 sustain God's people through life's fiercest storms. I've written for the cancer patient questioning God's goodness, the struggling believer haunted by past failures, the young Christian wondering if their salvation is secure, and the mature saint longing for deeper assurance of God's love.

My prayer is that you'll discover in these pages what countless believers have found before you: that Romans 8 offers more than theological information; it provides supernatural transformation. When Paul's words penetrate your heart by the Spirit's power, you'll never again wonder if God truly loves you. You'll face trials knowing they serve His purpose. You'll battle temptation confident of His help. You'll look forward to glory with unshakeable hope.

The truths in this chapter aren't merely ancient words written to first-century Romans. They're living promises for twenty-first-century believers. They're God's answer to your deepest fears and your soul's greatest longings. They're the foundation for unshakeable faith in a world that shakes everything not firmly anchored.

Come, let's explore together what it means to live with no condemnation, to be more than conquerors, and to rest secure in a love from which nothing can separate us.

Bruce W. Newcomer, ThD. 2025

Introduction

Historical and Literary Context

Romans chapter 8 stands as the magnificent pinnacle of Paul's theological masterpiece. Written around AD 57 while the apostle was in Corinth, the letter to the Romans represents his most comprehensive and systematic presentation of the gospel. Though Paul had never visited the Roman church, he wrote to establish a theological foundation before his planned journey to Spain, hoping the Roman believers would support his missionary endeavors.

The historical context of the Roman church helps us understand Paul's emphases in chapter 8. The congregation consisted of both Jewish and Gentile believers, with tensions existing between these groups following the return of Jewish Christians after Emperor Claudius's expulsion order had been lifted. The church faced external pressures from the pagan culture of Rome and internal challenges of unity across ethnic divides. Within this context, Romans 8 offers powerful assurance that transcends all human distinctions and circumstances.

Literarily, chapter 8 serves as the triumphant conclusion to the first major section of Romans. In chapters 1-3, Paul established universal human guilt before God. In chapters 4-5, he explained justification by faith alone through the work of Christ. In chapters 6-7, he addressed sanctification and the ongoing struggle with sin. Now in chapter 8, Paul unfolds the absolute security of believers and the certainty of their final glorification.

This chapter's position within Romans gives it special significance. It follows directly after Paul's agonizing description in chapter 7 of the believer's struggle with indwelling sin, where he cried out, "Wretched man that I am! Who will deliver me from this body of death?" (Romans 7:24). Chapter 8 provides the glorious answer to that desperate question, beginning with the declaration that there is "no condemnation" and concluding with the certainty that nothing can "separate us from the love of God in Christ Jesus our Lord" (Romans 8:39).

Structure and Flow

Romans 8 can be divided into five major sections, each building upon the previous one to create a comprehensive picture of the believer's security in Christ:

1. Life in the Spirit (verses 1-13): Beginning with the declaration of "no condemnation," Paul contrasts life according to the flesh with life according to the Spirit.

2. Adoption as Children of God (verses 14-17): Believers are identified as God's children, led by His Spirit, with all the privileges and responsibilities of divine sonship.

3. Present Suffering and Future Glory (verses 18-25): The current groaning of creation and believers points toward the certain hope of future redemption.

4. The Spirit's Work in Prayer (verses 26-30): In our weakness, the Spirit intercedes for us according to God's will, working all things together for our good.

5. The Believer's Ultimate Security (verses 31-39): Nothing can separate believers from God's love in Christ Jesus.

The chapter's structure reveals a deliberate progression from justification to glorification, from the Spirit's present work to the final resurrection, from the believer's current struggles to ultimate triumph. Each section builds upon what precedes it, creating an ascending argument that culminates in one of Scripture's most magnificent declarations of security in God's love.

Major Theological Themes
The Believer's Freedom from Condemnation

Romans 8 opens with what may be the most comforting words in all of Scripture: "There is therefore now no condemnation for those who are in Christ Jesus" (Romans 8:1). This declaration flows directly from the justification Paul has been explaining throughout the letter. Those united to Christ by faith are completely free from the penalty of sin. The judicial verdict has been rendered, and it is final: not guilty.

This freedom from condemnation doesn't result from our moral improvement or religious performance. It comes "through Christ Jesus" who has "set you free from the law of sin and death" (Romans 8:2). Where the law could not save because of human weakness, God accomplished salvation by sending "his own Son in the likeness of sinful flesh" to condemn sin and fulfill the law's righteous requirement (Romans 8:3-4).

In Reformed theology, this freedom represents the fruit of Christ's substitutionary atonement and the imputation of His righteousness to believers. Our justification is complete and irreversible because it rests not on our works but on Christ's finished work. We stand before God clothed in Christ's perfect righteousness, with all our sins: past, present, and future fully atoned for at Calvary.

The Spirit's Work in Sanctification

While justification forms the foundation of Romans 8, the chapter's central focus concerns the Holy Spirit's work in believers' lives. Paul mentions the Spirit no fewer than 19 times in this chapter, more than in any other chapter in his writings. This emphasis highlights the crucial role of the Spirit in applying Christ's redemptive work to believers.

Paul contrasts those who "live according to the flesh" with those who "live according to the Spirit" (Romans 8:5). The difference isn't merely behavioral but concerns fundamental orientation and identity. Those in the flesh cannot please God, but believers are "not in the flesh but in the Spirit" because God's Spirit dwells in them (Romans 8:8-9).

This indwelling Spirit produces several effects in believers:

He gives spiritual life to mortal bodies (verse 11)

He enables the putting to death of sinful deeds (verse 13)

He leads believers as God's children (verse 14)

He bears witness to our adoption (verse 16)

He helps us in our weakness and intercedes for us (verses 26-27)

Reformed theology recognizes sanctification as God's work, not merely human effort. While believers actively participate in growth toward Christlikeness, the power and direction come from the Spirit. We work out our salvation precisely because God is at work in us (Philippians 2:12-13). The Spirit who begins the good work of sanctification will bring it to completion (Philippians 1:6).

Adoption into God's Family

One of Romans 8's most profound themes concerns the believer's adoption into God's family. Paul declares that "all who are led by the Spirit of God are sons of God" who have "received the Spirit of adoption as sons" (Romans 8:14-15). This adoption isn't metaphorical but legal and real, giving believers the right to address God intimately as "Abba! Father!" (Romans 8:15).

This familial relationship carries both privileges and responsibilities. As children, we are "heirs of God and fellow heirs with Christ," but this inheritance comes with the condition that "we suffer with him in order that we may also be glorified with him" (Romans 8:17). Our sonship connects us both to Christ's suffering and to His glory.

In the Reformed understanding, adoption represents a distinct blessing beyond justification. While justification changes our legal status from condemned to righteous, adoption changes our relational status from enemies to beloved children. This adoption flows from God's electing love and results in a permanent family relationship that cannot be broken.

The Present Suffering and Future Glory

Paul doesn't minimize the reality of suffering in the Christian life. Instead, he places it within the context of redemptive history and God's ultimate purpose. The "sufferings of this present time are not worth comparing with the glory that is to be revealed to us" (Romans 8:18). Present difficulties serve a purpose within God's plan.

This suffering extends beyond believers to all creation, which "waits with eager longing" and "groans" under the weight of the curse (Romans 8:19, 22). Believers themselves "groan inwardly as we wait eagerly for adoption as sons, the redemption of our bodies" (Romans 8:23). Even the Holy Spirit joins this groaning through His wordless intercession on our behalf (Romans 8:26).

This universal groaning isn't aimless but directed toward the certain hope of resurrection and renewal. Creation will be "set free from its bondage to corruption" (Romans 8:21). Believers will receive glorified bodies. What we now possess as "firstfruits of the Spirit" will come to full harvest in the resurrection (Romans 8:23).

Reformed theology places this suffering within God's sovereign purpose. Our trials aren't random accidents but divinely appointed means of conforming us to Christ's image. God works "all things" together for our good, including the things that cause us pain (Romans 8:28). This perspective doesn't eliminate suffering but transforms how we understand and endure it.

Divine Election and Predestination

In verses 29-30, Paul provides one of Scripture's clearest statements on God's sovereign election: "For those whom he foreknew he also predestined to be conformed to the image of his Son... And those whom he predestined he also called, and those whom he called he also justified, and those whom he justified he also glorified" (Romans 8:29-30).

This "golden chain of redemption" links five divine actions that secure the believer's salvation from beginning to end. God's foreknowledge represents not merely advance awareness but covenant love set upon specific individuals before time began. His predestination determines their destiny in advance. His calling effectively brings them to faith. His justification declares them righteous. His glorification (spoken of in the past tense though future in experience) completes their salvation.

Reformed theology has consistently emphasized the doctrines of election and predestination as taught in this passage. These truths don't diminish human responsibility but establish it within the context of divine sovereignty. They don't produce complacency but profound gratitude and assurance. Knowing that salvation depends ultimately on God's unchangeable purpose rather than our fluctuating faithfulness produces both humility and confidence.

The Believer's Absolute Security

Romans 8 concludes with what may be Scripture's most magnificent declaration of the believer's security. Beginning with the rhetorical question "If God is for us, who can be against us?" (Romans 8:31), Paul systematically dismantles every threat to the believer's salvation:

No accusation can stand because God justifies (verse 33)

No condemnation can prevail because Christ intercedes (verse 34)

No separation can occur because God's love in Christ is invincible (verses 35-39)

The comprehensive list of potential separators, tribulation, distress, persecution, famine, nakedness, danger, sword, death, life, angels, rulers, present, future, powers, height, depth, anything in creation, demonstrates that nothing conceivable can separate believers from Christ's love. This absolute security flows not from believers' grip on God but from God's grip on them.

In the Reformed understanding, this passage powerfully expresses the doctrine of the perseverance of the saints. Genuine believers will persevere to the end not through their own strength but through God's preserving grace. The same love that chose them before creation will bring them safely to glory. Their security rests not on their performance but on God's promise, not on their faithfulness but on Christ's finished work.

Contemporary Relevance

Romans 8 speaks powerfully to contemporary believers facing various challenges. In an age of moral relativism, the chapter affirms that genuine freedom comes not from following our desires but from being led by the Spirit. In a culture obsessed with self-actualization, it reminds us that true identity comes from adoption into God's family. In a world full of suffering and injustice, it places our pain within the context of God's redemptive purpose and coming glory.

The chapter addresses the anxiety that characterizes modern life. Many believers struggle with uncertainty about their standing with God, doubting their salvation when they fail or suffer. Romans 8 provides rock-solid assurance based not on religious performance but on Christ's completed work and the Spirit's ongoing ministry. The security Paul describes doesn't depend on economic stability, political conditions, or personal circumstances but on the unchangeable love of God in Christ.

For churches divided by theological disputes or cultural differences, Romans 8 reminds us of what unites all true believers: the indwelling Spirit, adoption as God's children, and the unshakeable love of Christ. These truths transcend denominational boundaries, ethnic divisions, and socioeconomic distinctions, forming the foundation for genuine Christian unity.

Conclusion

Romans 8 presents the gospel in its fullest expression, moving from no condemnation in Christ to no separation from Christ's love. Between these twin pillars of assurance stands a comprehensive theology of the Spirit's work, the believer's adoption, the purpose of suffering, the hope of glory, and the certainty of God's sovereign purpose in salvation.

This chapter doesn't offer abstract theological concepts but practical, life-transforming truths that sustain believers through every trial. It answers the most fundamental human questions: Where do I stand with God? What purpose does suffering serve? How can I endure life's struggles? What hope exists beyond the present difficulties? The answers found in God's justifying grace, sanctifying Spirit, adopting love, and preserving power form the foundation for Christian living in every generation.

As we explore Romans 8 verse by verse in the chapters that follow, we'll unpack these magnificent truths in greater detail, seeing how they interconnect to form a cohesive vision of the Christian life. But even from this introductory overview, we can recognize why generations of believers have found in this chapter both their greatest comfort in trials and their strongest motivation for faithful service. Here, in these 39 verses, the gospel reaches its most glorious expression.

Chapter One

No Condemnation

**"There is therefore now no condemnation for those who are in Christ Jesus."
Romans 8:1**

These words have echoed through my heart countless times during my years of pastoral ministry and teaching. In just thirteen words, the apostle Paul captures the essence of our security in Christ. This single verse stands as a spiritual Gibraltar, an immovable rock of assurance for every believer.

I remember counseling a woman who had become convinced that God was perpetually disappointed with her. Despite her genuine faith, she lived under a cloud of divine disapproval. When we read Romans 8:1 together, tears streamed down her face. The Holy Spirit was illuminating this truth: her position in Christ meant freedom from condemnation. Not just partial freedom or temporary reprieve, but complete and permanent liberation from judgment.

The Power of Therefore

The opening word "therefore" connects this declaration to everything Paul has established in the preceding chapters. In Romans 1-3, he meticulously demonstrated that all humanity stands condemned under God's righteous judgment. Jews and Gentiles alike have violated God's law and fall short of His glory.

In Romans 3-5, Paul unveiled God's remedy: justification by faith alone in Christ alone. We receive the righteousness we could never achieve when we have faith in Jesus.

In Romans 6, he addressed how this grace relates to ongoing sin, showing that believers have died to sin's dominion. In Romans 7, he depicted the believer's struggle with indwelling sin.

Now, in Romans 8:1, Paul drives home the magnificent conclusion: despite our continued struggle with sin, our justification remains secure. The "therefore" gathers all these theological threads and weaves them into a banner of assurance.

The Power of Now

Notice Paul's emphasis on the present reality: "There is therefore now no condemnation." This isn't a future promise awaiting fulfillment. It's our current standing before God.

I've observed how easily believers slip into thinking of their justification as tenuous or provisional. We imagine God's approval fluctuating with our spiritual performance. But Paul's "now" refutes this misunderstanding. The moment we are united in Christ by faith, condemnation is removed, fully and immediately.

During my years in the Marines, I witnessed the moment when a court-martial verdict was announced. When the judgment was "not guilty," the accused was instantly freed from the threat of punishment. Similarly, God's verdict of "not guilty" over believers isn't pending or partial; it's present and complete.

The Nature of Condemnation

What exactly is this "condemnation" from which believers are freed? The Greek word *katakrima* appears only three times in the New Testament, all in Romans. It refers to the judicial verdict of "guilty" and the penalty that follows.

In Romans 5:16, Paul contrasts the condemnation that came through Adam's sin with the justification that comes through Christ. In Romans 5:18, he expands this contrast: "Therefore, as one trespass led to condemnation for all men, so one act of righteousness leads to justification and life for all men."

Condemnation involves both the verdict and the sentence. It's not merely being declared guilty; it's being consigned to punishment. When Paul says there is "no condemnation," he means believers face neither the verdict of guilt nor the penalty of eternal separation from God.

This doesn't mean believers never experience a conviction of sin. The Holy Spirit certainly convicts us when we stray (John 16:8). But conviction differs fundamentally from condemnation. Conviction is God's fatherly discipline aimed at restoration; condemnation is judicial punishment aimed at retribution.

The Qualifying Condition: In Christ Jesus

Paul's assurance isn't universal. This freedom from condemnation belongs specifically to those "who are in Christ Jesus." This phrase appears over 80 times in Paul's writings and describes the believer's mystical union with Christ.

To be "in Christ" means we are united to Him by faith. His death becomes our death; His resurrection becomes our resurrection; His righteousness becomes our righteousness. This union is the foundation of every spiritual blessing we receive.

I often use marriage as an analogy when teaching this concept. When my wife and I married, what belonged to me became hers, and what belonged to her became mine. Similarly, through our union with Christ, His righteous standing before the Father becomes ours.

This qualifying phrase reminds us that freedom from condemnation isn't automatic for all people. It's a special privilege of those united to Christ by faith. As Augustine said, "God does not condemn those who are in Christ Jesus, for if they are clothed with Christ, they are not seen in their sins."

The Theological Foundation

Why can Paul make such a sweeping declaration? The theological foundation lies in the doctrine of substitutionary atonement and double imputation.

Christ bore our condemnation on the cross. As Isaiah prophesied, "He was pierced for our transgressions; he was crushed for our iniquities" (Isaiah 53:5). Paul puts it this way in 2 Corinthians 5:21: "For our sake he made him to be sin who knew no sin, so that in him we might become the righteousness of God."

At Calvary, a great exchange occurred. God imputed our sin to Christ, and he imputed his righteousness to us. The condemnation we deserved fell on Him, so that the acceptance He deserved might fall on us.

I find it significant that in Romans 8:3, Paul explains that God "condemned sin in the flesh" of Jesus. Our Substitute already suffered the condemnation we feared. Divine justice is satisfied; the penalty is paid in full.

The Practical Implications

This theological truth has profound practical implications for daily Christian living. First, it liberates us from performance-based religion. Many believers live as though their standing with God rises and falls with their spiritual performance. They imagine God keeps a running tally of their failures and successes. Romans 8:1 demolishes this misconception. Our acceptance is based on Christ's perfect record, not our fluctuating obedience.

Second, it frees us from paralyzing guilt. Satan is called "the accuser of our brothers" (Revelation 12:10), and he excels at dredging up past sins to convince believers they remain under condemnation. But when accusations come, whether from Satan, others, or our own conscience, we can respond with Paul's triumphant question: "Who shall bring any charge against God's elect? It is God who justifies. Who is to condemn?" (Romans 8:33-34).

I've counseled countless believers tormented by guilt over past sins, even sins committed before conversion. The truth of Romans 8:1 is the antidote to this spiritual poison. If God has justified us, no accusation can stick.

Third, it empowers holy living. Some fear that emphasizing freedom from condemnation will promote moral laxity. But I've found the opposite to be true. When believers grasp that their acceptance is secure, they serve God from gratitude rather than fear. Love becomes their motivation, not dread of punishment.

As the chapter continues, Paul explains that the Spirit enables us to "put to death the deeds of the body" (Romans 8:13). Our freedom from condemnation doesn't make us indifferent to sin; it equips us to fight it more effectively, now motivated by love rather than fear.

Fourth, it produces spiritual boldness. When we know we stand before God without condemnation, we approach Him with confidence. Hebrews 4:16 urges us to "with confidence draw near to the throne of grace." This boldness isn't presumption; it's the appropriate response to our justification.

The Assurance of Perseverance

Romans 8:1 also assures us that our justification is permanent. Paul **doesn't say**, "There is therefore now no condemnation for those who are in Christ Jesus, as long as they maintain their faith and obedience." The freedom from condemnation isn't conditional or temporary; it's absolute.

This security flows from God's sovereign purpose in salvation. Later in the chapter, Paul unfolds the unbreakable chain of redemption: "Those whom he predestined he also called, and those whom he called he also justified, and those whom he justified he also glorified" (Romans 8:30). Notice the certainty expressed in these verbs. God completes what He begins.

During my years of ministry, I've seen believers shaken by the suggestion that they could lose their salvation. Romans 8:1 stands as a bulwark against such fears. If justification could be lost, Paul would have included conditions or warnings. Instead, he makes an unconditional declaration.

The Context of Romans 8

Understanding Romans 8:1 in context enhances its impact. This verse isn't an isolated statement; it's the opening declaration of what many consider the greatest chapter in Scripture, a chapter that climaxes with the certainty that nothing "will be able to separate us from the love of God in Christ Jesus our Lord" (Romans 8:39).

After establishing our freedom from condemnation, Paul explains how believers live according to the Spirit rather than the flesh (verses 2-17). He then addresses the role of suffering in the Christian life (verses 18-25), the Spirit's help in our weakness (verses 26-27), and God's sovereign purpose in salvation (verses 28-30). The chapter concludes with a magnificent celebration of our security in God's love (verses 31-39).

In this grand context, verse 1 serves as the foundation. Because there is no condemnation, we can walk by the Spirit, endure suffering, receive the Spirit's help, trust God's purpose, and rest secure in His love.

Conclusion

"There is therefore now no condemnation for those who are in Christ Jesus." These words have transformed countless lives throughout church history, including my own. They've lifted the burden of guilt, broken the power of fear, and inspired joyful obedience.

As believers, we don't minimize the reality of sin or our need for ongoing sanctification. But we face these challenges from a position of acceptance, not probation. We pursue holiness not to gain God's approval but because we already have it in Christ.

If you're in Christ today, hear this good news afresh: You are not condemned. The verdict is settled. The case is closed. Your advocate has prevailed. Your substitute has paid your debt. Your judge is now your Father.

Let this truth penetrate your heart and mind. Let it shape your identity and fuel your obedience. And let it fill you with the "joy unspeakable" that comes from knowing you are forever accepted in the Beloved.

Chapter Two

Freedom from the Law of Sin and Death

"For the law of the Spirit of life has set you free in Christ Jesus from the law of sin and death." Romans 8:2

After establishing the profound reality that there is no condemnation for those in Christ Jesus, Paul continues in Romans 8:2 with a statement that explains the basis for this freedom: "For the law of the Spirit of life has set you free in Christ Jesus from the law of sin and death".

This verse deserves careful meditation. During my years as a pastor and seminary professor, I've found that many believers miss the revolutionary implications of what Paul declares here.

This isn't simply a theological abstraction; it's the practical foundation for our daily experience of the Christian life.

Two Opposing Laws

First, let's understand what Paul means by these two "laws." He's not primarily referring to the Mosaic Law, though that connection exists. Rather, he's describing two powerful governing principles that operate in human experience.

The "law of sin and death" refers to the inevitable pattern where sin leads to death. We first see this principle enacted in Genesis, where Adam's disobedience led to death entering the human experience. Paul detailed this law's operation in Romans 7, where he portrayed his own struggle with sin's enslaving power.

I remember counseling a man addicted to pornography who exemplified this law's operation. "I hate what I'm doing," he confessed, "but I feel powerless to stop." Despite his best intentions and repeated commitments to change, he kept returning to his sin like a dog to its vomit. This is precisely what Paul describes in Romans 7:23-24: "I see in my members another law waging war against the law of my mind and making me captive to the law of sin that dwells in my members. Wretched man that I am! Who will deliver me from this body of death?"

The "law of the Spirit of life," in contrast, is the new governing principle introduced by the Holy Spirit. This isn't just a new set of commands but a new power, the very life of God working within us through the indwelling Spirit. Where the law of sin and death produces inevitable defeat, the law of the Spirit produces freedom and transformation.

The Meaning of Freedom

What does Paul mean when he says this new law has "set you free"? The Greek word *eleutherōsen* indicates a decisive, completed action. This isn't a gradual process but a definitive liberation that has already occurred for every believer.

This freedom operates on multiple levels. First, we're freed from sin's condemnation. Christ has fully paid the penalty of sin, as Paul emphasized in verse 1.

Second, we're freed from sin's dominion. While we still struggle with sin, we're no longer enslaved to it. Before Christ, we had no choice but to obey sin's impulses. Now through the Spirit, we have the power to choose righteousness.

During my Marine Corps years, I observed how rigorous training transformed ordinary civilians into disciplined warriors. What once seemed impossible became second nature through consistent training and the power of unit cohesion. How much more does the indwelling Spirit transform our spiritual capabilities!

Third, we're freed from sin's deception. Sin promises satisfaction but delivers misery. The Spirit enables us to see sin for what it truly is and to recognize the superior joy found in obedience to God.

The Means of Our Freedom

Notice that this freedom comes "in Christ Jesus." We do not achieve liberation through self-improvement or moral reform; instead, we achieve it through union with Christ. When we're joined to Him by faith, His victory over sin becomes our victory.

This truth transformed Martin Luther's understanding of the Christian life. After years of striving unsuccessfully for holiness through monastic disciplines, he discovered that Christ Himself is our sanctification. We don't achieve freedom through our efforts; we receive it as a gift through our union with Christ.

I've often illustrated this to my seminary students using the image of a spacesuit. An astronaut in the vacuum of space doesn't survive by holding their breath or through extraordinary personal discipline. They survive because they're enclosed within a life-support system that provides everything they need. Likewise, we don't overcome sin by trying harder but by remaining "in Christ," who supplies the spiritual atmosphere we need to thrive.

The Agent of Our Freedom

Paul specifies that this freedom comes through "the law of the Spirit of life." The Holy Spirit is the active agent who applies Christ's work to our lives. Without the Spirit's operation, the objective work of Christ would remain external to us.

I believe Paul echoes Genesis 2, where God breathed the "breath of life" into Adam. Just as that divine breath animated the first Adam, the Spirit now breathes spiritual life into those who are in the last Adam, Christ.

This helps us understand why legalism always fails as a strategy for sanctification. Rules and regulations, even biblical ones, can't produce life. Only the Spirit can do that. As Paul writes elsewhere, "the letter kills, but the Spirit gives life" (2 Corinthians 3:6).

The Relationship of the Mosaic Law

Although Paul isn't focusing on the Mosaic Law in this verse, we should consider how his statement relates to that Law. In Romans 7:12, Paul affirmed that "the law is holy, and the commandment is holy and righteous and good." The problem wasn't with God's Law but with our inability to keep it due to our sinful nature.

The Mosaic Law served several crucial purposes in God's redemptive plan. It revealed God's holy character, exposed our sin, and foreshadowed Christ. But it was never intended as the means of our justification or sanctification. It diagnosed our spiritual disease without providing the cure.

Christ fulfilled the Law's righteous requirements on our behalf. When we're united to Him by faith, His perfect obedience is credited to us. More than that, the Spirit writes God's law on our hearts (Jeremiah 31:33), transforming our desires so that we begin to love what God loves and hate what He hates.

During my pastoral ministry, I've seen how this truth liberates believers from the pendulum swing between legalism and license. Those who understand that the Spirit produces obedience as the fruit of our union with Christ neither dismiss God's moral standards nor try to achieve them through self-effort.

The Practical Implications

What difference does this theological truth make in everyday Christian living? Let me suggest several practical implications.

First, it changes our approach to temptation and sin. Rather than merely trying to resist sin through willpower, we learn to rely on the Spirit's power working through our union with Christ. Victory over sin isn't achieved by focusing on the sin but by focusing on Christ and our identity in Him.

I recall a man in my congregation who had struggled with alcoholism for decades. After multiple failed attempts at sobriety, he experienced lasting transformation when he began to understand his identity in Christ. Rather than saying, "I'm an alcoholic trying to stay sober," he began saying, "I'm a new creation in Christ who no longer needs alcohol." This wasn't mere positive thinking; it was living out the reality that Paul describes in Romans 8:2.

Second, it transforms our motivation for obedience. We obey not to earn God's favor but because we already have it in Christ. Our obedience becomes a response of gratitude rather than an attempt to secure God's love.

Third, it gives us confidence in our spiritual growth. If our progress depended entirely on our own determination, we would have reason to despair. But since it's the Spirit who produces transformation, we can be confident that "he who began a good work in you will bring it to completion at the day of Jesus Christ" (Philippians 1:6).

Fourth, it reminds us of the essential role of the Holy Spirit in our sanctification. We can't produce spiritual fruit through fleshly means. Just as we received Christ by faith, we must walk in Him by faith, relying on the Spirit's power moment by moment.

The Ongoing Reality

While Romans 8:2 speaks of our freedom as an accomplished reality, we must acknowledge that we don't always experience this freedom completely in our daily lives. We still struggle with sin and sometimes feel its enslaving power.

This apparent contradiction is explained by the "already/not yet" nature of our salvation. We are already freed from sin's condemnation and dominion, but we don't yet experience the full manifestation of that freedom. We live in the overlap of the ages, where the old creation is passing away and the new creation is breaking in.

Paul acknowledges this tension throughout his writings. In Romans 6, he tells believers to "consider yourselves dead to sin and alive to God in Christ Jesus" (v. 11). This indicates that we must actively live out a reality that is already true of us in Christ.

In my own spiritual journey, I've found that growth often involves deepening my understanding and experience of freedom that is already mine in Christ, rather than trying to achieve a freedom I don't yet possess. The more I grasp what Christ has already accomplished, the more I experience the freedom He has secured.

Conclusion

"For the law of the Spirit of life has set you free in Christ Jesus from the law of sin and death." This declaration stands as one of the most liberating truths in all of Scripture. It announces that through Christ and by the Spirit, we have been transferred from one realm to another, from death to life, from bondage to freedom, from defeat to victory.

This freedom isn't something we achieve; it's something we receive through faith in Christ. It's not a distant goal to be reached through spiritual disciplines but a present reality to be lived out through dependence on the Spirit.

As you navigate the challenges of the Christian life, remember this fundamental truth: In Christ, you are already free. The Spirit of life dwells within you, empowering you to live according to God's design. You may still feel the pull of sin, but Christ has broken its dominion over you. You may still experience failure, but your identity as God's beloved child remains secure.

Live today in the freedom Christ has secured for you. Walk according to the Spirit rather than the flesh. And rejoice that the same Spirit who raised Christ from the dead dwells in you, guaranteeing that sin and death will not have the final word in your story.

Chapter Three

What the Law Could Not Do

"For God has done what the law, weakened by the flesh, could not do. By sending his own Son in the likeness of sinful flesh and for sin, he condemned sin in the flesh," Romans 8:3

Romans 8:3 stands as one of the most profound declarations in Scripture regarding the limitations of the Law and the triumph of God's grace through Christ. The apostle Paul writes, "For God has done what the law, weakened by the flesh, could not do. By sending his own Son in the likeness of sinful flesh and for sin, he condemned sin in the flesh" (Romans 8:3).

As I've studied this verse throughout my years as both a pastor and seminary professor, I've come to see it as a theological cornerstone that illuminates the magnificent grace of God against the backdrop of human inability. Let me walk you through what I believe this powerful verse reveals to us.

The Inherent Limitation of the Law

The Law of God, given through Moses, stands as a perfect expression of God's holy character and righteous requirements. During my years of ministry, I've encountered many sincere believers who struggled to understand why something God Himself gave could be described as having limitations. The key insight is that the limitation was never in the Law itself, but rather in us.

When Paul writes the Law was "weakened by the flesh," he pinpoints the genuine problem. The Law, in its divine perfection, collided with our fallen human nature. I recall counseling a young man who was desperately trying to overcome a persistent sin through sheer willpower and rule-following. Frustration, defeat, and doubt about his faith consumed him. What he failed to understand was that the Law was never designed to provide the power for its own fulfillment.

This is precisely what Paul means. The Law could diagnose our spiritual disease with perfect accuracy, but it could not provide the cure. It could reveal sin, but it could not remove sin. It could command righteousness, but it could not create righteousness within us.

Three Things the Law Could Not Do

As I've reflected on this passage over decades of study, I've identified three critical functions that the Law, though perfect in itself, could never accomplish due to the weakness of our flesh.

1. The Law Could Not Justify Us Before God

First and foremost, the Law could never serve as our path to justification. In Romans 3:20, Paul makes this abundantly clear:

"For by works of the law no human being will be justified in his sight, since through the law comes knowledge of sin."

During my time as a Marine, I learned the importance of standards and regulations. Every aspect of military life was governed by clear rules and expectations. But I quickly discovered that even in that structured environment, perfect compliance was impossible. How much more impossible is perfect compliance with God's infinitely higher standard!

The Law demands flawless, perpetual obedience, a standard no fallen human could ever meet. James 2:10 reminds us that "whoever keeps the whole law but fails in one point has become guilty of all of it." One transgression renders us lawbreakers, and all of us have transgressed countless times. The mathematics of justification by Law-keeping simply doesn't compute for fallen humanity.

2. The Law Could Not Transform Our Hearts

Second, while the Law could command external compliance, it lacked the power to transform our hearts. In my years of pastoral ministry, I've observed this reality time and time again. External behavior modification without heart transformation inevitably leads either to self-righteousness or to despair.

The Law could say, "Do not covet," but it could not remove covetousness from our hearts. It could command, "Love the Lord your God with all your heart," but it could not produce that love within us. It could prohibit idolatry, but it could not eliminate our idolatrous tendencies.

Ezekiel prophesied of a future solution to this problem when he declared God's promise: "I will give you a new heart, and a new spirit I will put within you. And I will remove the heart of stone from your flesh and give you a heart of flesh. And I will put my Spirit within you, and cause you to walk in my statutes and be careful to obey my rules" (Ezekiel 36:26-27). The Law could prescribe the rules, but only the Spirit could provide the power and desire to follow them.

3. The Law Could Not Defeat the Power of Sin

Third, the Law was powerless to break sin's dominion over us. In fact, Paul makes the startling claim in Romans 7:8-9 that the Law actually aroused sinful passions: "But sin, seizing an opportunity through the commandment, produced in me all kinds of covetousness. For apart from the law, sin lies dead. I was once alive apart from the law, but when the commandment came, sin came alive and I died."

I remember teaching this concept to seminary students, who were initially shocked by it. How could God's holy Law increase sin? I explained that the Law doesn't create sin, but rather exposes and even provokes our rebellious nature. Tell a child not to touch something, and suddenly touching that object becomes their greatest desire! The Law functions like a dam against a river; it provides resistance but cannot stop the flow of water; in fact, the water builds up against it with even greater pressure.

The Law lacks the power to defeat sin because it works externally while sin operates internally. It can forbid sinful actions but cannot extinguish sinful desires. It can condemn the sinner but cannot conquer sin.

What God Did That the Law Could Not Do

The brilliance of Romans 8:3 is that it doesn't merely highlight the Law's limitations; it proclaims God's solution. "For God has done what the law, weakened by the flesh, could not do. By sending his own Son in the likeness of sinful flesh and for sin, he condemned sin in the flesh."

In this powerful declaration, Paul reveals how God accomplished what the Law never could. Let me unpack this magnificent truth.

1. God Sent His Own Son

First, notice the personal nature of God's intervention. He didn't send an angel or a prophet, He sent "his own Son." This speaks both to the severity of our condition and to the depth of God's love. Nothing less than the incarnation of the Second Person of the Trinity would suffice.

I've often reflected on what this means for our understanding of God's character. The Father was willing to send His beloved Son into a hostile world. The Son was willing to leave heaven's glory and take on human flesh. This is love beyond comprehension.

2. In the Likeness of Sinful Flesh

Second, Paul carefully articulates the nature of Christ's incarnation. Jesus came "in the likeness of sinful flesh." This precise wording affirms both Christ's genuine humanity and His sinlessness. He possessed real human flesh, yet without sin's corruption.

During my years of theological study, I've come to appreciate the critical importance of this distinction. Had Jesus come merely in the appearance of humanity (as some early heretics claimed), He could not truly represent us. Had He come with a sinful nature, He could not have served as our perfect sacrifice. Instead, He came fully human yet without sin, uniquely qualified to be our representative and substitute.

3. For Sin

Third, Christ came "for sin" a phrase that echoes the language of sacrifice throughout the Old Testament. Jesus came as the final and sufficient sin offering, fulfilling what all the animal sacrifices could only foreshadow.

When I teach on this text, I often remind students that the phrase "for sin" carries the weight of divine purpose. Christ's coming wasn't accidental or merely responsive; it was intentional and purposeful from eternity past. As Peter declares, He was "foreknown before the foundation of the world" (1 Peter 1:20) as the remedy for sin.

4. He Condemned Sin in the Flesh

Finally, through Christ, God "condemned sin in the flesh." This is perhaps the most remarkable statement of all. Sin, which had condemned us, was itself condemned through Christ's perfect life and sacrificial death. The execution of the judgment that should have fallen on us fell on Him instead.

In my pastoral ministry, I've seen countless individuals liberated by this truth. Sin's condemnation has been fully satisfied in Christ. The legal demands of God's holy Law have been met completely. The power of sin has been decisively broken.

The Implications for Believers Today

Understanding what the Law could not do and what God has done through Christ transforms how we live as believers. Let me share several implications I've seen work themselves out in both my life and the lives of those I've shepherded.

1. Freedom from Performance-Based Righteousness

First, we escape the crushing burden of performance-based righteousness. I recall counseling a woman who had spent decades trying to earn God's favor through religious observance. She lived under constant fear and guilt, never certain she had done enough. When she finally grasped that Christ had done what she could never do, tears of relief streamed down her face.

The gospel assures us that our right standing with God depends not on our perfect Law-keeping but on Christ's perfect work on our behalf. As Paul declares in Romans 8:1, "There is therefore now no condemnation for those who are in Christ Jesus." This is not a license for lawlessness but the foundation for grateful obedience.

2. A New Relationship with the Law

Second, understanding Romans 8:3 establishes a new relationship with God's Law. The Law remains "holy and righteous and good" (Romans 7:12), but it is no longer our means of justification or sanctification.

Instead, filled with the Spirit, we now delight in the Law as a guide for godly living. The same commandments that once condemned us now instruct us in righteousness. We obey not to become righteous but because Christ declared us righteous, and His Spirit makes us righteous.

3. Hope in our Ongoing Struggle with Sin

Finally, this truth offers profound hope in our ongoing struggle with sin. Though the Law could not defeat sin's power, Christ has! And while we still battle the presence of sin in our lives, its dominion has been broken.

During my years in the Marines, I learned that victory in battle doesn't always mean the immediate cessation of all conflict. Often, it means a decisive turning point that guarantees the final outcome. So it is with Christ's victory over sin. The war has been decisively won, even though individual battles continue.

Conclusion

Romans 8:3 stands as a testament to both human inability and divine sufficiency. The Law, though perfect in itself, could not justify us, transform us, or defeat sin's power because of our weakness. But God, in His infinite wisdom and love, accomplished through Christ what the Law could never do.

As believers, we now live in the freedom of this truth. We are justified by faith in Christ, transformed by His indwelling Spirit, and progressively delivered from sin's power. The Law could command but not enable; Christ both commands and enables through His Spirit.

This is the heart of the gospel, not self-improvement or moral reformation, but divine intervention and spiritual transformation. Not what we must do, but what God has done. Not our feeble attempts at righteousness, but Christ's perfect righteousness imputed to us and worked in us.

What the Law could not do, God has done. And for this, we offer our endless praise.

Chapter Four

Fullfillment of the Law's Righteous Requirements

"In order that the righteous requirement of the law might be fulfilled in us, who walk not according to the flesh but according to the Spirit." Romans 8:4

Having explored what the Law could not do and what God accomplished through Christ in Romans 8:3, we now turn to the glorious purpose behind it all. As Paul transitions to verse 4, we encounter one of the most profound and practical statements in all of Scripture regarding the Christian life. It answers the crucial question: What was God's ultimate aim in sending His Son?

The opening phrase "in order that" signals purpose. To achieve this, everything discussed in verse 3 was intended: "that the righteous requirement of the law might be fulfilled in us." This statement has generated considerable discussion throughout church history, and rightly so. It strikes at the heart of how the gospel transforms our relationship to God's Law.

What is the Righteous Requirement of the Law

What is "the righteous requirement of the law"? In my years of pastoral ministry, I've found this question often creates confusion. Some interpret it to mean the Law's demand for perfect obedience, which Christ fulfilled on our behalf. Others see it as the Law's moral standards, now fulfilled in believers through the Spirit's work. Both perspectives contain important truths.

The Greek term *dikaiōma* (translated "righteous requirement") is singular, suggesting the Law's unified demand rather than its individual commandments. What is this singular demand? Jesus Himself identified it: "'You shall love the Lord your God with all your heart and with all your soul and with all your mind. This is the great and first commandment. And a second is like it: You shall love your neighbor as yourself. On these two commandments depend all the Law and the Prophets" (Matthew 22:37-40).

Love, then, is the righteous requirement of the Law. As Paul states elsewhere, "Love is the fulfilling of the law" (Romans 13:10).

How is the Requirement Fulfilled in Us

How is this requirement "fulfilled in us"? Notice carefully the passive construction: "might be fulfilled in us." Paul doesn't say we fulfill the Law, but that its requirement is fulfilled in us. This distinction is crucial for understanding the gospel's transformative power.

During my military service, I learned that success in combat depends not on individual prowess but on proper equipping and leadership. Similarly, the fulfillment of the Law's righteous requirement depends not on our striving but on God's empowering grace working in us.

This fulfillment occurs in two complementary ways. First, it happens through justification, Christ's perfect righteousness imputed to us. When we place faith in Christ, His Law-keeping is credited to our account. The Law demanded perfect obedience; Christ provided it on our behalf. This is what theologians call "passive obedience" not because Christ was passive, but because we passively receive His righteousness by faith.

I remember counseling a man who had spent decades trying to earn God's favor through religious performance. When he finally understood that Christ had already fulfilled the Law's demands for him, his countenance transformed. The burden of impossibility lifted from his shoulders.

Second, this fulfillment occurs through sanctification, Christ's righteousness being formed in us by the Spirit. This is the Law written on our hearts, as promised in the New Covenant (Jeremiah 31:33). Through the Spirit's indwelling power, we begin to fulfill the Law's essential requirement of love.

Who Experiences this Fulfillment

Paul is specific about who experiences this fulfillment: those "who walk not according to the flesh but according to the Spirit." This isn't describing two categories of Christians but the defining characteristic of all true believers. To be in Christ means to have the Spirit and to "walk" according to His guidance.

The Greek word *peripateo* "walk" denotes our habitual conduct, our manner of life. It's not occasional behavior but a consistent direction. Just as my Marine training influenced how I responded to situations, so the Spirit shapes our natural responses to align with God's character.

The Two Ways of Walking

In this verse, Paul introduces a contrast that will dominate the rest of the chapter: walking according to the flesh versus walking according to the Spirit. This distinction is fundamental to understanding the Christian life.

Walking According to the Flesh

Walking "according to the flesh" means living under the control of our fallen human nature with its self-centered desires. It's autonomy from God, attempting to navigate life by our own wisdom and strength.

I've witnessed the destructive power of flesh-walking throughout my ministry. The seminary student, whose private addiction eventually destroyed his family. Ethical compromise resulted from the businessman's pursuit of success. The church member whose unresolved bitterness poisoned relationships throughout the congregation. In each case, the underlying issue wasn't simply bad behavior but a fundamental orientation toward self-rule rather than Spirit-rule.

Walking according to the flesh isn't limited to obvious immorality. It includes religious flesh-walking, attempting to please God through self-effort rather than faith-filled dependence. The Pharisees exemplified this approach, and many sincere Christians fall into the same trap today.

Walking According to the Spirit

By contrast, walking "according to the Spirit" means living under the Spirit's guidance and empowerment. It's surrendering control to God and depending on His resources rather than our own.

This walk doesn't happen automatically. Even as believers, we must consciously yield to the Spirit's leading. As Paul will later command, "If we live by the Spirit, let us also keep in step with the Spirit" (Galatians 5:25).

In my pastoral experience, I've observed that Spirit-walking involves three key elements:

1. Saturation in Scripture.

The Spirit primarily leads us through the Word He inspired. When we immerse ourselves in Scripture, our minds are renewed, and our spiritual discernment sharpened.

2. Surrender in prayer.

Through honest, dependent prayer, we acknowledge our need and invite the Spirit's work in specific areas of struggle.

3. Submission in community.

The Spirit often speaks through the counsel and correction of other believers. Isolation hinders Spirit-sensitivity.

When these elements become habitual, walking according to the Spirit becomes increasingly natural, not through self-effort but through growing responsiveness to the Spirit's presence.

The Miracle of Fulfillment

Let's step back and marvel at what Paul is saying: the very Law that once condemned us is now being fulfilled in us. This is nothing short of miraculous. The impossible has become possible, not by lowering the standard but by transforming the participants.

I often use the analogy of heart transplantation with my congregations. Before salvation, we had "hearts of stone" unresponsive to God's commands. Through regeneration, God has given us "hearts of flesh" spiritually alive and responsive to His will (Ezekiel 36:26). The commands haven't changed, but we have.

This transformation addresses a common misconception about grace. Some fear that emphasizing grace leads to lawlessness. "If we're not under law but under grace," they reason, "won't people just sin freely?" Paul's answer is emphatically no! Grace doesn't abolish the Law's righteous requirement; it fulfills it through the Spirit's work.

The Ongoing Process

It's important to acknowledge that this fulfillment is both already accomplished and still progressing. In justification, the Law's requirement is fully met through Christ's imputed righteousness. In sanctification, it's being progressively realized through the Spirit's transforming work.

This explains the tension many of us experience in our Christian walk. We're simultaneously righteous in Christ and being made righteous by the Spirit. The gap between these realities, between our position and our practice, creates holy dissatisfaction that propels spiritual growth.

During my military career, I observed how new Marines gradually embodied the Corps' values and disciplines. What began as external conformity eventually became internal identity. Similarly, as we walk according to the Spirit, God's Law increasingly becomes not just an external standard but our internal delight.

Practical Applications

How does Romans 8:4 transform our daily lives as believers? Let me suggest several applications:

1. It Liberates Us from Legalism

Understanding that the Law's fulfillment comes through the Spirit frees us from the burden of legalistic performance. Our standing with God doesn't depend on our perfect obedience but on Christ's perfect work applied to us by faith.

I recall a woman in my congregation who lived under constant guilt, feeling she never measured up to God's standards. When she grasped that Christ had fulfilled the Law's righteous requirement for her, and that the Spirit was working to fulfill it in her, the relief was visible. "For the first time," she told me, "I feel like I can breathe."

2. It Elevates Our View of Holiness

Far from diminishing holiness, Romans 8:4 elevates it by connecting it to the Spirit's supernatural work rather than mere human effort. True holiness isn't achieved through willpower but through surrender to the Spirit.

This perspective transforms spiritual disciplines from attempts to earn God's favor into means of experiencing the Spirit's empowering presence. Prayer, Scripture reading, worship, and fellowship become channels of grace rather than works of merit.

3. It Provides Hope in Struggle

Perhaps most practically, this verse offers profound hope in our ongoing struggle against sin. When we fail, and we will, we're reminded that our justification rests on Christ's fulfillment of the Law, not our own performance.

Simultaneously, it assures us that the Spirit is actively working to conform us to Christ's image. Our transformation isn't optional or peripheral to salvation; it's the very purpose for which Christ died. As Paul will later declare, "For those whom he foreknew he also predestined to be conformed to the image of his Son" (Romans 8:29).

Conclusion

Romans 8:4 captures the beautiful purpose behind Christ's redemptive work: "that the righteous requirement of the law might be fulfilled in us, who walk not according to the flesh but according to the Spirit." Here we find the perfect balance between grace and holiness, between what Christ has done for us and what the Spirit is doing in us.

The Law's demand for perfect love toward God and neighbor, impossible for us in our fallen state, is now being fulfilled through the supernatural work of the Spirit in believers. What was once our condemnation has become through Christ our joyful direction.

As we walk this path, let us remember that both legalism and lawlessness miss the gospel's transformative power. Legalism attempts to fulfill the Law's requirement through human effort; lawlessness abandons the requirement altogether. The gospel fulfills the requirement through the Spirit's empowering presence.

May we, as those indwelt by the Spirit, walk daily in the freedom and power He provides, experiencing the progressive fulfillment of the Law's righteous requirement in our lives, not to earn God's favor but as a response to the favor already received in Christ.

Chapter Five

Two Ways of Thinking

"For those who live according to the flesh set their minds on the things of the flesh, but those who live according to the Spirit set their minds on the things of the Spirit." Romans 8:5

I've often found that how we think determines how we live. This profound connection between mind and action is precisely what the Apostle Paul addresses in Romans 8:5. In this verse, Paul presents us with two contrasting mindsets that produce two radically different ways of living. Let's examine these two ways of thinking and their implications for our Christian walk.

The Mind Set on the Flesh

Paul begins by describing those who "live according to the flesh" and consequently "set their minds on the things of the flesh." The word translated "set their minds" (*phronousin* in Greek) refers to a settled pattern of thinking, not just passing thoughts but a sustained orientation of the mind.

When I served as a Marine, I observed how military training works to reorient a person's entire thought pattern. The goal wasn't merely to change external behaviors but to transform the way Marines think about themselves, their mission, and their responsibilities. Similarly, the fleshly mindset isn't just about individual sinful thoughts but an entire worldview and value system opposed to God.

What characterizes this fleshly mindset? From Scripture, we can identify several key attributes:

1. Self-Centeredness

The mind of the flesh revolves around self: my rights, my comforts, my desires, my will. I've counseled countless individuals whose spiritual struggles stemmed from this fundamental self-orientation. Even religious activities can become expressions of the flesh when performed to glorify self rather than God.

In Reformed theology, we recognize this self-centeredness as a direct consequence of the Fall. As descendants of Adam, we are born with a nature inclined toward self-worship rather than God-worship. As Augustine famously put it, sin is being "curved in upon oneself" (*incurvatus in se* in Latin).

2. Present-Focused

The fleshly mind fixates on immediate gratification rather than eternal values. During my pastoral ministry, I witnessed many believers struggling with decisions that pitted momentary pleasure against long-term spiritual good. The mind that is set on the flesh consistently chooses the immediate over the eternal.

3. Autonomy-Seeking

At its core, the fleshly mind seeks independence from God. It's the mindset that says, "I will determine my own truth, my own morality, my own purpose." This autonomy-seeking posture began in Eden with the temptation to "be like God" and continues today in countless forms.

4. Death-Producing

Paul will go on to say in verse 6 that "to set the mind on the flesh is death." This mindset leads not just to physical death but to spiritual death, separation from God and the life He offers. I've watched with sorrow as people following fleshly thinking progressively distanced themselves from the Lord, experiencing the deadening of their spiritual sensitivities.

The Mind Set on the Spirit

In beautiful contrast, Paul describes those who "live according to the Spirit" and therefore "set their minds on the things of the Spirit." This mindset represents the renewed thinking that the Holy Spirit produces in believers.

What characterizes this spiritual mindset?

1. God-Centeredness

The mindset on the Spirit revolves around God, His glory, His kingdom, His will. I've had the privilege of knowing many believers whose thoughts consistently gravitate toward the Lord, who filter decisions through the question: "How will this honor Christ?"

This God-centeredness doesn't come naturally to any of us. It's the fruit of the Spirit's regenerating work, giving us new hearts that desire God above all else. As Reformed theology emphasizes, this transformation is entirely of grace, not something we produce but something God works in us.

2. Eternally-Focused

The spiritual mind weighs decisions in light of eternity rather than merely the present moment. I remember a young couple in my congregation who declined a lucrative job opportunity because they discerned it would hinder their spiritual growth and ministry effectiveness. They were thinking with eternity in view, setting their minds on the things of the Spirit.

3. Submission-Embracing

Contrary to the flesh's quest for autonomy, the mind set on the Spirit embraces submission to God's authority. It says with Christ, "Not my will, but yours be done." This submission isn't begrudging but joyful, recognizing God's way as the path of true freedom and flourishing.

4. Life-Producing

Paul continues in verse 6 that "to set the mind on the Spirit is life and peace." The spiritual mindset leads to spiritual vitality, communion with God, joy in His presence, and the peace that transcends understanding. I've observed that believers who consistently set their minds on spiritual things radiate a life and peace that cannot be explained by their circumstances.

The Sovereign Work of God

As we consider these two ways of thinking, we must recognize a crucial theological truth: the transition from fleshly thinking to spiritual thinking is not something we accomplish through sheer willpower. In Reformed theology, we understand that this transformation is God's sovereign work of grace.

By nature, all of us are born with minds set on the flesh. As Paul states in Ephesians 2:3, we were "by nature children of wrath, like the rest of mankind." Our natural disposition is toward fleshly thinking, and we cannot change this orientation by our own efforts.

The shift to a mindset on the Spirit begins with regeneration, God's work of giving spiritual life to those who are spiritually dead. When the Holy Spirit regenerates us, He gives us new hearts capable of desiring God and new minds capable of spiritual thinking.

This doesn't mean the battle is over. Even as regenerate believers, we still struggle with fleshly thinking. Paul's exhortation in Romans 12:2 to "be transformed by the renewal of your mind" indicates an ongoing process. The Spirit has begun this transformation, but we must cooperate with His work through the spiritual disciplines, Scripture meditation, prayer, worship, and fellowship.

Practical Applications

How does understanding these two ways of thinking change our daily lives? Let me suggest several practical applications:

1. It Calls us to Vigilant Self-Examination

Paul's teaching invites us to regularly examine our thought patterns. Are we consistently setting our minds on fleshly things or spiritual things? During my years of ministry, I developed the habit of periodically asking myself: "What have I been thinking about most this week? Where has my mind naturally gravitated?" These questions often reveal whether I'm walking according to the flesh or the Spirit.

2. It Directs Our Attention to the Mind's Role in Sanctification

While many Christians focus exclusively on changing behaviors, Paul directs our attention to the mind's crucial role in sanctification. If we want to live according to the Spirit, we must think according to the Spirit. Behavior modification that doesn't address underlying thought patterns will inevitably fail.

I've found that helping believers identify and challenge fleshly thought patterns is often more effective than simply prescribing new behaviors. When our thinking changes, our actions naturally follow.

3. It Guides Our Media Consumption

Paul's teaching has significant implications for what we allow into our minds through media. The entertainment, news, and social media we consume shape our thinking patterns, either reinforcing fleshly mindsets or encouraging spiritual ones.

I've counseled many Christians struggling with spiritual growth who never considered how their media diet was cultivating fleshly thinking. When they began intentionally consuming content that set their minds on spiritual things, their spiritual lives flourished.

4. It Informs Our Understanding of Christian Community

Romans 8:5 also helps us understand the importance of Christian fellowship. Those with whom we spend time significantly influence us. Surrounding ourselves with believers who set their minds on the Spirit helps us do the same.

My most spiritually formative relationships have been with men and women whose minds consistently focused on spiritual things. Their conversation naturally gravitated toward the Lord, His Word, and His work, which helped orient my own thinking in the same direction.

The Hope of Progressive Transformation

As we conclude our exploration of Romans 8:5, I want to emphasize the hope this verse offers. While we all struggle with fleshly thinking patterns, the indwelling Spirit is actively working to transform our minds. This transformation isn't instantaneous but progressive, a lifelong journey of having our minds increasingly set on the things of the Spirit.

I've witnessed this progressive transformation in countless believers over my years of ministry and seminary. People who once thought almost exclusively about fleshly concerns gradually developed minds increasingly fixed on spiritual realities. The change wasn't overnight, but over years of walking with the Spirit, their default thought patterns shifted remarkably.

This gives me tremendous hope for my own spiritual journey and for yours. Though we still battle fleshly thinking, the Spirit is working within us, renewing our minds day by day. And one day, when we see Christ face to face, our transformation will be complete. We will perfectly set our minds on the things of the Spirit, and we will never again be distracted by fleshly concerns.

Until that day, let us cooperate with the Spirit's work by intentionally setting our minds on spiritual things, fixing our thoughts on what is true, honorable, just, pure, lovely, commendable, excellent, and praiseworthy (Philippians 4:8). As our thinking changes, our living will follow, increasingly reflecting the life of the Spirit rather than the way of the flesh.

May the Lord grant us minds that are consistently set on the things of the Spirit, producing the life and peace that come from walking in step with Him.

Chapter Six

The Consequence of Mindset

"For to set the mind on the flesh is death, but to set the mind on the Spirit is life and peace." Romans 8:6

In our exploration of Romans 8, we've seen Paul's clear distinction between those who live according to the flesh and those who live according to the Spirit. Now in verse 6, the apostle reveals the profound consequences of these two mindsets. This verse strikes me as one of the most sobering yet hope-filled declarations in all of Scripture. In these few words, Paul lays before us the ultimate outcome of our thought patterns, either death or life and peace. There is no middle ground, no third option. The consequences couldn't be more stark.

The Mindset of the Flesh Leads to Death

Let's first consider what Paul means when he says, "to set the mind on the flesh is death." The term "death" in Scripture carries multiple dimensions, and I believe Paul has all of these in view.

Spiritual Death

At its core, the fleshly mindset perpetuates spiritual death, separation from God. When our minds fixate on fleshly concerns, we remain alienated from the life of God. I've counseled countless individuals who wondered why God seemed distant, only to discover their minds were thoroughly consumed with worldly concerns. As Jesus taught in Matthew 6:24, "No one can serve two masters." When our minds serve the flesh, communion with God inevitably suffers.

This spiritual death isn't merely a future reality but a present condition. Paul reminds us in Ephesians 2:1 that before Christ, we "were dead in the trespasses and sins." The mind set on the flesh perpetuates this state of spiritual deadness even in those who profess faith.

Relational Death

The fleshly mindset also brings death to our relationships. I've witnessed how self-centered thinking, a hallmark of the fleshly mind, poisons marriages, fractures friendships, and divides churches. Pride, jealousy, bitterness, and unforgiveness, all fruits of the flesh, create relational graveyards around those who nurture them.

During my pastoral ministry, I counseled a man whose marriage was crumbling. Through our conversations, it became clear his mind was consumed with his rights, his needs, and his grievances. This fleshly mindset was literally killing his marriage. Only when he began to set his mind on the things of the Spirit, sacrificial love, forgiveness, and humble service, did his relationship begin to revive.

Ethical Death

A mind set on the flesh also leads to moral and ethical decay. Paul elaborates on this in Galatians 5:19-21, where he catalogs the "works of the flesh" as "sexual immorality, impurity, sensuality, idolatry, sorcery, enmity, strife, jealousy, fits of anger, rivalries, dissensions, divisions, envy, drunkenness, orgies, and things like these." These behaviors don't suddenly appear in our lives; they germinate first in fleshly thought patterns.

I've observed that no one suddenly falls into grievous sin. There's always a progression that begins with the mind. The man who commits adultery first entertained lustful thoughts. The woman who destroys her witness through deceit first rationalized small dishonesty in her thinking. A mind set on flesh produces actions that bring death to our moral character.

Eternal Death

Finally, we cannot ignore that Paul ultimately has eternal death in view. Later in Romans 8:13, he explicitly states, "For if you live according to the flesh you will die." This refers to the second death described in Revelation 20:14-15, eternal separation from God.

While true believers are secure in Christ, this warning serves as a sober reminder that a persistently fleshly mindset may indicate someone has never truly been born again. As Jesus warned, "Not everyone who says to me, 'Lord, Lord,' will enter the kingdom of heaven" (Matthew 7:21). A consistently fleshly mindset should prompt serious self-examination regarding the authenticity of one's faith.

The Mindset of the Spirit Produces Life and Peace

In glorious contrast to the death that comes from a fleshly mindset, Paul proclaims that "to set the mind on the Spirit is life and peace." These twin blessings, life and peace, encompass God's greatest gifts to humanity.

Life in All Its Dimensions

The "life" Paul references is not merely biological existence but in Greek *zōē*, abundant, eternal life. This life begins the moment we trust Christ and continues throughout eternity. Jesus declared in John 10:10, "I came that they may have life and have it abundantly."

I've observed that when believers consistently set their minds on spiritual things, they experience this life in all its dimensions:

First, they enjoy spiritual vitality, an ongoing communion with God that infuses every aspect of existence with meaning and purpose. Their Bible reading becomes life-giving rather than dutiful. Their prayers flow from relationship rather than obligation. Worship stirs their hearts rather than merely occupying their time.

Second, they manifest ethical vitality, growing in Christlikeness and bearing spiritual fruit. Galatians 5:22-23 describes this fruit as "love, joy, peace, patience, kindness, goodness, faithfulness, gentleness, self-control." These qualities naturally emerge from a mind saturated with spiritual thoughts.

Third, they demonstrate missional vitality, becoming channels of God's life to others. I've noticed that those whose minds dwell on spiritual realities naturally share the gospel more frequently and serve others more joyfully. They don't need to be cajoled into ministry; it flows from their Spirit-oriented thinking.

Finally, they anticipate eternal vitality, living with confident hope in God's promises regarding the life to come. This eternal perspective transforms how they view present sufferings and challenges. As Paul declares in Romans 8:18, "For I consider that the sufferings of this present time are not worth comparing with the glory that is to be revealed to us."

Peace That Surpasses Understanding

Alongside life, Paul mentions peace as the consequence of a spiritually oriented mind. This peace has multiple dimensions as well.

First and foremost, it includes peace with God. Romans 5:1 states, "Therefore, since we have been justified by faith, we have peace with God through our Lord Jesus Christ." The Spirit-oriented mind rests in this reconciled relationship, free from the burden of earning God's favor.

Beyond this foundational peace, there's also the peace of God—that inner tranquility that remains even amid life's storms. This is what Paul describes in Philippians 4:7 as "the peace of God, which surpasses all understanding."

During my years of ministry, I've sat with believers facing terminal diagnoses, devastating losses, and shattered dreams. What struck me most about those with Spirit-oriented minds was their supernatural peace. Their circumstances were no less difficult, but they possessed an inner stillness that testified to God's sustaining grace.

This peace extends to our relationships as well. Those who set their minds on the Spirit cultivate what Romans 14:19 calls "the things that make for peace and for mutual up-building." I've observed that spiritually-minded Christians are typically the peacemakers in their families, workplaces, and churches.

Practical Implications for the Believer

Paul's teaching in Romans 8:6 carries profound implications for our daily lives as followers of Christ. Let me share several practical applications:

1. The Mind as the Battleground of Sanctification

First, this verse highlights the mind as the primary battleground of our sanctification. While many Christians focus exclusively on changing behaviors, Paul directs our attention to the mind as the source of either death or life and peace. If we want to experience the abundant life Christ promised, we must win the battle for our thoughts.

This understanding revolutionized my approach to spiritual formation, both personally and in my ministry. Rather than merely prescribing behavioral changes, I began helping believers identify and challenge fleshly thought patterns while cultivating spiritual ones. When our thinking changes, our actions naturally follow.

2. The Need for Intentional Thought Management

Second, Romans 8:6 underscores the necessity of intentionally managing our thought lives. The mind naturally gravitates toward fleshly concerns unless we deliberately redirect it toward spiritual matters.

I've developed several practices that help me maintain a spiritually-oriented mind:

Beginning each day with Scripture meditation rather than immediately checking news or social media

Strategically placing Bible verses in locations where my mind tends to wander (my car dashboard, computer screen, etc.)

Regularly evaluating my thought patterns using Philippians 4:8 as a filter: "Whatever is true, whatever is honorable, whatever is just, whatever is pure, whatever is lovely, whatever is commendable, if there is any excellence, if there is anything worthy of praise, think about these things"

Cultivating friendship with spiritually-minded believers whose conversation naturally gravitates toward godly topics

3. The Warning Against Spiritual Complacency

Third, this verse warns against spiritual complacency. The consequences of our thought patterns, either death or life and peace, are too significant to approach casually. We cannot afford to be passive about what occupies our minds.

I've witnessed the tragic results of believers who became complacent about their thought lives. Slowly, imperceptibly, their minds became increasingly occupied with fleshly concerns. Eventually, this fleshly thinking produced the fruit of death in various aspects of their lives, strained relationships, ethical compromises, and diminished spiritual vitality.

4. The Hope of Progressive Transformation

Finally, Romans 8:6 offers tremendous hope for believers struggling with fleshly thought patterns. While none of us has perfectly spiritual minds this side of heaven, the indwelling Spirit is working to progressively transform our thinking.

I take great encouragement from Paul's words in 2 Corinthians 3:18: "And we all, with unveiled face, beholding the glory of the Lord, are being transformed into the same image from one degree of glory to another. For this comes from the Lord who is the Spirit." The same Spirit who raised Christ from the dead is working within us, gradually reorienting our minds toward spiritual things.

Conclusion

As we conclude our examination of Romans 8:6, I'm struck by the elegance of Paul's teaching. In this single verse, he captures both the problem of human existence, minds oriented toward death-producing flesh, and its solution, minds reoriented toward the life-giving Spirit.

The choice before us is clear. Will we set our minds on the flesh and experience the various dimensions of death? Or will we set our minds on the Spirit and enjoy the life and peace God intends for us?

By God's grace, may we increasingly think according to the Spirit, not occasionally but habitually. May our default mental orientation be toward spiritual realities rather than fleshly concerns. And may we experience, in ever-increasing measure, the life and peace that come from minds set on the things of the Spirit.

Chapter Seven

Conflict with God

"For the mind that is set on the flesh is hostile to God, for it does not submit to God's law; indeed, it cannot." Romans 8:7

Having explored the stark contrast between the mind set on the flesh and the mind set on the Spirit in Romans 8:6, we now turn to verse 7, where Paul deepens his analysis of the fleshly mind.

This verse delivers a sobering diagnosis of humanity's natural condition. As I've studied this passage over my time in ministry, I've come to see it as one of the most penetrating analyzes of the human predicament in all of Scripture. Paul isn't merely suggesting that the unbeliever occasionally has disagreements with God or periodically rebels against His commands. Rather, he's asserting something far more fundamental: the very orientation of the natural human mind stands in direct opposition to its Creator.

The Hostility of the Fleshly Mind

The first part of Romans 8:7 declares that "the mind that is set on the flesh is hostile to God." The Greek word translated "hostile" (*echthra*) denotes active enmity or antagonism. It's the same word used elsewhere in Scripture to describe the state of hostility between enemies.

I remember counseling a man years ago who struggled to accept this biblical truth. "Pastor Bruce," he protested, "I know plenty of non-Christians who are good, decent people. They donate to charities, love their families, and live moral lives. How can you say their minds are hostile toward God?"

His question reflects a common misunderstanding of Paul's teaching. The hostility Paul describes isn't necessarily manifested in outward acts of rebellion or hatred toward religion. Rather, it's a fundamental orientation of the heart and mind that may exist alongside many outwardly commendable qualities.

Let me illustrate. When I served in the Marines, I understood what genuine hostility between opposing forces looked like. Two nations can be at war even during periods when no shots are being fired. The hostility exists at the fundamental level of allegiance and authority, even when circumstances temporarily prevent open conflict.

Similarly, the natural human mind is set in opposition to God's rightful authority, even when this opposition isn't always expressing itself in obvious ways. This hostility manifests in many forms:

1. Intellectual resistance to divine truth - The natural mind constructs elaborate systems of thought that exclude God or redefine Him according to human preferences.

2. Moral resistance to divine standards - The natural mind resents God's absolute moral claims and asserts its right to determine its own standards of right and wrong.

3. Volitional resistance to divine authority - The natural mind insists on autonomy and self-determination, rejecting God's rightful lordship.

4. Affectional resistance to divine glory - The natural mind loves created things more than the Creator and fails to find its greatest delight in God.

This comprehensive opposition to God isn't limited to the most depraved individuals in society. It characterizes every human heart apart from divine grace. As Reformed theology has consistently emphasized, the Fall affected every aspect of human nature, including our intellectual and moral capacities. Total depravity doesn't mean we're as bad as we could be, but rather that no part of our being has escaped the corrupting effects of sin.

The Insubordination of the Fleshly Mind

Paul doesn't stop with declaring the fleshly mind's hostility. He explains how this hostility manifests: "for it does not submit to God's law." The word translated "submit" (*hypotassō*) carries military connotations of arranging oneself under proper authority. The natural mind refuses to take its proper place under God's authority as expressed in His law.

This refusal to submit isn't just about breaking specific rules. It's about rejecting the very idea that God has the right to give us rules in the first place. At its core, sin is not primarily about violating divine commands but about usurping divine authority.

I witnessed this rebellion countless times during my military service. The most problematic recruits weren't necessarily those who occasionally failed to execute an order correctly but those who fundamentally rejected the chain of command. Similarly, the deepest problem with the fleshly mind isn't that it occasionally sins but that it rejects God's fundamental right to rule.

This insubordination began in the Garden of Eden when our first parents chose to define good and evil for themselves rather than submitting to God's determination. Their external disobedience flowed from an internal rebellion, a mind set on the flesh rather than on the Spirit. Every human sin since then has followed the same pattern.

I've observed this pattern in my own heart as well. When I'm honest with myself, I must admit that my most persistent struggles with sin stem not from ignorance of God's will but from a desire for autonomy. In those moments, my mind is set on the flesh, and I'm functioning according to the rebellious pattern Paul describes in this verse.

The Inability of the Fleshly Mind

Paul's analysis grows even more sobering as he adds, "indeed, it cannot." The fleshly mind not only does not submit to God's law; it cannot do so. This inability isn't a physical constraint but a moral and spiritual one. The natural mind lacks both the desire and the capacity to truly submit to divine authority.

This teaching aligns with what theologians in the Reformed tradition have called "the bondage of the will." Apart from God's intervening grace, human beings remain free to choose according to their desires, but their desires themselves are corrupted by sin. The fleshly mind freely chooses against God because it wants to, and it cannot do otherwise because it has no contrary desire.

Jesus expressed this same truth when He said, "No one can come to me unless the Father who sent me draws him" (John 6:44). Paul elsewhere declares that "the natural person does not accept the things of the Spirit of God, for they are folly to him, and he is not able to understand them because they are spiritually discerned" (1 Corinthians 2:14).

This inability explains why mere moral exhortation or intellectual argumentation never suffices to transform a human heart. Education, while valuable, cannot solve humanity's fundamental problem. Our need goes far deeper than information; we need regeneration, a supernatural work of God's Spirit to transform our minds from fleshly to spiritual.

Implications for Christian Life and Ministry

Paul's stark assessment of the fleshly mind carries profound implications for how we understand ourselves and our mission as believers:

1. It Humbles Us Regarding Our Own Salvation

First, Romans 8:7 reminds us that our salvation resulted not from our own spiritual insight or moral superiority but from God's sovereign grace. If the natural mind cannot submit to God's law, then our conversion must be attributed entirely to divine intervention.

I remember vividly the moment this truth gripped my heart. I had been a believer for several years but still harbored a subtle pride about my decision to follow Christ. While studying this passage during seminary, I was confronted with the reality that my very ability to respond to the gospel was itself a gift from God. This realization produced in me a deeper gratitude and a more profound worship of the God who overcame my natural hostility toward Him.

2. It Explains Our Ongoing Struggle with Sin

Second, this verse helps explain the persistent struggle with sin that even mature believers experience. Though we've been fundamentally transformed by God's Spirit, remnants of the flesh remain within us. When we set our minds on the flesh rather than the Spirit, we temporarily operate according to the hostile, insubordinate pattern Paul describes.

This understanding has been invaluable in my pastoral counseling. Many Christians become discouraged by their continued struggles with sin, wondering if their conversion was genuine. I've helped them see that these struggles, while painful, actually confirm Paul's teaching about the two mindsets warring within the believer. The very fact that they experience this conflict as painful rather than pleasant, demonstrates that they've been given a new nature that desires holiness.

3. It Shapes Our Approach to Evangelism

Third, Romans 8:7 profoundly shapes how we approach evangelism. If the natural mind is hostile to God and incapable of submission, then we must recognize our utter dependence on the Holy Spirit to open hearts to the gospel.

This realization transformed my approach to ministry. I stopped relying on clever arguments or emotional appeals to persuade people into the kingdom. Instead, I began to prioritize prayer, recognizing that only God's Spirit can overcome the natural hostility of the human heart. I still presented the gospel as clearly and compellingly as possible, but I did so with the awareness that spiritual transformation requires divine power.

4. It Underscores the Need for Ongoing Renewal

Finally, this verse highlights our need for continual renewal of our minds. Romans 12:2 exhorts us, "Do not be conformed to this world, but be transformed by the renewal of your mind." Since our default orientation is fleshly, we must actively cultivate spiritual mindedness through Scripture meditation, prayer, and fellowship with other believers.

I've made this a central focus in my own spiritual disciplines. Each morning, I deliberately set my mind on the things of the

Spirit through extended time in God's Word. Throughout the day, I regularly remind myself of gospel truths to counteract the natural drift toward fleshly thinking. This practice isn't about earning God's favor but about living in alignment with my new identity in Christ.

Conclusion

Romans 8:7 delivers a humbling diagnosis of our natural condition: "For the mind that is set on the flesh is hostile to God, for it does not submit to God's law; indeed, it cannot." This verse shatters any illusion of human self-sufficiency or moral neutrality. It reveals that, apart from divine grace, our very minds stand in active opposition to our Creator.

Yet, this sobering assessment makes the gospel all the more glorious. The same God toward whom we were hostile has provided the remedy for our condition. Through Christ's atoning work and the Spirit's transforming power, minds that were once bent on rebellion can be reoriented toward submission and love.

As believers, we've experienced this miraculous transformation, yet we continue to battle the remnants of the flesh within us. Our ongoing spiritual growth depends on continually setting our minds on the Spirit rather than the flesh. As we do so, the hostility that once characterized our relationship with God is increasingly replaced by joyful submission to His perfect will.

Chapter Eight

Inability to Please God

"Those who are in the flesh cannot please God." Romans 8:8

After examining the profound implications of Romans 8:7, we now turn our attention to the logical conclusion Paul draws in verse 8. This statement, though brief, contains theological depth that deserves careful consideration. As we unpack this verse, we'll discover both challenging and comforting truths about our relationship with our Creator.

The Blunt Reality of Romans 8:8

"Those who are in the flesh cannot please God." The apostle Paul doesn't mince words here. The statement is absolute and uncompromising. I've often found that this verse stands in stark contrast to the positive-thinking spirituality so prevalent in our culture today. Paul isn't suggesting that those in the flesh find it difficult to please God or that they occasionally fail in their attempts. Rather, he declares their complete inability to do so.

When I first encountered this verse as a young seminary student, it struck me as unnecessarily harsh. Surely, I thought, even unbelievers can do things that please God, acts of charity, selfless sacrifice, or moral behavior. But as I studied Reformed theology more deeply, I came to understand that Paul is addressing something more fundamental than isolated good deeds. He's speaking about the orientation of a person's entire being toward God.

What Does It Mean to Be "In the Flesh"?

To understand Romans 8:8, we must first clarify what Paul means by being "in the flesh." This phrase doesn't merely refer to having a physical body or experiencing natural desires. After all, Jesus himself took on human flesh, yet without sin. Rather, being "in the flesh" describes the natural state of fallen humanity, a condition in which the sin nature dominates and controls a person's thoughts, desires, and actions.

When I teach this concept, I often use the analogy of a fish in water. The fish is so completely surrounded by water that it has no awareness of any other environment. Similarly, those "in the flesh" are so immersed in their fallen nature that they cannot perceive spiritual realities correctly. They operate entirely within the limited parameters of their sinful condition.

This understanding helps us see why those in the flesh cannot please God. It's not primarily a matter of behavior but of nature. A person in the flesh is, by definition, oriented away from God and toward self. Even their seemingly good deeds spring from motivations that ultimately fail to give God his proper place.

The Impossibility of Pleasing God Apart from Faith

In Hebrews 11:6, we read: "And without faith it is impossible to please him, for whoever would draw near to God must believe that he exists and that he rewards those who seek him." This verse provides a helpful companion to Romans 8:8, showing that the fundamental barrier to pleasing God is not primarily moral failure but a lack of faith.

I recall counseling a church member who was devastated by repeated moral failures. "I just can't seem to please God," he confessed tearfully. I directed him to these passages, explaining that his primary problem wasn't his individual sins but the fact that he was trying to please God through his own efforts rather than resting in Christ's finished work. His breakthrough came not through increased moral effort but through embracing his complete dependence on God's grace.

Those in the flesh may perform outwardly good actions, but they cannot do so from the faith that pleases God. They may be motivated by social approval, guilt, fear, or self-interest, but not by love for God or desire for His glory. This is what Reformed theologians have traditionally called "civic virtue" which are actions that benefit society but lack the spiritual foundation that would make them pleasing to God.

Why This Inability Exists

Why can't those in the flesh please God? I believe there are several interconnected reasons:

1. The Problem of Corrupt Motives

First, those in the flesh inevitably act from corrupted motives. Even their best deeds are tainted by selfish intentions. I'm reminded of Augustine's description of the virtues of unbelievers as "splendid vices" outwardly impressive but inwardly flawed.

During my years as a Marine, I witnessed many acts of courage and sacrifice by men who had no Christian faith.

These actions were commendable from a human perspective, but they weren't performed for God's glory. Reformed theology teaches that God looks not only at the outward action but at the heart behind it. As 1 Samuel 16:7 reminds us, "Man looks on the outward appearance, but the LORD looks on the heart."

2. The Requirement of Spiritual Life

Second, pleasing God requires spiritual life, which those in the flesh don't possess. Jesus said, "It is the Spirit who gives life; the flesh is no help at all" (John 6:63). Those in the flesh are, according to Ephesians 2:1, "dead in trespasses and sins." A dead person cannot perform living actions.

I've often illustrated this point by comparing it to expecting a corpse to run a marathon. No amount of external motivation can enable a dead body to run. Similarly, no amount of moral exhortation can enable a spiritually dead person to produce actions that please God. Life must precede action.

3. The Inability to Submit to God's Law

Third, as we saw in Romans 8:7, the mind set on the flesh "does not submit to God's law; indeed, it cannot." If a person cannot submit to God's law, they certainly cannot please the Lawgiver. Every attempt to please God apart from submission to His revealed will is doomed to failure.

I've observed this principle at work in my own heart. Before my conversion, I occasionally tried to "be good" or "do the right thing," but I did so on my own terms, selecting which parts of God's standards I would follow. This selective obedience is actually disobedience, revealing a heart that places itself above God's authority.

4. The Absence of Christ's Mediation

Finally, nothing we do can please God apart from the mediating work of Christ. Our approaches to God must come through the "new and living way" opened for us by Jesus (Hebrews 10:20). Those in the flesh attempt to approach God on their own terms, without the covering of Christ's righteousness.

When I pastored, I often encountered people who believed their good deeds would make them acceptable to God. I would gently explain that no amount of good works can bridge the infinite gap between a holy God and sinful humanity. Only Christ can do that. As 1 Peter 2:5 tells us, our spiritual offerings are "acceptable to God through Jesus Christ."

The Pastoral Implications

Understanding Romans 8:8 has profound implications for pastoral ministry and personal spiritual growth. Let me share several ways this verse has shaped my approach to ministry and my own walk with Christ.

1. It Eliminates the Ground for Boasting

First, this verse demolishes any basis for human pride or boasting. If those in the flesh cannot please God, then our ability to please Him must come entirely from His grace. As Paul writes elsewhere, "What do you have that you did not receive? If then you received it, why do you boast as if you did not receive it?" (1 Corinthians 4:7).

I've found this truth particularly liberating in my own life. There was a time when I subtly took credit for my spiritual growth, as if it resulted primarily from my discipline and commitment. Romans 8:8 reminds me that my very ability to please God is itself a gift, not an achievement.

2. It Shapes Our Approach to Evangelism

Second, this verse profoundly influences how we approach evangelism. If unbelievers cannot please God in their current state, then our primary goal cannot be to help them become "better people." Rather, they need new life altogether.

This understanding transformed my preaching and evangelistic efforts. Instead of merely calling people to improve their behavior, I began emphasizing their need for radical spiritual rebirth. Moral reformation, while beneficial, cannot substitute for regeneration. As Jesus told Nicodemus, "You must be born again" (John 3:7).

3. It Increases Our Gratitude for Grace

Third, Romans 8:8 deepens our appreciation for God's grace. When we realize the impossibility of pleasing God through our own efforts, we more fully value the gift of justification and sanctification.

I remember visiting a man on his deathbed who had recently come to faith after decades of rejecting Christ. "I wasted so many years," he lamented. "Nothing I did during all that time pleased God." I shared with him the wonder of grace, that through faith in Christ, his remaining days could be genuinely pleasing to his Creator, regardless of how few they might be. This truth brought him immense comfort in his last hours.

4. It Explains the Necessity of Regeneration

Fourth, this verse helps us understand why regeneration must precede faith and obedience. If those in the flesh cannot please God, then something must happen to transfer us from the realm of the flesh to the realm of the Spirit before we can respond appropriately to God.

This is precisely what Reformed theology means by "irresistible grace" or "effectual calling" God's sovereign work of bringing spiritual life to those who are dead in sin. Without this divine intervention, we would remain perpetually incapable of pleasing God.

The Comfort Within the Challenge

While Romans 8:8 initially appears discouraging, it actually contains profound comfort for believers. Consider the inverse of Paul's statement: if those in the flesh cannot please God, then those in the Spirit can please Him! The verse implies that through the Spirit's work, we who were once incapable of pleasing God can now live in ways that bring Him delight.

This realization transformed my understanding of the Christian life. I once viewed godly living primarily as a burden, a constant struggle to avoid disappointing God. Now I see it as a privilege, the opportunity to please the One who, in Christ, has made me pleasing to Himself.

Ephesians 5:8-10 captures this beautifully: "For at one time you were darkness, but now you are light in the Lord. Walk as children of light (for the fruit of light is found in all that is good and right and true), and try to discern what is pleasing to the Lord." Notice the connection: because we have been transferred from darkness to light, we can now discern and do what pleases the Lord.

Conclusion

Romans 8:8 delivers a sobering assessment of the human condition: "Those who are in the flesh cannot please God." This verse confronts us with the utter bankruptcy of human effort and self-righteousness. It reminds us that apart from God's grace in Christ, we stand in a state of absolute spiritual inability.

Yet, this same verse points us toward the glorious solution found in the gospel. Through faith in Christ, we are transferred from the realm of the flesh to the realm of the Spirit. What was once impossible, pleasing God, becomes possible, not through our own strength but through the Spirit who dwells within us.

As believers, we no longer live under the sentence of Romans 8:8. Instead, we can embrace the promise of 2 Corinthians 5:9: "So whether we are at home or away, we make it our aim to please him." This is the miracle of grace, that those who were once incapable of pleasing God can now make pleasing Him the central purpose of their lives.

In my journey, this understanding has produced both humility and confidence, humility because I recognize my complete dependence on God's grace, and confidence because I know that through Christ, my life can truly bring pleasure to my heavenly Father. May we all live in the freedom and joy of this remarkable truth.

Chapter Nine

Indwelling Presence: Marked by the Spirit

"You, however, are not in the flesh but in the Spirit, if in fact the Spirit of God dwells in you. Anyone who does not have the Spirit of Christ does not belong to him." Romans 8:9

In my years of pastoral ministry and theological study, few verses have captured the essence of Christian identity more powerfully than Romans 8:9. After exploring the sobering reality that "those who are in the flesh cannot please God" (Romans 8:8), Paul pivots to a glorious declaration that transforms our understanding of who we are in Christ. Romans 8:9 draws a clear line of demarcation between those who belong to Christ and those who don't, the indwelling presence of the Holy Spirit.

The Radical Shift: "Not in the Flesh but in the Spirit"

The opening phrase, "You, however, are not in the flesh but in the Spirit" reveals a complete transformation of our spiritual condition. Paul isn't simply describing a behavioral improvement but a fundamental change in our spiritual location and identity.

During my military service, I witnessed how a change in uniform signaled a complete change in identity and allegiance. When I put on that uniform, I was no longer simply Bruce the civilian but a Marine representing something greater than myself. Similarly, when the Spirit takes up residence in our lives, we're no longer defined by our fallen human nature (the flesh) but by the Spirit who now indwells us.

This shift isn't merely cosmetic or behavioral. It concerns the very essence of who we are. We haven't just received new guidance or inspiration; we've experienced a supernatural transformation of our fundamental identity. As Paul states elsewhere, "If anyone is in Christ, he is a new creation. The old has passed away; behold, the new has come" (2 Corinthians 5:17).

I remember counseling a young man struggling with persistent sin. He kept lamenting, "This is just who I am." His identity was firmly rooted in his fallen nature. My response was to direct him to Romans 8:9: "No, that's who you were. If you are in Christ, you are not in the flesh but in the Spirit. Your identity has fundamentally changed."

The Divine Indwelling: "If in fact the Spirit of God dwells in you"

The conditional statement that follows, "if in fact the Spirit of God dwells in you" should not be read as casting doubt on the Roman Christians' salvation. Rather, it's Paul's way of highlighting the non-negotiable reality of the Spirit's presence in every true believer.

The word "dwells" (*oikeō* in Greek) carries the sense of taking up permanent residence. This isn't a temporary visitation or occasional influence. The Spirit of God has moved in and made our bodies His temple (1 Corinthians 6:19).

I'm reminded of buying our first home. The difference between visiting a house and owning it is profound. As visitors, we're careful not to move things or make changes. But once we take ownership, we rearrange, renovate, and transform the space according to our purposes. When the Spirit dwells in us, He doesn't come as a guest but as the rightful owner, molding every aspect of our lives to the image of Christ.

This indwelling is not something we achieve through spiritual disciplines or moral effort. It's God's sovereign work in us. As Calvin noted, "It is not from us that we begin to be the temples of God, but from His calling." The Spirit's presence is not the reward for our spiritual progress; it's the cause of it.

The Sobering Reality: "Anyone who does not have the Spirit of Christ does not belong to him"

In this verse, the final statement makes a stark distinction: possessing Christ's Spirit means belonging to Him, and not possessing it means not belonging. There is no third category, no middle ground.

Notice how Paul seamlessly shifts from "the Spirit of God" to "the Spirit of Christ," highlighting the Trinitarian nature of our salvation. The Spirit who indwells us is both the Spirit of the Father and the Spirit of the Son, a beautiful reminder that our salvation involves the work of all three persons of the Trinity.

The phrase "does not belong to him" carries profound implications. In the original Greek, it literally means "is not of him" suggesting not merely a lack of relationship but a lack of essential connection. Those without the Spirit are not merely estranged from Christ; they have no part in Him whatsoever.

I recall a funeral I conducted for a man who had attended church for decades but showed no evidence of spiritual life. His family sought comfort in the fact that he had been "religious." But religion without regeneration offers false hope. The distinguishing mark of those who belong to Christ is not religious activity but the indwelling presence of the Holy Spirit.

Four Implications of This Truth

1. The Spirit's Presence Is the Defining Mark of a Christian

First and foremost, Romans 8:9 teaches us that the indwelling Spirit, not external religious performance, defines Christian identity. This liberates us from both legalism and licentiousness.

I once counseled a couple torn apart by the husband's religious performance. He attended every church function, maintained rigid personal disciplines, and criticized his wife's "spiritual laziness." Yet his life displayed none of the Spirit's fruit: love, joy, peace, patience, kindness, goodness, faithfulness, gentleness, and self-control (Galatians 5:22-23). His religion had become a form of self-righteousness that damaged his relationship with both God and his wife.

Romans 8:9 reminds us that Christianity is fundamentally about a divine presence, not human performance. The question is not "How religious are you?" but "Does the Spirit of God dwell in you?"

2. The Spirit's Presence Is Universal in All Believers

This verse also teaches that all true believers have the Holy Spirit. There is no such thing as a "second blessing" that divides Christians into those who have the Spirit and those who don't. The Spirit's indwelling is not reserved for spiritual elites or those who have undergone special experiences.

In my early ministry, I encountered teachings suggesting that speaking in tongues was the necessary evidence of having received the Spirit. But Romans 8:9 makes clear that all who belong to Christ have His Spirit. The evidence of the Spirit's presence is not any particular spiritual gift but the fruit of transformed character and the internal witness that we are God's children (Romans 8:16).

3. The Spirit's Presence Is Transformative

While the Spirit's indwelling is immediate upon conversion, His transforming work is progressive. Being "in the Spirit" means we now have the capacity and calling to "walk according to the Spirit" (Romans 8:4).

I've witnessed this reality countless times in my years of ministry. A hardened, self-centered businessman comes to Christ and gradually becomes generous and compassionate. A bitter, resentful woman slowly discovers the freedom of forgiveness. A young man trapped in addiction finds progressive victory through the Spirit's power. These transformations are not instantaneous, but they are inevitable where the Spirit truly dwells.

As the Puritan John Owen wrote, "The Spirit never so dwells in any in this world as to transform them perfectly into the image of Christ." Yet where He dwells, He is always at work, conforming us to Christ's image from one degree of glory to another (2 Corinthians 3:18).

4. The Spirit's Presence Provides Assurance

Finally, this verse offers profound assurance to believers while challenging the complacency of mere professors. If you have trusted in Christ, you can know with certainty that you belong to Him because His Spirit dwells in you.

During a particularly difficult time of ministry, I found myself battling doubts about my own salvation. Was I truly regenerated, or was I just going through religious motions? In my distress, the Lord drew me back to Romans 8:9-16, reminding me that the very concern I felt was evidence of the Spirit's work in my life. My desire to please God, my grief over sin, my love for Christ and His people; these were manifestations of the Spirit's indwelling presence.

How Do We Know If the Spirit Dwells in Us?

This question naturally arises from our text. Since the Spirit's presence is invisible, how can we be certain He dwells in us? Scripture provides several evidences:

New spiritual desires and affections: Those indwelt by the Spirit desire the things of God (Romans 8:5).

Internal witness: "The Spirit himself bears witness with our spirit that we are children of God" (Romans 8:16).

Conviction of sin: The Spirit convicts us when we stray from God's path (John 16:8).

Fruit of the Spirit: love, joy, peace, patience, kindness, goodness, faithfulness, gentleness, and self-control gradually appear in our lives (Galatians 5:22-23).

Faith in Christ: The very ability to trust in Christ as Lord and Savior comes from the Spirit (1 Corinthians 12:3).

These evidences aren't about perfection but direction. No believer perfectly displays these qualities, but all true believers exhibit them in increasing measure over time.

Conclusion: The Wonder of Divine Indwelling

Romans 8:9 presents us with both comfort and challenge. The comfort lies in knowing that if we have trusted Christ; we are no longer defined by our fallen nature but by the Spirit who indwells us. We belong to Christ, and nothing can separate us from His love.

The challenge comes in recognizing that this indwelling presence must manifest itself in transformed lives. As the Spirit takes up residence in us, He inevitably begins the work of renovation, conforming us to the image of Christ.

I find myself continually amazed at this reality. The God who created the universe, who spoke galaxies into existence, has chosen to dwell within frail human vessels like us. And His presence is not merely a theological abstraction but a living reality that transforms us from the inside out.

In my time of ministry, I've never found a more profound truth than this: if you belong to Christ, you are not in the flesh but in the Spirit, because the Spirit of God dwells in you. This is the heart of Christian identity and the foundation of Christian hope. May we live each day in the conscious awareness of this indwelling presence, yielding ourselves to the Spirit's transforming work until we are fully conformed to the image of Christ.

Chapter Ten

Spirit-Life Amid Mortal Bodies

"But if Christ is in you, although the body is dead because of sin, the Spirit is life because of righteousness." Romans 8:10

As I continue our journey through Paul's magnificent eighth chapter of Romans, I find myself standing before yet another profound spiritual reality. Having established in verse 9 that the Holy Spirit indwells true believers, Paul now explores the tension of our present existence, living with the Spirit of life within bodies still subject to death.

The Present Reality: "The Body is Dead Because of Sin"

When Paul writes that "the body is dead because of sin," he isn't suggesting our physical bodies are currently lifeless. Rather, he's acknowledging a sobering reality: our bodies bear the sentence of death. Like a terminal patient whose diagnosis is certain though the end hasn't yet come, our physical frames exist under death's inescapable decree.

I remember visiting a dear saint in our congregation during her final days. Though her body was failing rapidly, her spirit remained vibrant with faith. "Pastor Bruce," she whispered, "this old tent is collapsing, but I'm more alive in Christ than ever before." Her words perfectly captured the paradox Paul describes in this verse.

Sin has done this to us all. From the moment Adam transgressed in the garden, death entered the human experience as sin's bitter wage (Romans 6:23). No scientific advancement, medical breakthrough, or health regimen can ultimately prevent our bodies from returning to the dust from which they came. The mortality rate remains stubbornly fixed at 100 percent.

This truth confronted me powerfully during my years as a Marine. I witnessed the fragility of human life in a way that left indelible impressions. Strong young men, seemingly invincible in their prime, could be reduced to lifeless forms in mere moments. Later, as a pastor, I stood beside graves, committing bodies to the earth while speaking words of resurrection hope. Our bodies are indeed "dead because of sin" not merely dying, but existing under death's inescapable sentence.

Yet, this somber diagnosis sets the stage for the glorious contrast Paul presents next.

The Spiritual Reality: "The Spirit is Life Because of Righteousness"

Against the backdrop of our body's mortality stands the vibrant reality of the Spirit's life within us. Notice Paul doesn't just say the Spirit gives life (though that's certainly true); the indwelling Spirit Himself constitutes the very life-principle of the believer.

The phrase "because of righteousness" refers primarily to the righteousness we receive through faith in Christ. It's not our personal righteousness that brings spiritual life, but the perfect righteousness of Jesus imputed to us. As the Reformers rightly insisted, we are justified by faith alone, but the faith that justifies is never alone; it produces the fruit of righteousness in our lives.

I've observed this principle countless times throughout my ministry. When a person truly encounters Christ and receives His righteousness as a gift, the Spirit brings an unmistakable vitality to their entire being. Eyes that once were dull with spiritual death begin to sparkle with divine life. The heart that was cold and indifferent to God's glory now beats with holy affections. The mind once darkened by sin is progressively illuminated by truth.

During my time teaching at the seminary, I often witnessed this transformation in my students. One young man arrived spiritually lethargic and academically disinterested. But after a profound encounter with God's grace during a campus revival, everything changed. His studies became acts of worship. His relationships reflected Christ's love. His ministry flowed with Spirit-empowered effectiveness. Though his body remained subject to the same physical limitations, his spirit pulsated with the life of God.

The Practical Implications of This Tension

Living between these realities, the body's mortality and the Spirit's vitality, creates a unique tension in the Christian experience. Let me explore several implications this has for our daily walk with Christ:

1. We Must Accept Our Physical Limitations

First, Paul's teaching reminds us to humbly accept our physical limitations. Despite the Spirit's presence within us, our bodies remain subject to weakness, aging, illness, and eventually death. Some prosperity teachers falsely claim that Christians should never be sick or experience physical decline if they have enough faith. But Paul's words here offer no such promise.

I learned this lesson during a health crisis my own life. After pushing myself beyond reasonable limits, I collapsed and needed back surgery. During that humbling season, the Lord gently reminded me that acknowledging my body's limitations wasn't spiritual weakness but stewardly wisdom. Even as the Spirit brings abundant life to our inner being, our outer nature wastes away (2 Corinthians 4:16).

2. We Must Cultivate Spiritual Vitality

Second, while accepting our physical limitations, we must actively cultivate the spiritual life the indwelling Spirit offers. If the Spirit truly is life within us, shouldn't this vitality be evident in our daily experience?

The 17th century Puritan John Owen wisely noted, "The vigor and power of our spiritual life depends on the mortification of the deeds of the flesh." In other words, we experience the Spirit's life most abundantly when we put to death the sinful tendencies that remain within us. This requires intentional discipline, regular communion with God through His Word and prayer, fellowship with other believers, and vigilant resistance against sin's pull.

I've found in my own spiritual journey that neglecting these disciplines quickly leads to spiritual lethargy. Though the Spirit's life is always present in the believer, neglect or disobedience can tragically diminish our experience of that life.

3. We Must Live with Eternal Perspective

Third, understanding the tension between our mortal bodies and the eternal life within us cultivates a proper eternal perspective. We learn to hold the temporal loosely while gripping the eternal firmly.

Paul captures this mindset beautifully in 2 Corinthians 4:17-18: "For this light momentary affliction is preparing for us an eternal weight of glory beyond all comparison, as we look not to the things that are seen but to the things that are unseen. For the things that are seen are transient, but the things that are unseen are eternal."

When my wife and I experienced the heartbreak of losing our oldest son, this eternal perspective became our lifeline. As we mourned his loss, we clung to the assurance that the Spirit of life within him could never be extinguished. Death might claim his body temporarily, but it could not touch the eternal life he possessed in Christ.

4. We Should Anticipate the Final Resolution

Finally, this tension points us forward to its ultimate resolution, the redemption of our bodies. Though Paul doesn't explicitly mention this hope until verse 23, it hovers implicitly over our present text.

The indwelling Spirit is not only life for our present experience but also the guarantee of our future bodily resurrection. As Paul declares elsewhere, "If the Spirit of him who raised Jesus from the dead dwells in you, he who raised Christ Jesus from the dead will also give life to your mortal bodies through his Spirit who dwells in you" (Romans 8:11).

During my pastoral years, I found this truth particularly meaningful when ministering to aging saints. As they faced the increasing limitations and discomforts of their failing bodies, I would remind them: "The same Spirit who gives life to your soul today will one day give resurrection life to your body. The best is yet to come!"

Practical Application: Living in the Tension

How then shall we live in this tension between our mortal bodies and the Spirit's life within us? Let me offer several practical suggestions:

First, care for your physical body as a steward, not as an owner. Though your body is "dead because of sin," it remains God's temple and your ministry instrument for however long your earthly pilgrimage lasts. Proper nutrition, adequate rest, reasonable exercise, and necessary medical care honor the Lord who purchased you with His blood.

Second, nourish your spiritual life daily through communion with Christ. Jonathan Edwards wisely observed that the Spirit typically works through means, not mystical shortcuts. Regular Bible reading, thoughtful meditation, fervent prayer, corporate worship, and faithful service create channels through which the Spirit's life flows abundantly.

Third, view suffering through the lens of sanctification. When physical pain, limitation, or decline comes (and it will), receive it as an opportunity for the Spirit's life to shine more brightly through your weakness. Some of the most spiritually vibrant believers I've known were those whose bodies were most thoroughly broken.

Fourth, meditate regularly on your future hope. The Spirit's presence within you guarantees that your current experience of spiritual life will eventually extend to your body as well. The same voice that called, "Lazarus, come forth!" will one day summon your mortal remains to glorious immortality.

Conclusion: The Spirit's Life Sustains Us Now

As I reflect on Romans 8:10, I'm struck by the profound pastoral wisdom in Paul's teaching. He minimizes neither the reality of our physical mortality nor diminishes the wonder of the Spirit's life within us. Instead, he holds these truths in perfect tension, offering both realistic acknowledgment of our present condition and triumphant hope for our eternal destiny.

In this present age, we live as those who have tasted the powers of the age to come (Hebrews 6:5). The spiritual life we now experience through the indwelling Spirit is but the firstfruits of the full harvest awaiting us in eternity. Though our bodies remain subject to weakness, disease, aging, and death, the life-giving Spirit within us guarantees that death will not have the final word.

As Augustine beautifully expressed: "We are talking about God. What wonder is it that you do not understand? If you do understand, then it is not God." So it is with this profound tension of the Spirit's life within our mortal bodies. We may not fully comprehend it, but we can fully experience its reality as we walk by faith, not by sight, until faith becomes sight and mortality is swallowed up by life.

In the meantime, we press on, outwardly wasting away yet inwardly being renewed day by day, confident that the same Spirit who raised Christ from the dead dwells within us, making us alive to God both now and forevermore.

Chapter Eleven

Resurrection Power: Life from the Spirit

"If the Spirit of him who raised Jesus from the dead dwells in you, he who raised Christ Jesus from the dead will also give life to your mortal bodies through his Spirit who dwells in you." Romans 8:11

In the previous passage, we examined the profound tension between our mortal bodies and the Spirit's life within us. Now, as we move to Romans 8:11, Paul deepens this truth by connecting our present spiritual life to our future bodily resurrection. This single verse contains an extraordinary promise that deserves careful unpacking. As we examine it, we'll discover how the resurrection power that brought Jesus from the tomb is the same power that dwells within every believer, guaranteeing our future bodily resurrection.

The Divine Symmetry of Resurrection

Paul's argument here follows a beautiful theological symmetry. Let me outline the logical progression:

1. God the Father raised Jesus from the dead through the Holy Spirit.

2. This same Holy Spirit now dwells in believers.

3. Therefore, God will raise believers' bodies through this same Spirit.

Notice the perfection of God's redemptive plan. The same power that conquered death in Christ is now resident within us, not only for present spiritual vitality but also as the guarantee of our future bodily resurrection.

During my years as a Marine, I witnessed the importance of symmetry in military operations. A well-executed plan requires consistency from beginning to end. God's redemptive plan displays this divine symmetry: what He began in Christ's resurrection, He will complete in ours.

The Spirit as the Agent of Resurrection

Paul's language is precise and significant. He refers to "the Spirit of him who raised Jesus from the dead." This description highlights the Spirit's role in the resurrection of Christ. While Scripture often attributes Jesus' resurrection to the Father (Acts 2:24; Galatians 1:1), here Paul emphasizes the Spirit's agency in this miraculous event.

This is consistent with other passages that connect the Spirit to resurrection power. In 1 Peter 3:18, we read that Christ was "put to death in the flesh but made alive in the spirit." Similarly, Romans 1:4 states that Jesus was "declared to be the Son of God in power according to the Spirit of holiness by his resurrection from the dead."

The Holy Spirit, then, was the divine power through which God raised Jesus from the dead. This same Spirit now dwells within believers, linking us to the resurrection power that conquered death itself.

I recall visiting Arlington National Cemetery during my military service, standing among thousands of white markers representing fallen soldiers. The finality of death felt overwhelming. Yet Paul reminds us that the Spirit within us is stronger than death itself. The same power that left an empty tomb in Jerusalem now resides in every believer.

The Present Reality: "The Spirit... Dwells in You"

Paul's argument hinges on a crucial present reality: "the Spirit... dwells in you." This indwelling is not potential or theoretical but actual and experiential for every genuine believer.

Throughout my pastoral ministry, I encountered many Christians who doubted their salvation because they didn't feel particularly spiritual. I would often point them to this passage, reminding them that the Spirit's indwelling isn't primarily about feelings but about God's faithfulness to His covenant promises.

The Spirit's indwelling is an objective reality for every person who has trusted in Christ. As Paul stated in Romans 8:9, "Anyone who does not have the Spirit of Christ does not belong to him." Conversely, everyone who belongs to Christ has the Spirit dwelling within them.

This indwelling marks the fulfillment of the prophetic promise in Ezekiel 36:26-27: "And I will give you a new heart, and a new spirit I will put within you. And I will remove the heart of stone from your flesh and give you a heart of flesh.

And I will put my Spirit within you, and cause you to walk in my statutes and be careful to obey my rules."

What the prophets anticipated has become reality for believers in the new covenant. The very Spirit who raised Jesus from the dead has taken up residence within us. This indwelling is the distinguishing mark of God's covenant people in the present age.

The Future Promise: "Will Also Give Life to Your Mortal Bodies"

Based on this present reality, Paul points to a future certainty: the resurrection of our mortal bodies. The logic is compelling: if God's Spirit raised Jesus from death, and this same Spirit now dwells in us, then our bodies will experience the same resurrection power.

Notice that Paul specifies "your mortal bodies." He's not speaking of a disembodied spiritual existence but the resurrection of our physical bodies. Christianity does not promise escape from materiality but rather its redemption and transformation.

I remember standing at the bedside of a dear saint in my congregation as cancer ravaged her body. Her once-vibrant frame had become thin and weak, her voice barely audible. Yet her eyes shone with the confidence of this promise: "Pastor Bruce," she whispered, "soon this broken body will be made new." Death may have claimed her temporarily, but it couldn't touch the eternal life she possessed in Christ.

The resurrection Paul promises isn't merely resuscitation, a return to the same frail existence we currently experience. Rather, it's transformation into an existence like Christ's resurrected body: imperishable, powerful, and spiritual (1 Corinthians 15:42-44). As Paul declares in Philippians 3:21, Christ "will transform our lowly body to be like his glorious body, by the power that enables him even to subject all things to himself."

The Vital Connection: "Through His Spirit Who Dwells in You"

Paul concludes by emphasizing the means by which this resurrection will occur: "through his Spirit who dwells in you." The indwelling Spirit forms the vital connection between Christ's resurrection and ours.

This phrase highlights an important theological truth: our resurrection isn't merely an arbitrary divine decision but the natural outworking of our union with Christ through the Spirit. Because we are united to Christ by the Spirit, what happened to Him will happen to us. His resurrection secures and guarantees ours.

In seminary, I often explained this concept to my students using the image of a train. Christ is the locomotive, and we are the cars connected to Him. Where He goes, we necessarily follow. His passage through death and resurrection blazes the trail that we will inevitably travel because we are connected to Him by the Spirit.

Theological Implications of Romans 8:11

This rich verse contains several profound theological implications that shape our understanding of the Christian life.

1. The Trinitarian Nature of Our Salvation

First, notice the Trinitarian dimensions of our salvation. The Father initiates the resurrection ("him who raised Jesus"), the Son is the firstfruits of resurrection ("raised Christ Jesus"), and the Spirit is the agent who accomplishes resurrection both in Christ and in us.

Our salvation is the work of the triune God from beginning to end. The Father plans, the Son accomplishes, and the Spirit applies. This Trinitarian pattern appears throughout Scripture's presentation of redemption.

During my years of teaching systematic theology, I emphasized that salvation is never the work of just one divine person but always the harmonious operation of all three persons of the Godhead. The doctrine of the Trinity isn't an abstract philosophical puzzle but the very structure of the gospel itself.

2. The Certainty of Our Hope

Second, this verse establishes the absolute certainty of our resurrection hope. Our future resurrection isn't merely possible or probable but guaranteed by God's past action in raising Christ and His present action in indwelling us by His Spirit.

The indwelling Spirit serves as what Paul elsewhere calls the "guarantee" or "down payment" of our inheritance (2 Corinthians 1:22; 5:5; Ephesians 1:14). Just as a down payment legally obligates the completion of a transaction, so the Spirit's presence within us legally obligates God (by His own covenant faithfulness) to complete our redemption through bodily resurrection.

I've counseled many believers facing death, both their own, and that of loved ones. The comfort I've offered isn't philosophical speculation about the afterlife but the solid certainty of God's promise. The same God who kept His word in raising Jesus will keep His word in raising us.

3. The Holistic Nature of Redemption

Third, this verse underscores the holistic nature of God's redemptive purposes. God intends to redeem not just our souls but our bodies as well. Christianity rejects both materialism (which reduces humans to mere physical entities) and spiritualism (which devalues the physical in favor of the spiritual).

Instead, biblical Christianity affirms the goodness of God's physical creation and His intention to redeem it completely.

Our bodies are not prisons from which we seek escape but divine creations that will be gloriously renewed.

This holistic vision has profound implications for how we view our bodies now. They are not disposable containers but the temple of the Holy Spirit (1 Corinthians 6:19), destined for glorious resurrection. This should motivate both appropriate care for our physical health and appropriate use of our bodies in God's service.

Practical Applications for Christian Living

How does this magnificent truth about resurrection power apply to our daily Christian experience? Let me suggest several practical applications.

1. Live with Resurrection Confidence

First, this verse calls us to live with resurrection confidence in the face of death. The resurrection power that dwells within us is stronger than death itself. We need not fear death as those without hope (1 Thessalonians 4:13).

I've observed a marked difference between the deaths of believers and unbelievers. Those without Christ often approach death with desperate denial or grim resignation. Believers, however, can face death with peaceful confidence, knowing it is not the end but merely a transition to fuller life.

2. Embrace Physical Stewardship

Second, the promise of bodily resurrection should motivate proper stewardship of our physical bodies. While avoiding both the extremes of asceticism and indulgence, we should care for our bodies as temples of the Holy Spirit and instruments for God's service.

This doesn't mean obsessing over physical appearance or health to the neglect of spiritual priorities. Rather, it means recognizing that how we treat our bodies matters to God because He values the physical creation and intends to redeem it.

3. Find Comfort in Physical Suffering

Third, this promise offers profound comfort in times of physical suffering. Whether facing the pain of disease, the limitations of disability, or the decline of aging, we can endure with hope knowing that these afflictions are temporary.

I remember visiting a church member who had suffered a devastating stroke that left him paralyzed and unable to speak. On his communication board, he had written out Romans 8:11. Each time I visited, he would point to this verse, his eyes communicating what his lips could not: "This broken body will be made new."

4. Serve with Resurrection Power

Fourth, we should recognize that the same Spirit who will raise our bodies in the future empowers our service in the present. The resurrection power within us isn't dormant until the last day but active now in sanctification and ministry.

As Paul prays in Ephesians 1:19-20, may we know "what is the immeasurable greatness of his power toward us who believe, according to the working of his great might that he worked in Christ when he raised him from the dead." This resurrection power enables us to live beyond our natural abilities and limitations for God's glory.

Conclusion: Living in Resurrection Hope

As I reflect on Romans 8:11, I'm struck by the perfect balance of Paul's theology. He minimizes neither the reality of our present physical mortality nor diminishes the certainty of our future physical resurrection. Instead, he grounds both in the person and work of the Holy Spirit, who connects us to Christ's resurrection.

The Spirit's indwelling isn't merely a subjective religious experience but the objective guarantee of our future bodily resurrection. What God began in raising Christ from the dead, He will complete by raising us as well through the same Spirit.

This truth has sustained me through many dark valleys, standing beside countless gravesides, witnessing the ravages of disease in beloved church members, and facing my own mortality. In each case, the promise of Romans 8:11 has shone like a beacon: the Spirit who raised Jesus dwells in us and will give life to our mortal bodies.

So let us live as resurrection people, confident in God's promise, faithful in present service, and hopeful in future expectation. For the same power that left an empty tomb in Jerusalem now dwells within us, guaranteeing that death will not have the final word.

Chapter Twelve

Obligation Redefined: The Debt We No Longer Owe

"So then, brothers, we are debtors, not to the flesh, to live according to the flesh."
Romans 8:12

As we continue our journey through Romans 8, we arrive at verse 12. This verse marks a critical transition in Paul's argument, moving from the glorious promise of resurrection to the practical implications for our daily lives.

I've often thought about how masterfully Paul structures his theology. He never leaves us floating in abstract doctrinal concepts but always brings us back to concrete application.

Here, after establishing the indwelling of the Spirit as our guarantee of resurrection, he immediately addresses how this reality should transform our present conduct.

Notice how Paul frames this application in terms of obligation. The word "debtors" (*opheiletēs* in Greek) carries the sense of being under obligation, of owing something. But what makes this verse particularly striking is that Paul defines our obligation negatively. He tells us what we do not owe rather than what we do owe.

No Longer in Debt to the Flesh

"We are debtors, not to the flesh, to live according to the flesh." This statement represents a profound reorientation of our understanding of obligation.

In my years of ministry, I've encountered countless people living under a crushing sense of obligation to their sinful desires. The alcoholic who feels he must have another drink. The porn addict who believes he can't go a day without viewing explicit material. The materialist who is driven to acquire more possessions. The approval-seeker who feels compelled to please everyone. Each lives as though they owe something to these fleshly desires, as though they must satisfy them.

But Paul declares with apostolic authority: you do not owe the flesh anything. You have no obligation to fulfill its demands. You are not indebted to your sinful nature.

This declaration of freedom strikes at the heart of how sin operates in our lives. Sin often functions through a kind of psychological extortion. It whispers, "You owe me this. You need this. You can't be happy without this." Paul exposes this lie. The flesh has no legitimate claim on us. We have no obligation to satisfy its demands.

Breaking the False Narrative

When I was a young Marine, I remember how easy it was to fall into patterns of sin during deployments away from home. There was a prevailing narrative that "what happens on deployment stays on deployment" and that certain indulgences were simply part of military life. Many of us lived as though we owed something to our fleshly desires, as though satisfying them was an obligation we couldn't escape.

It wasn't until I encountered the liberating truth of Romans 8:12 that I realized this was a false narrative. I didn't owe my flesh anything. I had no obligation to live according to its dictates. This realization was profoundly freeing. Sin lost much of its power when I recognized it had no legitimate claim on me.

The Basis of Our Freedom

What gives Paul the confidence to declare we have no obligation to the flesh? The answer lies in the preceding verses. Because the Spirit of him who raised Jesus from the dead dwells in us (v. 11), we are no longer controlled by the flesh but by the Spirit (v. 9). The indwelling Spirit has severed our obligation to the flesh.

Think of it this way: When a debt is paid in full, the debtor no longer has any obligation to the creditor. Christ has paid our debt to sin in full. As Paul says in Romans 6:18, "having been set free from sin, [we] have become slaves of righteousness." The transaction is complete. Our account with sin has been settled.

A New Obligation Implied

While Paul explicitly states what we don't owe, he implies what we do owe. By stating that we are debtors, but not to the flesh, he suggests there is someone to whom we do owe an obligation. Though he doesn't explicitly name this creditor in verse 12, the context makes it clear: we are debtors to God and specifically to the Holy Spirit who dwells within us.

Indebted to Grace

Our debt to God is not a burden but a joyful response to grace. It's not that we must pay God back for salvation; that would contradict the very nature of grace. Rather, we owe Him our allegiance, obedience, and worship because He has freed us from sin's tyranny at the cost of His Son's life.

I often think of the parable Jesus told about the servant who was forgiven a massive debt by his master, only to turn around and demand payment from a fellow servant who owed him a trivial amount (Matthew 18:23-35). The first servant failed to recognize that being forgiven placed him under a new kind of obligation, not to repay, which was impossible, but to extend the same grace he had received.

Similarly, we who have been forgiven our debt of sin stand under a new obligation, not to earn or maintain our salvation, but to live in grateful response to the One who saved us.

Indebted to the Spirit

More specifically in this context, Paul is pointing to our obligation to live according to the Spirit who dwells within us. If the Spirit has given us life (v. 11), then we owe it to Him to live by His direction and power.

This is not a burden but a blessing. The Spirit's guidance leads to life and peace (v. 6), while the flesh leads only to death. Living according to our obligation to the Spirit is the path to true fulfillment and joy.

The Practical Implications

Understanding that we are no longer obligated to the flesh but are instead obligated to God through His Spirit has profound practical implications for Christian living.

1. Freedom from Sin's Tyranny

First, it means we can reject sin's demands with confidence. When temptation comes knocking, claiming we owe it our attention and compliance, we can firmly respond, "I owe you nothing. My debt to you has been paid in full by Christ."

I've counseled many believers struggling with habitual sin who feel trapped in a cycle of guilt and obligation. They sin, feel guilty, and then sin again to escape the guilt, creating a downward spiral. Breaking this cycle begins with embracing the truth that they have no obligation to the flesh. They can say no to sin not merely because it's wrong but because they owe it nothing.

2. Freedom for Joyful Obedience

Second, our new obligation to God is not a form of legalistic bondage but of joyful freedom. We obey not to earn God's favor but because we already have it. Our obedience flows from gratitude, not fear.

In my pastoral ministry, I've observed that believers who grasp this distinction serve God with remarkably different attitudes than those who don't. Those who see obedience as paying off a debt to God often serve with resentment, anxiety, and spiritual exhaustion. Those who see obedience as a grateful response to grace already received serve with joy, creativity, and perseverance.

3. A New Perspective on Temptation

Third, this understanding transforms how we view temptation. Rather than seeing temptation as an overwhelming force we can't resist, we can recognize it as an illegitimate demand from a creditor to whom we owe nothing.

I remember counseling a young man struggling with sexual addiction who had repeatedly failed in his attempts to overcome it. His breakthrough came when he stopped viewing his temptations as irresistible urges he was obligated to satisfy and started seeing them as demands from a tyrant who had no legitimate authority over him. This shift in perspective, grounded in the truth of Romans 8:12, gave him new strength to resist.

Living Out Our True Obligation

So how do we practically live as those who are no longer obligated to the flesh but to the Spirit? Let me suggest several applications.

1. Consciously Reject False Obligations

When temptation comes, consciously remind yourself: "I owe sin nothing. I have no obligation to satisfy this desire in a sinful way." Speak this truth to yourself before temptation strikes, not just during its assault.

2. Cultivate Gratitude for Grace

Regularly meditate on the grace that has freed you from sin's debt. A heart filled with gratitude to God has little room for allegiance to the flesh. As the Puritan John Owen wisely observed, "Be killing sin or it will be killing you." The way we kill sin is by filling our hearts with the grace of God.

3. Acknowledge Your True Obligation

Recognize daily that you do owe something to God, not payment for salvation but the grateful response of a life lived for His glory. This is not a burden but a privilege. As Jesus said, "My yoke is easy, and my burden is light" (Matthew 11:30).

4. Live in the Spirit's Power

Remember that the same Spirit who guarantees your future resurrection empowers your present obedience. You're not left to fight the flesh in your own strength. The indwelling Spirit provides all the resources you need to fulfill your obligation to God.

Conclusion: The Path to True Freedom

In Romans 8:12, Paul redefines obligation in a way that leads to true freedom. By declaring that we are not debtors to the flesh, he liberates us from sin's false claims on our lives. By implying that we are instead debtors to God and His Spirit, he points us to the path of joyful, grateful obedience.

As I reflect on my own journey from being a young Marine captive to sin's demands to being a pastor helping others find freedom in Christ, I'm deeply grateful for this redefined understanding of obligation. It has been transformative in my life and in the lives of countless believers I've had the privilege to serve.

The flesh has no claim on us. We owe it nothing. Instead, we joyfully embrace our obligation to the God who has given us everything in Christ. This is the essence of Christian freedom, not freedom to sin but freedom from sin's false obligations and freedom for grateful service to our true Master.

As we continue our journey through Romans 8, let us walk in the confidence that we are no longer debtors to the flesh but beloved children of God, empowered by His Spirit to live for His glory.

Chapter Thirteen

Life Through the Spirit

"For if you live according to the flesh you will die, but if by the Spirit you put to death the deeds of the body, you will live." Romans 8:13

Having established in Romans 8:12 that we are not debtors to the flesh, Paul continues with a solemn warning and a glorious promise in verse 13. As I've studied this verse over my time in ministry, I've come to see it as one of the most crucial passages in understanding the Christian life. It presents both the deadly danger of sin and the life-giving power of the Spirit with stark clarity.

The Deadly Consequence of Living According to the Flesh

Paul begins with a sobering reality: "For if you live according to the flesh you will die." The "for" connects this verse directly to the previous one, explaining why we are not debtors to the flesh. We owe the flesh nothing because living according to its dictates leads to death.

But what does Paul mean by "death" here? Since he's addressing believers who already possess eternal life, he's not referring to physical death, which comes to all, nor to eternal separation from God, from which true believers are forever secured. Rather, he's speaking of what theologians sometimes call "spiritual death," the deadening of our communion with God, the withering of spiritual vitality, and ultimately, if persisted in without repentance, evidence that regeneration never truly occurred.

I'm reminded of James 1:15, which describes this deadly progression: "Then desire when it has conceived gives birth to sin, and sin when it is fully grown brings forth death." Sin is never static; it's always moving toward death. Like a spiritual cancer, it spreads and destroys everything in its path if left untreated.

During my time as a Marine, I witnessed the destructive power of unaddressed sin. Men with promising futures threw everything away for momentary pleasures. Later, as a pastor, I counseled countless individuals whose lives were devastated by choosing to live according to the flesh. The pattern was always the same. What began as "harmless" indulgence eventually consumed and destroyed.

Living according to the flesh means allowing our unredeemed human nature to dictate our choices, priorities, and actions. It means following desires that oppose God's will rather than submitting those desires to His authority. This way of living is incompatible with genuine spiritual life because it fundamentally contradicts the new nature imparted to believers at regeneration.

The Life-Giving Power of the Spirit

But Paul doesn't leave us in despair. He presents the glorious alternative: "but if by the Spirit you put to death the deeds of the body, you will live." Here is the pathway to true life, not passive resignation to sin but active resistance through the power of the Spirit. Notice several crucial elements in this promise:

1. The Personal Responsibility: "you put to death"

While we depend entirely on the Spirit's power, we are not passive in sanctification. The verb "put to death" (in Greek, *thanatoo*) is in the active voice. We are called to be ruthless executioners of sin in our lives. As John Owen famously stated, "Be killing sin or it will be killing you."

This imagery of execution is intentionally violent. Sin is not to be coddled, managed, or tolerated. It is to be put to death. During my military service, I learned that in combat, hesitation toward an enemy often proves fatal. The same principle applies in spiritual warfare. We cannot negotiate with sin; we must eliminate it.

2. The Divine Empowerment: "by the Spirit"

While we are responsible for putting sin to death, we cannot do so in our own strength. The phrase "by the Spirit" indicates the means by which this mortification occurs. Just as we were regenerated by the Spirit, we are sanctified by the Spirit.

This truth guards against both passive quietism ("let go and let God") and self-reliant moralism. We work, but we work in the strength that God supplies. As Philippians 2:12-13 beautifully expresses this paradox: "Work out your own salvation with fear and trembling, for it is God who works in you, both to will and to work for his good pleasure."

I remember counseling a man struggling with pornography who had tried everything to break free, accountability software, support groups, behavior modification techniques. Yet nothing worked until he began to actively rely on the Spirit's power through prayer, Scripture meditation, and purposeful walking in the light with fellow believers. The change was remarkable, not immediate perfection, but genuine progress and eventual victory.

3. The Specific Target: "the deeds of the body"

Paul identifies what is to be put to death: "the deeds of the body." These are the sinful actions that flow from our yet-unredeemed physical existence. Though believers are spiritually regenerated, our bodies remain affected by sin's corruption until our final redemption (Romans 8:23).

It's important to note that Paul isn't advocating asceticism or teaching that the body itself is evil. Rather, he's addressing those actions performed through the body that express the sinful nature. We are to put to death not our bodies but the sinful deeds done through them.

4. The Promised Result: "you will live"

The conclusion offers magnificent hope: "you will live." This "life" is not merely future eternal existence but present spiritual vitality. It's the abundant life Jesus promised in John 10:10. It's experiencing the reality of being united with the living Christ right now.

In my pastoral ministry, I've observed that the most joyful, peace-filled, and purposeful Christians are not those who have the fewest problems or the most comfortable circumstances. Rather, they are those who actively wage war against sin through the Spirit's power. Their spiritual vibrancy stands in stark contrast to the deadness evident in those who have made peace with their sin.

The Practical Application: How Do We Put Sin to Death by the Spirit?

Understanding this verse is one thing; applying it is another. How do we practically "by the Spirit put to death the deeds of the body"? Let me offer several biblical strategies:

1. Recognize the Presence and Danger of Sin

We cannot fight what we do not acknowledge. Many believers live in denial about the sin in their lives, either through self-deception or because they've redefined sin to accommodate their desires. The first step in mortification is an honest recognition of sin for what it is, rebellion against God that leads to death.

During my seminary teaching years, I often encountered students who could articulate sophisticated theological concepts yet remained blind to obvious sin patterns in their lives. True spiritual growth begins with the humility to see ourselves as we truly are.

2. Rely Consciously on the Holy Spirit

Mortification is impossible in our own strength. We must deliberately depend on the Spirit, crying out for His help in our weakness (Romans 8:26). This means regular prayer that acknowledges our dependence, asking specifically for the Spirit's power to overcome particular sins.

I've developed the habit of beginning each day with a simple prayer: "Holy Spirit, I cannot live this day righteously in my own strength. I need Your power to put to death sin and to walk in obedience. Lead me, empower me, and produce Your fruit in my life today."

3. Renew Your Mind with God's Word

Romans 12:2 instructs us to "be transformed by the renewal of your mind." The Spirit primarily works through the Word of God to transform our thinking, which then transforms our actions. Regular, thoughtful engagement with Scripture is essential for mortification.

In counseling situations, I've often found that persistent sin patterns correlate directly with neglect of God's Word. The mind unrenewed by Scripture remains vulnerable to the deceptions that make sin appear attractive.

4. Remove Yourself from Unnecessary Temptation

While we cannot escape all temptation in this world, we are foolish to deliberately place ourselves in situations that inflame our particular weaknesses. Jesus taught us to pray, "Lead us not into temptation" (Matthew 6:13), indicating that avoiding temptation when possible is part of godly wisdom.

I've known believers who claimed to trust the Spirit's power while needlessly exposing themselves to influences that stirred sinful desires. This isn't faith but presumption. The Spirit empowers us to overcome unavoidable temptation, not to rescue us from foolish choices.

5. Remember Your Identity in Christ

Romans 6:11 instructs us to "consider yourselves dead to sin and alive to God in Christ Jesus." Our fundamental identity has changed; we are no longer defined by sin but by our union with Christ. This truth gives us both the motivation and the confidence to put sin to death.

I often counsel believers to speak this truth to themselves daily: "I am in Christ. Sin is no longer my master. Through the Spirit's power, I can say no to sin and yes to righteousness."

6. Remain in Christian Community

God has designed the Christian life to be lived in community. We need the encouragement, accountability, and support of fellow believers in our battle against sin. Hebrews 3:13 commands us to "exhort one another every day... that none of you may be hardened by the deceitfulness of sin."

In both my military and pastoral experience, I've observed that isolation almost invariably precedes moral failure. The lone soldier is vulnerable in battle; the lone Christian is vulnerable to sin.

Conclusion: The Life-Giving Path of Mortification

Romans 8:13 presents us with two paths, one leading to death, the other to life. The path of life involves the painful but ultimately liberating process of putting sin to death through the Spirit's power.

This mortification is not an optional advanced teaching for especially committed Christians. It is essential to authentic Christian living. As J.I. Packer rightly observed, "Mortification is not an extra feature in the Christian life for super-spiritual people; it is basic Christianity."

The good news is that we are not left with this task alone. The same Spirit who raised Jesus from the dead dwells within us, empowering us to put sin to death and experience the abundant life that is ours in Christ. This is not a hopeless struggle but a fight we are guaranteed to win if we persevere, for God Himself is working in us both to will and to work for His good pleasure.

As I reflect on decades of walking with Christ, through the disciplined environment of military service, the intellectual challenges of seminary teaching, and the pastoral care of countless souls, I can testify that this truth has proven itself reliable. Where sin is consistently mortified through the Spirit's power, true life flourishes. Where sin is tolerated and accommodated, spiritual death inevitably follows.

May we choose the path of life, putting to death the deeds of the body by the Spirit, and thereby experiencing the vibrant, abundant life that is our inheritance in Christ.

Chapter Fourteen

Led by the Spirit: The Mark of God's Children

"For all who are led by the Spirit of God are sons of God." Romans 8:14

This single verse, seemingly simple in its declaration, contains a profound reality that defines authentic Christian existence. Throughout my years of pastoral ministry and theological instruction, I've found Romans 8:14 to be both a source of tremendous comfort and a searching diagnostic tool for the soul. It stands as a divine marker, drawing a clear line between those who merely profess faith and those who genuinely possess it.

The Context of Romans 8:14

To understand the full weight of this verse, we must situate it within Paul's unfolding argument in Romans 8. The apostle has just delivered the solemn warning of verse 13: "For if you live according to the flesh you will die, but if by the Spirit you put to death the deeds of the body, you will live." Paul then presents verse 14 as a logical continuation: "For all who are led by the Spirit of God are sons of God."

The small conjunction "for" is significant. It indicates that verse 14 explains the preceding statement. In other words, those who "by the Spirit put to death the deeds of the body" are precisely those who are "led by the Spirit of God" and thus proven to be "sons of God." This connection establishes a crucial truth: Spirit-led mortification of sin is not just one optional aspect of Christian living; it is the distinguishing mark of divine sonship.

What It Means to Be "Led by the Spirit"

During my time teaching at the seminary, I often found students confused about what it means to be "led by the Spirit." Many had absorbed notions of mystical promptings, subjective impressions, or extraordinary divine guidance. While I wouldn't deny that the Spirit occasionally can work in such ways, Paul's meaning here is far more fundamental and consistent.

To be "led by the Spirit" in Romans 8:14 refers primarily to the Spirit's governance of our moral and ethical lives. This leading isn't primarily about divine guidance for decisions (though the Spirit certainly provides this) but about the Spirit's authoritative direction of our character and conduct. The Spirit leads us into holiness, conforming us to Christ's image.

I recall counseling a young man who claimed the Spirit was "leading him" to leave his wife for another woman. With gentle firmness, I opened Romans 8 and explained that the Spirit's leading never contradicts God's revealed moral will. True spiritual leading always aligns with Scripture and moves us toward greater holiness, not away from it.

The Greek word for "led" (*agontai*) carries the sense of being conducted or guided, but also implies a measure of compulsion or carrying. The Spirit doesn't merely suggest a direction; He actively moves us along the path of righteousness, sometimes against our natural inclinations. This isn't a violation of our will but a transformation of it. As Augustine famously prayed, "Command what You will, and grant what You command."

The Nature of Divine Sonship

Paul declares that those led by the Spirit "are sons of God." The Greek term "sons" (*huioi*) shouldn't be understood in a gender-exclusive sense but rather in its cultural context. In the ancient world, "sons" were legal heirs with full inheritance rights. By using this term, Paul emphasizes our full legal standing as God's children with all accompanying privileges and responsibilities.

Throughout my military career, I witnessed the special relationship between fathers and sons, the pride, the legacy, the shared identity. Yet even the strongest earthly father-son bond pales in comparison to our relationship with God. Divine sonship is not merely sentimental or metaphorical; it is a profound spiritual reality with transformative implications.

Paul elaborates on this sonship in verses 15-16: "For you did not receive the spirit of slavery to fall back into fear, but you have received the Spirit of adoption as sons, by whom we cry, 'Abba! Father!' The Spirit himself bears witness with our spirit that we are children of God." Our sonship isn't characterized by fearful servitude but by intimate fellowship with God as our Abba, our dear Father.

The Universal Application: "All Who Are Led"

Notice the universal scope of Paul's statement: "ALL who are led by the Spirit of God are sons of God." There are no exceptions, no special categories of Christians who are exempt from the Spirit's leading. Every genuine believer experiences this divine guidance toward holiness.

This universal principle works in both directions. Positively, all who are truly led by the Spirit are certainly God's children. Negatively (by implication), those not led by the Spirit cannot rightfully claim to be God's children, regardless of their profession of faith, church attendance, or religious credentials.

During my pastoral years, I encountered many who claimed Christian identity without evidence of the Spirit's leading in their lives. With compassionate honesty, I had to help them understand that genuine faith always produces fruit. As Jesus taught, "Thus you will recognize them by their fruits" (Matthew 7:20).

The Certainty of Our Standing

This verse offers tremendous assurance to the believer genuinely struggling against sin. If you find yourself being led by the Spirit, even imperfectly and with stumbles along the way, you have objective evidence of your standing as God's child. Your desire for holiness and your active cooperation with the Spirit's sanctifying work testify to your authentic spiritual life.

I remember a faithful church member who came to my office in tears, doubting her salvation because of continued struggles with a particular sin. "Pastor," she said, "if I were really saved, wouldn't I have victory by now?" I directed her to Romans 8:14 and asked, "Do you find yourself being led by the Spirit to fight against this sin, even when you fail?" When she affirmed this was true, I explained that her very struggle was evidence of the Spirit's work in her life, not a reason to doubt it.

At the same time, this verse challenges comfortable, nominal Christianity that makes no demands on behavior. In many American churches today, I've observed a dangerous disconnect between professed faith and practical living. Romans 8:14 confronts this disconnect head-on: where there is no Spirit-led movement toward holiness, there is legitimate reason to question whether someone is truly a child of God.

What the Spirit Leads Us Toward

The Spirit's leading is not aimless or abstract. He leads us toward specific expressions of Christlikeness:

1. The Spirit Leads Us to Truth

Jesus promised that "when the Spirit of truth comes, he will guide you into all the truth" (John 16:13). The Spirit consistently leads believers to embrace biblical truth and sound doctrine. When someone consistently rejects clear biblical teaching while claiming to be Spirit-led, we have reason to be concerned.

In seminary, I occasionally encountered students who claimed, "The Spirit has shown me a new interpretation" that contradicted established biblical understanding. I would gently remind them that the same Spirit who inspired Scripture would never lead us to interpretations that undermine its clear meaning.

2. The Spirit Leads Us to Holiness

The Spirit is, after all, the Holy Spirit. His fundamental work is to make us holy as God is holy. He leads us away from sin and toward righteousness. This doesn't mean instant perfection, but it does mean a progressive movement toward greater conformity to Christ's character.

3. The Spirit Leads Us to Love

Paul writes in Galatians 5:22 that "the fruit of the Spirit is love." The Spirit invariably leads God's children to greater love for God and neighbor. Where bitterness, unforgiveness, and hatred persist unchallenged, we must question whether we are truly following the Spirit's leading.

During my years as a Marine, I witnessed how combat and hardship could either harden a man's heart or soften it toward his comrades. Similarly, life's trials either embitter us or, through the Spirit's work, expand our capacity for compassion and love.

4. The Spirit Leads Us to Witness

Jesus said, "You will receive power when the Holy Spirit has come upon you, and you will be my witnesses" (Acts 1:8). The Spirit leads believers to share Christ with others. This doesn't mean everyone becomes an evangelist by gifting, but all Spirit-led believers will have some desire to see others come to know Christ.

Practical Evidences of Being Led by the Spirit

How can we discern whether we are truly being led by the Spirit? Let me suggest several practical evidences:

1. An Increasing Sensitivity to Sin

Those led by the Spirit become increasingly sensitive to sin in their lives. What once seemed insignificant now troubles the conscience. I've observed that spiritual growth often involves feeling more sinful, not less, not because we're sinning more, but because we're more aware of sin's presence.

2. A Growing Desire for God's Word

The Spirit who authored Scripture naturally draws believers to love and study the Bible. Consistent indifference toward Scripture should raise concerns about one's spiritual condition.

3. An Ongoing Battle Against Sin

The Spirit leads us to actively resist sin, not passively accommodate it. This battle may be difficult and marked by temporary setbacks, but the war continues throughout the believer's life.

4. A Deepening Prayer Life

The Spirit leads God's children to cry, "Abba! Father!" (Romans 8:15). He creates in us a desire for communion with God that expresses itself in prayer.

5. A Growing Love for God's People

John writes, "We know that we have passed out of death into life, because we love the brothers" (1 John 3:14). The Spirit leads believers to genuine love for other Christians, especially those different from themselves.

When We Resist the Spirit's Leading

Even as God's children, we sometimes resist the Spirit's leading. This grieving of the Spirit (Ephesians 4:30) doesn't revoke our status as God's children, but it does disrupt our fellowship with God and impede our spiritual growth.

In my pastoral experience, I've observed that prolonged resistance to the Spirit's leading often results in three consequences: loss of joy, diminished spiritual perception, and increased vulnerability to sin's deception. The Spirit never abandons God's true children, but He may withdraw His manifest presence until we return to the path of obedience.

Conclusion: The Privilege and Responsibility of Divine Sonship

Romans 8:14 presents both immense privilege and solemn responsibility. The privilege is clear; we are children of the living God, heirs to all His promises, recipients of His fatherly care. What greater honor could there be?

Yet with this privilege comes responsibility. As God's children, we are called to follow the Spirit's leading in every area of life. We are to "walk by the Spirit" (Galatians 5:16) and "keep in step with the Spirit" (Galatians 5:25). This is not burdensome legalism but the joyful response of beloved children to a perfect Father.

As I reflect on my own journey of faith through military service, pastoral ministry, and theological education, I can testify that the Spirit's leading has been my greatest comfort and strongest anchor. In times of doubt, the evidence of His work in my life has reassured me of my standing as God's child. In times of temptation, His gentle yet firm guidance has kept me from countless sins and sorrows.

Dear reader, if you sense the Spirit's leading in your life, His convicting, guiding, sanctifying work, take heart. This is the unmistakable mark of God's children. But if you find yourself consistently resisting or ignoring the Spirit's direction, I urge you to examine your faith. True children of God are led by His Spirit, not perfectly, but progressively and persistently.

May we all embrace both the privilege and responsibility of being "led by the Spirit of God" as beloved "sons of God."

Chapter Fifteen

Spirit of Adoption: Freedom from Fear

"For you did not receive the spirit of slavery to fall back into fear, but you have received the Spirit of adoption as sons, by whom we cry, "Abba! Father!"" Romans 8:15

In Romans 8:15, this single verse contains a theological treasure trove that has transformed my understanding of the Christian life and continues to shape my daily walk with the Lord.

Two Contrasting Spirits

Paul begins by establishing a stark contrast: "For you did not receive the spirit of slavery to fall back into fear, but you have received the Spirit of adoption." This contrast deserves careful consideration. The "spirit of slavery" and the "Spirit of adoption" represent two fundamentally different ways of relating to God.

When I reflect on the "spirit of slavery," I'm reminded of my early religious experiences. I viewed God primarily as a stern taskmaster, keeping meticulous records of my failures. My relationship with Him was dominated by obligation and fear, fear of punishment, fear of disappointment, fear of rejection. This "spirit of slavery" produces what I call "checklist Christianity," an anxious attempt to accumulate enough spiritual merit to offset our demerits.

I've counseled countless believers trapped in this mindset. One particular seminary student comes to mind. Despite his extensive theological knowledge, he lived in constant spiritual anxiety. "I know God is gracious," he once told me, "but I never feel like I've done enough to deserve that grace." His words revealed the fundamental contradiction of merit-based religion: grace, by definition, cannot be deserved.

The "spirit of slavery" isn't limited to non-Christians. Many genuine believers, especially those from legalistic backgrounds, struggle with this fear-based relationship with God. They've been justified by faith but continue living as though their standing before God depends on their performance.

The Spirit of Adoption

In contrast, Paul declares that believers have received "the Spirit of adoption." This isn't merely a different attitude or perspective; it's the Holy Spirit Himself, functioning in a specific role in our lives. The same Spirit who regenerates us, who indwells us, who sanctifies us, is also the Spirit of adoption.

What does this mean? In Roman culture, adoption was even more significant than in our modern context. An adopted son received full legal standing in the family, with all the rights and privileges of a natural-born son. In fact, Roman adoption was often used to secure suitable heirs for important families, sometimes bypassing natural-born children deemed unworthy.

When God adopts us into His family, He doesn't create a second-class category of children. We aren't God's foster children, temporarily taken in but lacking full family status. We are fully and permanently His, with all the rights and privileges that accompany this new relationship.

No Falling Back into Fear

Paul specifically states that we haven't received the spirit of slavery "to fall back into fear." This phrase suggests that fear was the previous condition of believers before receiving the Spirit of adoption. This aligns perfectly with the biblical testimony about humanity's natural condition.

Throughout Scripture, we see fear as a consequence of sin. After Adam and Eve disobeyed God, they hid themselves, saying, "I heard the sound of you in the garden, and I was afraid" (Genesis 3:10). Fear entered the human experience at the very moment of the Fall, and it has characterized our natural relationship with God ever since.

In my pastoral ministry, I've observed how deeply this fear can be entrenched. One elderly woman who had served faithfully in her church for over sixty years confessed to me her terror about meeting God. "I'm not sure I've done enough," she whispered, tears streaming down her face. Despite decades of Christian service, she remained enslaved to fear.

But the gospel declares that in Christ, we need not fall back into this fear. The Spirit of adoption creates a fundamentally different relationship with God, one characterized by intimacy rather than terror, confidence rather than anxiety.

The Cry of the Heart

Paul continues by saying that through the Spirit of adoption, we "cry, 'Abba! Father!'" This dual address, combining both Aramaic and Greek terms for father, emphasizes the intimacy of our relationship with God.

"Abba" was the Aramaic term used by Jewish children to address their fathers. It was a term of intimacy and trust, roughly equivalent to our "Daddy" or "Papa." Jesus Himself used this term in His prayer in Gethsemane (Mark 14:36), revealing the deep intimacy He enjoyed with the Father.

What astounds me is that through the Spirit of adoption, we are invited into the same intimate relationship with God that Jesus Himself experienced. We approach God not as terrified subjects before a tyrannical king, but as beloved children running to a tender father.

I recall a powerful moment during a visit to a friend. His wife and him took a trip to an orphanage in Eastern Europe to adopt a young boy. This young boy, recently adopted after years in institutional care, was playing with his new father. The joy and security in that child's eyes spoke volumes about the transformation adoption had brought. Where once there had been anxiety and abandonment, there was now belonging and security. This, I realized, is what the Spirit of adoption creates in our relationship with God.

The Spirit's Testimony

It's crucial to understand that this cry of "Abba! Father!" is not something we generate through our own emotional efforts. Paul makes it clear that it is "by" the Spirit that we cry out. The Spirit of adoption creates this intimate address in our hearts.

In the next verse (Romans 8:16), Paul elaborates: "The Spirit himself bears witness with our spirit that we are children of God." This dual testimony, the Holy Spirit confirming to our human spirit, provides the basis for our assurance as God's children.

This has profound implications for how we understand assurance of salvation. Our confidence as God's children doesn't rest primarily on our feelings, our performance, or even our faith. It rests on the objective, ongoing testimony of the Holy Spirit to our spirits.

During a particularly dark time of my life, when doubt and spiritual dryness seemed to overwhelm me, this truth became my anchor. Despite my fluctuating emotions, the Spirit's testimony remained constant. Even when I could barely whisper "Father," I knew that this cry itself was evidence of His work within me.

Practical Implications

This theological truth has immense practical significance for our daily lives as believers. Let me highlight several implications:

1. Freedom from Performance-Based Acceptance

The Spirit of adoption liberates us from the crushing weight of trying to earn God's favor. Our standing as God's children isn't maintained by our spiritual performance, it's secured by the finished work of Christ and confirmed by the Spirit's presence.

I spent too many years on the spiritual treadmill, exhausting myself with religious activity designed to keep God pleased with me. The Spirit of adoption helped me step off that treadmill into the freedom of grace.

2. Confidence in Prayer

Understanding our adoption transforms our prayer life. We approach God not as nervous petitioners hoping to catch the attention of a distracted deity, but as beloved children who have our Father's full attention.

Jesus captured this beautifully in Matthew 7:11: "If you then, who are evil, know how to give good gifts to your children, how much more will your Father who is in heaven give good things to those who ask him!" Our prayers flow from our position as adopted children.

3. Security in Suffering

The Spirit of adoption provides profound security even in life's darkest moments. Suffering often triggers our deepest fears about God's disposition toward us. We wonder, "Is God punishing me? Has He abandoned me?"

But the Spirit continually witnesses to our spirit that we remain God's children even in suffering. In fact, Romans 8 goes on to connect our adoption with our suffering: "and if children, then heirs—heirs of God and fellow heirs with Christ, provided we suffer with him in order that we may also be glorified with him" (Romans 8:17).

4. Motivation for Obedience

Perhaps counterintuitively, the security of adoption creates the strongest motivation for obedience. We obey not to become children but because we already are children who love our Father and desire to please Him.

I've witnessed this principle in healthy families. Children who are secure in their parents' unconditional love naturally desire to please them, not from fear of rejection but from gratitude and love. Similarly, our obedience flows from our secure identity as God's adopted children.

Adoption and the Trinity

This doctrine of adoption through the Spirit connects us to the entire Trinity. We are adopted by the Father, through the redeeming work of the Son, by means of the Spirit. As Paul writes in Galatians 4:4-6: "But when the fullness of time had come, God sent forth his Son, born of woman, born under the law, to redeem those who were under the law, so that we might receive adoption as sons. And because you are sons, God has sent the Spirit of his Son into our hearts, crying, 'Abba! Father!'"

Each person of the Trinity participates in our adoption. The Father predestined us for adoption (Ephesians 1:5). The Son purchased our adoption through His redemptive work. The Spirit implements our adoption by uniting us to Christ and creating the filial cry in our hearts.

Conclusion: From Fear to Freedom

Romans 8:15 charts the trajectory of the believer's life: from the spirit of slavery with its accompanying fear to the Spirit of adoption with its cry of "Abba! Father!" This movement from fear to freedom, from distance to intimacy, from insecurity to confidence, encapsulates the heart of the gospel.

As I've walked with Christ over the decades, I've experienced this transformation not as a onetime event but as an ongoing process. The Spirit of adoption continues to displace remnants of the spirit of slavery in my heart, gradually but persistently deepening my experience of God as Father.

For those still struggling with fear in your relationship with God, I encourage you to meditate deeply on this truth: through Christ, you have received not the spirit of slavery leading to fear, but the Spirit of adoption by whom we cry, "Abba! Father!" Let the Spirit Himself bear witness with your spirit that you are a child of God. And in that secure identity, find freedom from fear.

Chapter Sixteen

Assurance from the Spirit: Children of God

"The Spirit himself bears witness with our spirit that we are children of God," Romans 8:16

Few verses in Scripture have brought me more comfort than this seemingly simple declaration. What appears straightforward on first reading contains depths of theological richness that have sustained saints through the darkest valleys of doubt. After exploring how we've been freed from the spirit of slavery to fear, Paul reveals the positive reality of our new relationship with God; we have received absolute assurance of our adoption.

The Dual Witness

Notice first the remarkable dual witness Paul describes: "The Spirit himself bears witness with our spirit." This isn't a one-sided declaration but a profound harmony of testimony. Two distinct witnesses collaborate to establish this truth.

In my years of pastoral ministry, I've encountered countless believers wrestling with doubt about their salvation. "How can I know for certain I'm saved?" they ask. Paul's answer is clear, we know because of a dual testimony. Our spirit testifies, and God's Spirit confirms that testimony.

The first witness is our own spirit. As believers, there develops within us an inner sense of belonging to God. We find ourselves drawn to Him in prayer, hungering for His Word, grieving when we sin, and delighting in obedience. These spiritual affections aren't manufactured but arise naturally from our regenerated hearts.

I remember my own journey after conversion. Though I couldn't articulate it theologically as a teenager, I knew something fundamental had changed. My desires were different. I found myself wanting to pray, eager to read Scripture, and sensitive to sin in ways I'd never experienced before. My spirit was bearing witness that I belonged to God.

But here's where the beauty of God's provision shines. Paul doesn't leave us with only a subjective internal witness that could be mistaken or manipulated. The second and primary witness is "the Spirit himself." The Holy Spirit, the third person of the Trinity, actively testifies to our adoption.

The Spirit's Testimony

How does the Spirit bear witness? This divine testimony isn't typically a thundering voice or spectacular sign but operates in several vital ways:

1. Through Scripture

The Spirit primarily testifies through the written Word He inspired. As I read promises like "Everyone who calls on the name of the Lord will be saved" (Romans 10:13) or "Whoever believes in him should not perish but have eternal life" (John 3:16), the Spirit applies these truths personally to my heart. He illuminates God's promises and helps me see that they apply to me specifically.

The Westminster Confession beautifully captures this reality when it speaks of "the inward evidence of those graces unto which these promises are made." When I see evidence of faith, repentance, and love for God in my life, graces the Spirit produces, I can look to the promises attached to these graces and find assurance.

2. Through Spiritual Fruit

The Spirit testifies by producing His fruit in our lives. Galatians 5:22-23 describes this fruit as "love, joy, peace, patience, kindness, goodness, faithfulness, gentleness, self-control." When I see these qualities emerging in my life, not perfectly, but progressively, I have evidence of the Spirit's work, confirming my adoption.

I've witnessed this countless times in my own life. When I respond with patience rather than anger, show love rather than indifference, or choose self-control rather than indulgence, I recognize these as the Spirit's fingerprints, not my natural inclinations.

3. Through Christian Affections

Jonathan Edwards, the towering theologian of the First Great Awakening, spoke eloquently of "religious affections," holy desires and emotions produced by the Spirit. The Spirit bears witness by creating in us a love for God, delight in His Word, grief over sin, and joy in Christ.

I've found that when my heart is most tender toward the Lord, perhaps during worship or private prayer, the Spirit often speaks His assurance most clearly. These moments aren't simply emotional experiences but the Spirit's testimony that I truly belong to God.

4. Through Prayer

Perhaps most directly, the Spirit testifies in our prayer life. Paul has just spoken of the Spirit enabling us to cry, "Abba! Father!" This intimate cry of a child to their father doesn't originate with us but is placed within us by the Spirit.

I've experienced moments in prayer when, despite my unworthiness, I've felt overwhelming confidence to approach God as Father. That confidence isn't natural to sinful humans; it's the Spirit bearing witness with my spirit.

The Content of the Testimony

What exactly does the Spirit testify? That "we are children of God." This simple phrase contains a universe of privilege and security.

First, note the present tense: "we are" not "we might become" or "we hopefully will be" but "we are" children of God. Our adoption isn't provisional or probationary but present and permanent.

For years, I misunderstood this. I lived as though my status as God's child fluctuated based on my spiritual performance. Good days meant secure standing; bad days meant questionable standing. But Paul declares a fixed reality: believers are children of God, a status secured by Christ and testified to by the Spirit.

Second, consider the relational nature of this testimony. We're not merely forgiven sinners or pardoned criminals, though we are certainly those things. We're children of God, brought into the most intimate family relationship possible.

In my years of pastoral ministry, I've counseled many who viewed God primarily as Judge, Lawgiver, or distant Deity. They struggled to embrace the familial intimacy Paul describes here. Yet this is precisely what the Spirit testifies; we've been brought into God's family with all the privileges that entails.

Assurance: The Spirit's Gift

This verse establishes that assurance of salvation isn't presumption but the Spirit's gift to God's children. Throughout church history, some have viewed assurance with suspicion, fearing it might lead to complacency. Others have demanded absolute certainty as the necessary mark of true faith.

Reformed theology takes a balanced approach, viewing assurance as the normal, though not universal, experience of believers, and as something that may fluctuate in strength.

The Westminster Confession wisely states: "This certainty is not a bare conjectural and probable persuasion grounded upon a fallible hope; but an infallible assurance of faith founded upon the divine truth of the promises of salvation, the inward evidence of those graces unto which these promises are made, the testimony of the Spirit of adoption witnessing with our spirits that we are the children of God."

I've witnessed this divine work in my own heart through times of both clarity and confusion. There have been times when the Spirit's witness was so clear that doubting my adoption seemed impossible. Other times brought struggles with assurance, requiring me to cling to the objective promises of God rather than subjective feelings.

This is why Paul's teaching on the dual witness is so important. When our spirit's witness grows weak, the objective testimony of the Spirit through Scripture remains. When emotions falter, the evidence of the Spirit's fruit still testifies. The Spirit's witness doesn't depend on our psychological state but on God's unchanging truth.

Distinguishing True and False Assurance

This leads to an important pastoral question: How can we distinguish between genuine spiritual assurance and false security? After all, Scripture warns about those who think they are saved but aren't (Matthew 7:21-23).

First, true assurance is Christ-centered. The Spirit always points to Jesus, not to our own merit or worthiness. If our confidence rests on our good works or religious performance rather than Christ's finished work, it's not the Spirit's testimony.

Second, true assurance produces holiness, not license. As John wrote, "And everyone who thus hopes in him purifies himself as he is pure" (1 John 3:3). The Spirit's assurance doesn't lead to spiritual laziness but to grateful obedience.

Third, true assurance acknowledges the ongoing struggle with sin while maintaining confidence in Christ's victory. The Spirit doesn't testify that we're sinless but that we're children despite our sins.

I've observed many cases of false assurance during my ministry, people confident in their salvation despite unrepentant sin and absence of spiritual fruit. This type of confidence doesn't stem from the Spirit's witness but from self-deception or superficial religion.

Practical Applications

How should this magnificent truth affect our daily lives?

First, we should actively seek the Spirit's assurance. While assurance is the Spirit's gift, we're not passive in the process. We cultivate attentiveness to the Spirit's voice through Scripture reading, prayer, worship, and fellowship with other believers.

Second, we should rest in our adoption rather than constantly questioning it. Many Christians live in perpetual insecurity, repeatedly asking, "Am I really saved?" While self-examination is biblical (2 Corinthians 13:5), endless introspection often reflects unbelief in the Spirit's testimony rather than spiritual vigilance.

Third, we should treasure assurance as one of God's precious gifts. In a world filled with uncertainty, the Spirit offers unshakable confidence about our most important relationship. This assurance becomes an anchor in life's storms and a source of courage in ministry.

Finally, we should let the Spirit's testimony transform our prayers and worship. When we truly grasp that we are God's children, our approach to God changes dramatically. Prayer becomes less formal and more familial. Worship becomes less performance and more the grateful response of a beloved child.

Conclusion: The Unshakable Foundation

As I reflect on Romans 8:16, I'm overwhelmed by God's provision for our assurance. He doesn't leave us to wonder about our standing or to construct shaky towers of self-confidence. Instead, He sends His Spirit to testify alongside our spirit that we truly are His children.

This dual witness provides an unshakable foundation for the Christian life. When Satan accuses, the Spirit testifies. When doubt clouds our minds, the Spirit clarifies. When sin tempts us to despair, the Spirit reminds us of our secure adoption.

In a world of uncertainty, this is certainty. In a culture of shifting identities, this is a fixed identity. In the midst of life's constant changes, this is the unchanging reality: we are children of God, and the Spirit himself bears witness to this glorious truth.

Chapter Seventeen

Heirs with Christ: Sharing in Glory and Suffering

"and if children, then heirs — heirs of God and fellow heirs with Christ, provided we suffer with him in order that we may also be glorified with him." Romans 8:17

As I've meditated on this verse through the years, I've come to see it as one of the most profound statements in all of Scripture about our identity and destiny as believers. Paul moves from the glorious truth of our adoption as God's children to its stunning implications: we are heirs of God and fellow heirs with Christ Himself.

The Staggering Logic of Inheritance

The apostle's reasoning in Romans 8:17 follows a clear and compelling logic. If we are God's children (as established by the Spirit's witness in verse 16), then we are also heirs. This inheritance isn't an afterthought or bonus to our salvation; it's the natural consequence of our adoption. In ancient Roman culture, which formed the background for Paul's readers, adopted children received full inheritance rights equal to biological children. In fact, Roman adoption was often undertaken specifically to secure proper heirs when biological offspring were lacking.

What strikes me most forcefully is the breathtaking scope of our inheritance. We aren't merely heirs to certain blessings or benefits; we are "heirs of God." Think about that phrase. We inherit God Himself, communion with Him, knowledge of Him, and participation in His very life. All that belongs to the Father becomes ours through Christ. The immensity of this truth overwhelms me each time I consider it.

Even more astonishing, we are "fellow heirs with Christ." The eternal Son, who by nature deserves all glory and honor, shares His inheritance with us who deserve nothing but judgment. Jesus isn't possessive of His privileges but welcomes us to share in everything the Father has given Him. This exemplifies the self-giving nature of our triune God.

The Connection Between Suffering and Glory

Yet Paul introduces a sobering qualification to this glorious promise: "provided we suffer with him in order that we may also be glorified with him." Here we encounter one of the great paradoxes of the Christian faith; the inseparable connection between suffering and glory.

Throughout my ministry, I've observed many believers struggle with this connection. Some adopt a "prosperity gospel" that promises glory without suffering, while others become so fixated on suffering that they lose sight of glory altogether. But Paul permits neither distortion. In God's economy, suffering and glory are linked in an unbreakable bond, just as they were in Christ's own experience.

When I served as a Marine, I learned something about the connection between hardship and honor. Those who endured the rigors of training and the challenges of deployment shared a special bond and dignity. That military experience provides a faint echo of the principle Paul describes here: glory comes through suffering, not apart from it.

The qualification "provided we suffer with him" doesn't suggest that our suffering earns or merits our glorification. Rather, it indicates that suffering with Christ is the pathway through which we reach glory. Just as Christ's path to glory led through Gethsemane and Golgotha, our path to glory leads through valleys of pain and sacrifice.

What Does It Mean to Suffer with Christ?

What exactly does it mean to "suffer with him"? I've encountered various interpretations in my years of study and teaching.

First, suffering with Christ includes suffering for Christ's sake, enduring persecution, rejection, or hardship because of our identification with Him. Jesus promised this would happen: "If they persecuted me, they will also persecute you" (John 15:20). Throughout church history and in many parts of the world today, believers experience direct opposition for bearing Christ's name.

I recall meeting a pastor from a restricted nation whose ministry had cost him imprisonment, torture, and family separation. He embodied this dimension of suffering with Christ in ways most Western believers rarely experience. Yet his countenance radiated joy despite his wounds. He understood that suffering with Christ is a privilege, not merely a burden.

Second, suffering with Christ includes participation in Christ's ongoing compassion for a broken world. When we weep with those who weep, bear others' burdens, and enter into the pain of the oppressed and marginalized, we share in Christ's own suffering love. The Christian who remains insulated from others' pain has not fully embraced suffering with Christ.

Third, suffering with Christ includes the painful process of sanctification, dying to sin and self. Paul describes this elsewhere as being "crucified with Christ" (Galatians 2:20) and as putting to death the deeds of the body (Romans 8:13). The mortification of sin is painful, like cutting off a hand or gouging out an eye, to use Jesus' vivid metaphors. Yet this suffering produces the peaceable fruit of righteousness.

Each of these dimensions reflects our union with Christ in His suffering. They aren't separate categories but overlapping aspects of what it means to follow a crucified Savior.

The Purpose of Shared Suffering

Why has God ordained that we must suffer with Christ? This question has confronted me during my own times of pain and while ministering to others in their affliction.

The text provides a clear purpose statement: "in order that we may also be glorified with him." Our suffering with Christ isn't pointless or arbitrary; it serves this magnificent purpose. Suffering is the pathway to glory, not because suffering itself has merit, but because God uses suffering to conform us to Christ's image.

The Reformed tradition has always emphasized that our union with Christ includes union with Him in both His humiliation and exaltation. We cannot have one without the other. Those who would reign with Him must also suffer with Him. The cross precedes the crown.

I'm reminded of what the Heidelberg Catechism teaches about providence: that all things, including suffering, come to us "not by chance but from his fatherly hand." This gives our suffering profound meaning. It isn't random misfortune but divinely ordained preparation for glory.

Moreover, our suffering with Christ demonstrates the authenticity of our faith. As Peter writes, the testing of our faith through suffering proves it to be genuine (1 Peter 1:6-7). Fair-weather disciples who abandon Christ when suffering comes reveal they were never truly His. True heirs persevere through suffering, not because of their own strength, but because the Spirit empowers their endurance.

The Glory That Awaits

Paul balances the sobering reality of suffering with the magnificent promise of glory. We suffer "in order that we may also be glorified with him." What does this glorification involve?

At its core, glorification means being conformed to Christ's perfect image. As Paul explains earlier in Romans, those whom God predestined "he also predestined to be conformed to the image of his Son" (Romans 8:29). The full restoration of God's image in us, marred by sin since the Fall, constitutes our ultimate glorification.

This glorification includes the redemption of our bodies (Romans 8:23), when "he will transform our lowly body to be like his glorious body" (Philippians 3:21). With no more disease, decay, or death, our resurrection bodies will reflect Christ's own glorious body, free from all corruption.

But glorification extends beyond individual transformation to our participation in Christ's reign. The saints will judge the world (1 Corinthians 6:2-3) and rule with Christ (2 Timothy 2:12; Revelation 20:6). The meek truly will inherit the earth (Matthew 5:5), and the last will be first (Matthew 20:16).

I find it remarkable that Scripture consistently presents glory as something shared, not solitary. We are glorified "with him." Our glorification isn't independent of Christ but flows from our union with Him. We will shine with His reflected glory, like the moon reflects the sun's light.

Suffering and Glory in Perspective

In the very next verse, Paul provides a crucial perspective on this suffering-glory relationship: "For I consider that the sufferings of this present time are not worth comparing with the glory that is to be revealed to us" (Romans 8:18).

This verse has sustained me through dark valleys. When my body ached with physical pain, when ministry brought heartbreak, when relationships fractured despite my best efforts, this verse reminded me that these sufferings, however intense, pale in comparison to coming glory.

Paul doesn't minimize suffering; he acknowledges its reality and intensity. But he places it on a scale with future glory and finds it "not worth comparing." The arithmetic of eternity reduces even lifelong suffering to a momentary affliction when weighed against "an eternal weight of glory" (2 Corinthians 4:17).

I've stood at the bedsides of dying saints who grasped this truth. Their physical pain was real, yet their eyes shone with anticipation of glory. They understood what Paul meant when he wrote that "this light momentary affliction is preparing for us an eternal weight of glory beyond all comparison" (2 Corinthians 4:17).

Practical Implications

How should this teaching on suffering and glory shape our daily Christian experience?

First, it cultivates realistic expectations. Following Christ doesn't exempt us from suffering but guarantees it. When affliction comes, we shouldn't be surprised, as though something strange were happening to us (1 Peter 4:12). Rather, we recognize suffering as part of the normal Christian life, our participation in Christ's own path to glory.

Second, it instills profound hope. Our suffering isn't meaningless but pregnant with purpose. It's not a detour from God's plan but integral to it. Every tear, every pain, every loss is being worked into a tapestry of glory we cannot yet imagine but will one day behold with awe.

Third, it fosters genuine community. Shared suffering creates bonds deeper than shared success ever could. When believers suffer together, bearing one another's burdens and weeping with those who weep, they experience communion that prefigures the perfect fellowship of glory.

Fourth, it inspires sacrificial ministry. Understanding that suffering precedes glory liberates us from self-protection and comfort-seeking. We become willing to pour ourselves out for others, knowing that self-giving love reflects Christ's own pattern.

Conclusion: The Privilege of Heirship

As I reflect on Romans 8:17, I'm struck by the immense privilege of our position. We who were once alienated from God, dead in our trespasses and sins, have been adopted as children, designated as heirs, and promised glory beyond imagination.

This inheritance isn't earned through our suffering. It's secured through Christ's suffering, in which we participate by faith. Our suffering doesn't merit glory but prepares us for it, shaping us into vessels capable of containing the glory God intends to reveal in us.

The path of suffering with Christ may seem daunting, but we walk it sustained by the Spirit, encouraged by fellow pilgrims, and animated by the hope of glory that awaits. Though momentarily obscured by clouds of pain, the brilliance of coming glory illuminates our way. And one day, when faith gives way to sight, we'll understand fully what Paul meant when he wrote that the sufferings of this present time aren't worthy to be compared with the glory that will be revealed in us.

As heirs with Christ, we follow where He has gone before, through suffering into glory, through the cross to the crown, through death to life everlasting. This is our inheritance, secured by His blood and guaranteed by His Spirit. It is the sure hope of every child of God.

Chapter Eighteen

Present Sufferings Versus Future Glory

"For I consider that the sufferings of this present time are not worth comparing with the glory that is to be revealed to us." **Romans 8:18**

As we contemplate our identity as children and heirs of God, we must confront a sobering reality. Paul makes it clear that our inheritance comes with a condition: "provided we suffer with him in order that we may also be glorified with him" (Romans 8:17). This divine pattern: suffering preceding glory, runs throughout Scripture like a golden thread, binding our experience to Christ's own journey.

The Divine Pattern: Suffering Before Glory

When I first encountered this passage as a young believer, I confess I found it troubling. Why must suffering be the pathway to glory? Couldn't God simply bestow glory without the painful prelude? Over decades of ministry and personal experience, I've come to understand that suffering isn't merely a prerequisite for glory; it's preparation for it.

Christ Himself embodied this pattern. Before His exaltation came humiliation. Before His crown came His cross. "Was it not necessary," He asked the disciples on the Emmaus road, "that the Christ should suffer these things and enter into his glory?" (Luke 24:26). The question was rhetorical because the divine pattern is inescapable.

When we suffer with Christ, we're not merely enduring similar experiences; we're participating in His sufferings. Peter tells us to "rejoice insofar as you share Christ's sufferings, that you may also rejoice and be glad when his glory is revealed" (1 Peter 4:13). Our suffering isn't identical to His redemptive work, but it connects us to His ongoing ministry in a fallen world.

In my years as a Marine, I learned that shared hardship creates bonds stronger than shared comfort ever could. Brothers who've bled together share a connection that transcends ordinary friendship. How much more profound is our fellowship with Christ when we participate in His sufferings!

The Suffering-Glory Calculation

Paul provides crucial perspective on this suffering-glory relationship: "For I consider that the sufferings of this present time are not worth comparing with the glory that is to be revealed to us" (Romans 8:18).

This verse has sustained me through dark valleys. When my body ached with physical pain, when ministry brought heartbreak, when relationships fractured despite my best efforts, this verse reminded me that these sufferings, however intense, pale in comparison to coming glory.

Paul doesn't minimize suffering; he acknowledges its reality and intensity. But he places it on a scale with future glory and finds it "not worth comparing." The arithmetic of eternity reduces even lifelong suffering to a momentary affliction when weighed against "an eternal weight of glory" (2 Corinthians 4:17).

I've stood at the bedsides of dying saints who grasped this truth. Their physical pain was real, yet their eyes shone with anticipation of glory. They understood what Paul meant when he wrote that "this light momentary affliction is preparing for us an eternal weight of glory beyond all comparison" (2 Corinthians 4:17).

The Nature of Our Present Sufferings

What constitutes the "sufferings of this present time" that Paul references? I believe they encompass at least four dimensions of Christian experience.

First, we suffer the universal consequences of living in a fallen world. Disease, natural disasters, aging, and death affect believers and unbelievers alike. When Paul speaks of creation groaning (Romans 8:22), he acknowledges that our physical environment and bodies remain subject to corruption.

Second, we experience opposition from a world system hostile to God. Jesus warned, "If they persecuted me, they will also persecute you" (John 15:20). This may range from subtle marginalization to outright persecution. As Western culture increasingly abandons its Christian moorings, believers face growing pressure to compromise biblical convictions or face social and professional consequences.

Third, we encounter spiritual warfare. Paul reminds us that "we do not wrestle against flesh and blood, but against...spi ritual forces of evil" (Ephesians 6:12). This battle manifests in temptation, accusation, and spiritual oppression.

Fourth, we experience the pain of sanctification as the Spirit works to conform us to Christ's image. Hebrews tells us that God "disciplines us for our good, that we may share his holiness" (Hebrews 12:10). This divine chiseling is painful but purposeful.

During my pastoral ministry, I counseled countless believers through these various dimensions of suffering. A young mother diagnosed with aggressive cancer. The faithful employee fired for declining to participate in activities that violated his conscience. A family under spiritual attack while pursuing ministry. The dedicated Christian struggling through painful sanctification in a persistent sin area. In each case, Paul's perspective proved transformative.

The Incomparable Glory to Be Revealed

If our present sufferings constitute one side of Paul's comparison, the "glory that is to be revealed to us" forms the other. What exactly is this glory that so outweighs our current trials?

The term "glory" (*doxa* in Greek) carries rich meaning in Scripture. It encompasses radiance, honor, splendor, and moral excellence. When applied to our future state, it signifies at least three dimensions of our eternal inheritance.

First, we will experience a physical transformation. Paul tells us that Christ "will transform our lowly body to be like his glorious body" (Philippians 3:21). Our resurrection bodies will be imperishable, powerful, and spiritual (1 Corinthians 15:42-44) free from pain, disease, and death.

Second, we will enjoy moral perfection. Sin's presence will be eradicated from our nature. John writes, "we shall be like him, because we shall see him as he is" (1 John 3:2). The sanctification that proceeds partially and painfully now will be completed instantaneously and perfectly then.

Third, we will share in Christ's reign. Revelation promises that we will "reign with him" (Revelation 20:6). The humiliations of this present age will give way to positions of honor in God's eternal kingdom.

I find it remarkable that Scripture consistently presents glory as something shared, not solitary. We are glorified "with him." Our glorification isn't independent of Christ but flows from our union with Him. We will shine with His reflected glory, like the moon reflects the sun's light.

The Practical Implications

How should this teaching on suffering and glory shape our daily Christian experience?

First, it cultivates realistic expectations. Following Christ doesn't exempt us from suffering but guarantees it. When affliction comes, we shouldn't be surprised, as though something strange were happening to us (1 Peter 4:12). Rather, we recognize suffering as part of the normal Christian life, our participation in Christ's own path to glory.

Second, it instills profound hope. Our suffering isn't meaningless but pregnant with purpose. It's not a detour from God's plan but integral to it. Every tear, every pain, every loss is being worked into a tapestry of glory we cannot yet imagine but will one day behold with awe.

Third, it fosters genuine community. Shared suffering creates bonds deeper than shared success ever could. When believers suffer together, bearing one another's burdens and weeping with those who weep, they experience communion that prefigures the perfect fellowship of glory.

Fourth, it inspires sacrificial ministry. Understanding that suffering precedes glory liberates us from self-protection and comfort-seeking. We become willing to pour ourselves out for others, knowing that self-giving love reflects Christ's own pattern.

A Personal Testimony

I still remember visiting Thomas, a member of my congregation battling terminal cancer. Disease and treatment ravaged his body, his strength nearly gone. Yet when I entered his hospital room, his face radiated a peace that transcended his circumstances.

"Pastor," he whispered, "I've been meditating on Romans 8:18 all morning."

I nodded, knowing the verse well. "For I consider that the sufferings of this present time are not worth comparing with the glory that is to be revealed to us."

"It's all here," he continued, gesturing weakly to his Bible. "The math of eternity. Paul did the calculation for us. Present suffering..." He paused, grimacing through a wave of pain. "Versus future glory. And it's not even close."

Thomas died three days later. At his memorial service, I shared his final testimony, how he had weighed his considerable sufferings against coming glory and found them "not worth comparing." His witness touched more lives in death than most touch in a lifetime of health.

In my own times of suffering, I've returned to Paul's divine calculation again and again. When chronic pain threatened to overwhelm me. When ministry criticism pierced deeply. When family trials seemed unbearable. Each time, I've found that focusing on the incomparable glory ahead doesn't eliminate present pain but places it in proper perspective.

Conclusion: The Privilege of Heirship

As I reflect on this, I'm struck by the immense privilege of our position. We who were once alienated from God, dead in our trespasses and sins, have been adopted as children, designated as heirs, and promised glory beyond imagination.

This inheritance isn't earned through our suffering. It's secured through Christ's suffering, in which we participate by faith. Our suffering doesn't merit glory but prepares us for it, shaping us into vessels capable of containing the glory God intends to reveal in us.

The path of suffering with Christ may seem daunting, but we walk it sustained by the Spirit, encouraged by fellow pilgrims, and animated by the hope of glory that awaits. Though momentarily obscured by clouds of pain, the brilliance of coming glory illuminates our way. And one day, when faith gives way to sight, we'll understand fully what Paul meant when he wrote that the sufferings of this present time aren't worthy to be compared with the glory that will be revealed in us.

As heirs with Christ, we follow where He has gone before, through suffering into glory, through the cross to crown, through death to life everlasting. This is our inheritance, secured by His blood and guaranteed by His Spirit. It is the sure hope of every child of God.

Chapter Nineteen

Creation's Eager Expectation

"For the creation waits with eager longing for the revealing of the sons of God."
Romans 8:19

The Apostle Paul, having established the profound connection between our present sufferings and future glory, now widens his lens to include all of creation in this cosmic drama of redemption. I've often paused at this verse, struck by its sweeping implications. Here Paul personifies creation itself, portraying it as waiting with "eager longing," a phrase that in Greek conveys the image of creation standing on tiptoe, neck stretched forward, eyes fixed on the horizon, earnestly waiting for something magnificent to appear. This isn't poetic hyperbole; it's theological truth about the created order's relationship to God's redemptive plan.

When I meditate on this verse, I'm reminded of a fundamental truth: creation's story is inseparably linked with humanity's story. What happened to us happened to the world around us.

Consider what took place in Genesis. When God created Adam and Eve, He placed them in a garden and gave them dominion over creation. They were to be creation's stewards, its caretakers, its priests. But when they fell into sin, creation fell with them. God's curse wasn't limited to humanity but extended to the ground itself: "Cursed is the ground because of you; in pain you shall eat of it all the days of your life; thorns and thistles it shall bring forth for you" (Genesis 3:17-18).

This helps us understand why creation "waits with eager longing." Creation suffers under the weight of humanity's sin, not because of any fault of its own, but because its destiny is tied to ours. Just as we were subjected to futility through Adam's sin, so too was the creation over which Adam was given dominion.

The Biblical View of Creation

Before we explore this further, it's essential to establish a biblical understanding of creation. In Reformed theology, we affirm that the material world is inherently good because God created it and declared it so (Genesis 1:31). Unlike some ancient philosophies that viewed matter as evil and spirit as good, Scripture teaches that the physical creation is valuable, purposeful, and beloved by God.

We also recognize that creation exists not merely as a backdrop for human drama but as an active participant in God's redemptive purposes. The Bible frequently portrays nature as responsive to God:

"The mountains and the hills shall break forth before you into singing, and all the trees of the field shall clap their hands" (Isaiah 55:12).

"Let the sea roar, and all that fills it; the world and those who dwell in it! Let the rivers clap their hands; let the hills sing for joy together" (Psalm 98:7-8).

This biblical perspective helps us understand Paul's anthropomorphic language in Romans 8:19. He's not merely using a literary device but expressing a theological reality: creation is personal, relational, and responsive to God's purposes.

Creation's Current State

What is creation's current condition that makes it long so eagerly for redemption? Paul describes it in the verses following our text:

"For the creation was subjected to futility, not willingly, but because of him who subjected it, in hope that the creation itself will be set free from its bondage to corruption and obtain the freedom of the glory of the children of God. For we know that the whole creation has been groaning together in the pains of childbirth until now" (Romans 8:20-22).

Three descriptions stand out to me: futility, bondage to corruption, and groaning. Futility speaks to creation's inability to fulfill its intended purpose. The word Paul uses (*mataiotes* in Greek) implies emptiness, frustration, or purposelessness. The natural world was designed to flourish in perfect harmony, reflecting God's glory without impediment. Sin introduced disorder into that design.

I've witnessed this futility firsthand. During my years of pastoring in a rural community, I saw farmers battle against unpredictable weather, invasive pests, and blighted crops. What should have been a partnership between human cultivation and natural abundance often became an exhausting struggle against thorns and thistles.

Bondage to corruption points to creation's enslavement to decay. The Greek word for corruption (*phthora*) indicates deterioration, wasting away, perishing. It's the relentless pull toward disorder that scientists call entropy. Every created thing is subject to this law of decay.

The groaning Paul mentions evokes the sound of creation's suffering. From forests devastated by wildfires to coastlines eroded by rising seas, from species driven to extinction to ecosystems thrown out of balance, creation groans under the weight of disorder.

Yet Paul's language also offers hope. These groans aren't death rattles but birth pangs. Creation isn't dying; it's in labor, awaiting something new.

What Creation Awaits

What exactly is creation waiting for with such eager expectation? Paul specifies: "the revealing of the sons of God." This phrase requires careful unpacking.

First, it refers to a future event, the final revelation of our status as God's children. While we are already God's children through faith in Christ, the full manifestation of this reality awaits Christ's return. As John writes, "Beloved, we are God's children now, and what we will be has not yet appeared; but we know that when he appears we shall be like him, because we shall see him as he is" (1 John 3:2).

Second, this revealing involves transformation. Our bodies will be redeemed, freed from weakness, decay, and death. Paul describes this in Philippians 3:20-21: "But our citizenship is in heaven, and from it we await a Savior, the Lord Jesus Christ, who will transform our lowly body to be like his glorious body."

Creation waits for this moment because its liberation is tied to ours. When we receive our glorified bodies, creation too will be transformed. It won't be destroyed but renewed, purged of curse and corruption.

The New Creation

Scripture gives us glimpses of what this renewed creation will be like. Isaiah prophesies a time when "the wolf shall dwell with the lamb, and the leopard shall lie down with the young goat... They shall not hurt or destroy in all my holy mountain" (Isaiah 11:6, 9). John's vision in Revelation includes "a new heaven and a new earth," with God dwelling among His people, wiping away every tear, and declaring, "Behold, I am making all things new" (Revelation 21:1-5).

This renewal isn't the annihilation of the present creation but its transformation. Just as our bodies will be raised and glorified, not discarded, so too the material world will be purified and renewed, not abandoned.

This understanding corrects two common misconceptions. First, that Christianity is concerned only with "saving souls" while disregarding the physical world. Scripture teaches God intends to redeem both. Second, that the earth's destiny is destruction. While Peter speaks of elements melting with fire (2 Peter 3:10), the context suggests purification, not annihilation, a cleansing fire that prepares for "new heavens and a new earth in which righteousness dwells" (2 Peter 3:13).

Practical Implications

Understanding creation's eager expectation transforms how we live in the present. Let me suggest several implications:

First, it grounds our environmental stewardship in redemptive hope. As Christians, we care for creation not merely because it's pragmatically wise but because creation is God's beloved handiwork, destined for restoration. Our ecological responsibility flows from theological conviction.

I recall walking through a once-polluted stream that church members had helped restore. As wildlife returned and waters ran clear, I sensed we were participating in a small foretaste of creation's future liberation, not achieving it ourselves, but honoring creation's God-given purpose.

Second, it helps us interpret creation's beauty rightly. When we stand awed before mountain majesty or ocean vastness, we're experiencing not just aesthetic pleasure but a whisper of creation's original glory and future restoration. These moments of wonder are signposts pointing to creation's ultimate purpose: displaying God's glory perfectly.

Third, it reshapes our understanding of redemption's scope. The gospel isn't just about saving individual souls but about God's comprehensive plan to restore all things in Christ. As Paul writes elsewhere, God's purpose is "to unite all things in him, things in heaven and things on earth" (Ephesians 1:10).

Fourth, it connects our bodily resurrection with creation's renewal. Our hope isn't to escape the material world but to inhabit transformed bodies in a transformed creation. This affirms the goodness of materiality and counters Gnostic tendencies to spiritualize Christian hope.

Conclusion: Joining Creation's Eager Expectation

As I reflect on creation's eager longing, I find my own hope strengthened and expanded. If even the non-rational creation waits expectantly for God's redemptive work to reach its culmination, how much more should we, who have tasted the firstfruits of the Spirit, live in active, hopeful anticipation?

Like creation, we too stand on tiptoe, straining forward to see the day when Christ returns, when our adoption is fully realized, when our bodies are redeemed, and when all creation is liberated from its bondage to decay.

Until that day, we join creation's groaning with our own, but we do so as those who have hope. We care for the earth as faithful stewards, knowing our efforts aren't futile but participate in God's sustaining grace. We marvel at creation's beauty as a foretaste of greater glory to come. And we proclaim a gospel big enough to encompass not just human souls but the entire created order.

In a world increasingly anxious about ecological crises, this biblical vision offers a unique perspective. Our hope isn't in human ingenuity alone but in God's promise to make all things new. This doesn't absolve us of responsibility but places our environmental stewardship within the larger story of God's redemptive work.

As sons and daughters of God, we look forward with creation to that great unveiling, when Christ returns and the words of the ancient prophet are fulfilled: "The earth will be filled with the knowledge of the glory of the LORD as the waters cover the sea" (Habakkuk 2:14).

Chapter Twenty

Creation Subjected in Hope

"For the creation was subjected to futility, not willingly, but because of him who subjected it, in hope" Romans 8:20

Standing in my study, surrounded by commentaries and Greek lexicons accumulated over decades of pastoral ministry and seminary teaching, I find myself drawn repeatedly to Romans 8:20, a verse that has challenged and enriched my understanding of God's sovereignty and redemptive plan. This single verse contains profound theological depths that speak to some of the most fundamental questions about suffering, sovereignty, and hope. As I've wrestled with these words through years of preaching and teaching, I've discovered that they reveal not just the scope of the fall's impact but the breathtaking extent of God's redemptive purposes.

The Nature of Subjection

The Greek word Paul uses for "subjected" is *hupetage*, which carries the idea of being placed under authority or control, not by choice, but by divine decree. This isn't voluntary submission but imposed subordination. Creation didn't choose its current state; it was placed there.

This passive construction is crucial for understanding Paul's theology. Creation didn't fall through its own moral failure but was subjected to futility as a consequence of humanity's rebellion. The earth didn't sin; Adam did. Yet creation bears the consequences of that primal disobedience.

During my Marine years, I witnessed the aftermath of human conflict on the natural world, landscapes scarred by war, ecosystems disrupted by violence. Even then, before my theological training, I sensed that nature itself was somehow caught up in humanity's brokenness. Romans 8:20 provides the biblical framework for that intuition.

The verb tense Paul employs indicates a specific, historical moment when this subjection occurred. This wasn't a gradual process but a decisive divine act corresponding to the fall recorded in Genesis 3. When God pronounced judgment on Adam's sin, creation itself was included in that judgment.

The Agent of Subjection

Paul's phrase "because of him who subjected it" raises an important question: who is the "him"? The Greek allows for two possible interpretations, each with significant theological implications.

Some interpreters argue that Adam is the one who subjected creation through his disobedience. This reading emphasizes human responsibility for creation's plight. Adam's federal headship over creation meant that his fall dragged the natural world down with him.

However, the more compelling interpretation, supported by the broader context and Paul's theological significance, identifies God as the one who subjected creation. This reading aligns with Reformed theology's emphasis on divine sovereignty over all events, including the consequences of sin.

This interpretation doesn't make God the author of sin but recognizes Him as the sovereign judge who determines sin's consequences. Just as God expelled Adam and Eve from Eden and cursed the ground (Genesis 3:17-19), so He subjected the entire creation to futility as part of His judicial response to human rebellion.

Understanding God as the agent of subjection preserves several crucial theological principles. First, it maintains God's absolute sovereignty over creation's destiny. Second, it ensures that even the fall and its consequences serve God's ultimate redemptive purposes. Third, it provides the foundation for hope. The same God who subjected creation in judgment can and will liberate it in redemption.

The Meaning of Futility

The word Paul chooses for "futility" (*mataiotes in Greek*) describes something empty, purposeless, or unable to achieve its intended goal. It's the same word the Septuagint uses to translate the Hebrew *hebel* in Ecclesiastes, often rendered "vanity" or "meaninglessness." This futility isn't moral corruption but functional frustration. Creation isn't evil; it's thwarted. The natural world continues to testify to God's glory and power (Romans 1:20), but it cannot achieve its ultimate purpose of perfectly mirroring His character or fully promoting human flourishing.

I've observed this futility countless times while hiking in the mountains. The breathtaking beauty of mountain meadows and towering peaks declares God's majesty, yet beneath the surface lies a world marked by death, decay, and destruction. Predators hunt prey, storms devastate landscapes, and entropy constantly works toward dissolution.

This isn't how creation was meant to function. In Eden, there was no death, no decay, no natural disasters. The lion lay down with the lamb, and humanity exercised dominion without exploitation. Creation's current state represents a cosmic holding pattern, magnificent yet incomplete, glorious yet groaning.

The futility extends beyond physical decay to creation's inability to achieve its teleological purpose. Created to serve as the perfect environment for God-imaging humanity to flourish in relationship with their Creator, creation now struggles under the weight of human sinfulness and divine judgment.

The Unwilling Nature of Subjection

Paul's clarification that creation was subjected "not willingly" emphasizes that the natural world bears consequences for choices it didn't make. Unlike humanity, which chose rebellion against God, creation had no moral agency in the fall. It was an innocent victim of humanity's cosmic treason.

This unwillingness creates what theologians call the "groaning" of creation, a deep, wordless longing for restoration that Paul describes in the following verses. Like a prisoner unjustly incarcerated, creation yearns for liberation from a bondage it didn't choose.

During my time as a pastor, I've counseled many people struggling with suffering that seemed unfair or undeserved. While each situation requires careful pastoral attention, Romans 8:20 reminds us that innocent suffering isn't foreign to God's creation. Even the natural world experiences consequences for sins it didn't commit.

This reality points to the interconnectedness of all creation under God's sovereign rule. Humanity's fall affected not just individual humans but the entire cosmic order. We see echoes of this principle throughout Scripture. When Israel sinned, the land suffered drought and famine; when David numbered the people, plague struck the nation.

Subjected in Hope

The phrase "in hope" transforms everything. The Greek preposition *epi* can mean "upon" or "on the basis of," suggesting that hope was the foundation upon which God subjected creation to futility. This wasn't arbitrary punishment but purposeful preparation for ultimate redemption. This hope isn't wishful thinking but confident expectation based on God's character and promises. The same God who subjected creation in judgment has planned and will accomplish its liberation. The futility is temporary; the hope is eternal.

Reformed theology emphasizes that God's purposes in history, including His response to sin, always serve His ultimate redemptive plan. The subjection of creation wasn't Plan B after the fall caught God off guard. From eternity, God purposed to display His glory through both judgment and redemption, both the cross and the resurrection.

This hope provides the theological foundation for what Paul describes in verse 21: "that the creation itself will be set free from its bondage to corruption and obtain the freedom of the glory of the children of God" (Romans 8:21). The subjection is purposeful, pointing toward ultimate liberation.

The Scope of Divine Sovereignty

Understanding creation's subjection in hope illuminates God's comprehensive sovereignty over all things. Nothing in creation's current state, neither its beauty nor its brokenness, falls outside God's sovereign control and redemptive purpose.

This doesn't mean God is the author of evil or that suffering is good. Rather, it means that even the consequences of sin serve God's ultimate purposes of displaying His justice, mercy, and glory. The darkness of the fall provides the backdrop against which God's redemptive light shines most brilliantly.

During my time teaching at the seminary, students often struggled with this aspect of divine sovereignty. How can a good God use evil circumstances for good purposes? The answer lies in understanding that God doesn't cause evil but sovereignly directs even evil's consequences toward redemptive ends.

Creation's subjection exemplifies this principle. God didn't cause the fall, but He did determine its consequence, including creation's subjection to futility, in such a way that they serve His ultimate plan to glorify Himself through the redemption of all things in Christ.

Implications for Theodicy

First, I should define theodicy. It is an attempt to explain how God remains perfectly good and sovereign even when we face evil and suffering, trusting that He works all things for His glory and our good.

Romans 8:20 provides crucial insight for addressing the problem of suffering and evil. If God subjected creation to futility in hope, then current suffering, while real and painful, isn't meaningless or purposeless. It serves God's greater redemptive design.

This doesn't minimize suffering's reality or suggest we should be passive in its face. Rather, it provides the theological framework for understanding how a sovereign, good God can permit a world filled with pain and death. The permission isn't arbitrary but purposeful, pointing toward ultimate restoration.

The verse also reminds us that suffering affects all creation, not just humanity. The theological problem isn't just human suffering but cosmic suffering. Paul's solution is equally cosmic, God's plan to redeem not just individuals, but the entire created order.

The Foundation of Environmental Stewardship

Understanding that God subjected creation in hope provides a Reformed foundation for environmental responsibility. If God has redemptive purposes for the natural world, then our care for creation participates in God's ongoing work of preservation and preparation for ultimate renewal.

This isn't environmental activism based on pantheistic nature worship but Christian stewardship grounded in biblical theology. We care for creation because God does, and because He has appointed us as His image-bearers to exercise dominion that reflects His character.

The hope dimension is crucial here. Our environmental efforts aren't attempts to save a doomed world but acts of faithful stewardship while we await God's ultimate renewal. We work to heal creation's wounds while recognizing that only God can accomplish final restoration.

Conclusion: Present Suffering and Future Glory

Romans 8:20 sets up Paul's magnificent declaration in verse 18: "For I consider that the sufferings of this present time are not worth comparing with the glory that is to be revealed to us." Creation's subjection in hope becomes the backdrop for understanding how present suffering relates to future glory.

If God subjected creation to serve redemptive purposes, then our current sufferings, while painful and real, must be understood within this larger framework of divine purpose and hope. This doesn't make suffering easy, but it does make it meaningful.

The "in hope" dimension reminds us that current conditions aren't permanent. God's purpose in subjecting creation point toward ultimate liberation and restoration. The futility is real but temporary; the hope is certain and eternal.

As I reflect on my years of pastoral ministry, I've seen how this hope transforms people's responses to suffering. When believers understand that their pain serves God's greater purposes and points toward ultimate redemption, they find strength to endure and grace to hope even in darkness.

Romans 8:20 thus becomes not just a theological statement about creation's past but a pastoral resource for present suffering and future hope. In subjecting creation to futility, God embedded hope into the very structure of fallen existence, ensuring that every groan points toward ultimate glory.

Chapter Twenty-One

Freedom from Decay

"that the creation itself will be set free from its bondage to corruption and obtain the freedom of the glory of the children of God." Romans 8:21

Romans 8:21 delivers one of Scripture's most magnificent promises about creation's ultimate destiny. This verse completes Paul's thought about creation's subjection in hope, revealing the specific content of that hope: complete liberation from decay and corruption.

The word "because" connects this promise directly to the preceding verse 20 about hope. Creation's subjection wasn't arbitrary or cruel but purposeful, aimed at this ultimate liberation. Paul reveals that God's plan encompasses not just human redemption but cosmic restoration, the freedom of all creation from the bondage that has characterized its existence since the fall.

The Nature of Corruption

The Greek word translated "corruption" (*phthora*) refers to decay, deterioration, and destruction. It describes the principle of entropy that governs our fallen world; everything tends toward breakdown and death. From the moment sin entered the world, creation became subject to this inexorable process of decline.

This corruption manifests in countless ways. Flowers wilt, bodies age, metals rust, wood rots, and stars burn out. The second law of thermodynamics describes scientifically what Scripture reveals theologically: our universe moves toward increasing disorder and decay. What God created as "very good" now groans under the weight of cosmic corruption.

During my years as a Marine, I witnessed this principle firsthand in ways that shaped my theological understanding. Equipment required constant maintenance to prevent deterioration. Human bodies broke down under stress and injury. Even the most beautiful landscapes bore scars of erosion, storm damage, and death. The created order itself testified to something fundamentally wrong with our world.

Yet Paul doesn't present corruption as creation's final destiny but as a temporary bondage from which it will be liberated. The decay we observe isn't permanent but provisional, serving God's purposes until the time of ultimate restoration.

Bondage and Liberation

Paul describes corruption as a form of "bondage" (*douleia* in Greek), using slavery terminology to convey creation's involuntary subjection to decay. Creation didn't choose this condition any more than a slave chooses slavery. The bondage was imposed through humanity's fall, and creation remains trapped until God acts to provide liberation.

This slavery imagery is crucial for understanding the scope of redemption. Just as human beings are born into bondage to sin and require divine liberation, creation itself exists in involuntary subjection to corruption and awaits divine deliverance. The parallel isn't accidental; Paul deliberately connects creation's need for freedom with humanity's need for salvation.

The promise of liberation reveals God's commitment to undoing completely the consequences of sin. Redemption isn't just about rescuing souls from hell but about restoring the entire created order to its intended glory. God's plan is as comprehensive as sin's devastation, addressing every aspect of reality corrupted by the fall.

This understanding transformed my approach to pastoral counseling during my ministry years. When believers struggled with physical illness, natural disasters, or environmental degradation, I could point them to this promise of cosmic liberation. Their current sufferings weren't meaningless but part of a larger story moving toward complete restoration.

The Freedom of Glory

Paul connects creation's future freedom to "the freedom of the glory of the children of God." This phrase reveals that creation's liberation is tied to humanity's ultimate glorification. When believers receive their resurrection bodies and final sanctification, creation will simultaneously experience its own form of liberation from corruption.

The "glory of the children of God" refers to the final state of redeemed humanity, resurrection bodies that are incorruptible, immortal, and perfectly conformed to Christ's image. First Corinthians 15:42-44 describes this transformation: "So is it with the resurrection of the dead. What is sown is perishable; what is raised is imperishable. It is sown in dishonor; it is raised in glory. It is sown in weakness; it is raised in power. It is sown a natural body; it is raised a spiritual body."

Creation's freedom will parallel this human glorification. Just as believers will receive bodies that are free from decay, disease, and death, creation itself will be liberated from the principle of corruption that currently governs its existence. The new heavens and new earth described in Revelation 21-22 represent this liberated creation, where "death shall be no more, neither shall there be mourning, nor crying, nor pain anymore, for the former things have passed away" (Revelation 21:4).

Theological Implications

Romans 8:21 carries profound implications for several key theological doctrines. First, it confirms the goodness of creation. If God plans to liberate creation rather than destroy it, then matter itself isn't inherently evil. The problem isn't with the physical world but with its subjection to corruption through sin.

This challenges both ancient Gnostic dualism, which viewed matter as evil, and modern secular materialism, which sees the physical world as all there is. Scripture presents a middle way. Creation is good but corrupted, destined for restoration rather than destruction or eternal existence in its current form.

Second, the verse establishes the cosmic scope of redemption. God's saving work addresses not just individual souls, but the entire created order. Sin's effects were cosmic, and salvation's reach is equally comprehensive. This prevents us from reducing Christianity to purely spiritual or individual concerns while affirming the ultimate importance of personal salvation.

Third, Paul's promise reveals the unity between human destiny and creation's destiny. We aren't saved from the world but with the world. Our glorification and creation's liberation occur together, suggesting an intimate connection between humanity and the rest of creation that reflects our original mandate to exercise dominion as God's image-bearers.

The Timing of Liberation

While Paul doesn't specify exactly when creation will be liberated from corruption, the connection to "the freedom of the glory of the children of God" suggests this occurs at the *eschaton*, the end times when Christ returns and believers receive their resurrection bodies.

Second Peter 3:10-13 provides additional insight: "But the day of the Lord will come like a thief, and then the heavens will pass away with a roar, and the heavenly bodies will be burned up and dissolved, and the earth and the works that are done on it will be exposed. Since all these things are thus to be dissolved, what sort of people ought you to be in lives of holiness and godliness, waiting for and hastening the coming of the day of God, because of which the heavens will be set on fire and dissolved, and the heavenly bodies will melt as they burn! But according to his promise we are waiting for new heavens and a new earth in which righteousness dwells."

This passage describes a process of purification and renewal rather than annihilation and replacement. The current creation will be transformed, not destroyed, liberated from corruption through divine fire that purges away all effects of sin and decay.

Revelation 21:1 confirms this interpretation: "Then I saw a new heaven and a new earth, for the first heaven and the first earth had passed away, and the sea was no more." The Greek word "new" (*kainos*) means renewed or qualitatively different, not brand new (*neos*). This suggests transformation of the existing creation rather than creation *ex nihilo* (Latin for out of nothing) of something entirely different.

Present Hope and Future Reality

Understanding creation's promised liberation provides believers with hope during present sufferings and motivation for current stewardship. If God plans to renew creation rather than discard it, then our care for the environment participates in God's ongoing work of preservation and preparation.

This doesn't mean environmental activism can bring about the promised liberation; only God can accomplish that through Christ's return and the general resurrection. But it does mean our stewardship efforts have eternal significance as acts of faithful dominion that anticipate creation's ultimate restoration.

During my teaching years, I often explained to students that Romans 8:21 provides the theological foundation for what some call "creation care." We protect and preserve the environment not because we worship nature but because we serve the God who created it and promises to renew it. Our environmental efforts become forms of worship and witness, demonstrating our faith in God's promises about creation's future.

The promise also transforms how we experience natural beauty and wonder. Every sunset, mountain vista, and moment of natural splendor becomes a preview of coming attractions, glimpses of the glory that will characterize liberated creation. The beauty we see now, despite corruption's effects, hints at the magnificent reality that awaits when decay is finally eliminated.

Creation's Eager Anticipation

Romans 8:19 speaks of creation's "eager longing" for the revelation of the sons of God, and verse 21 explains why, because that revelation will coincide with creation's own liberation. This personification of creation as eagerly anticipating freedom isn't mere poetic device but a theological truth about the interconnectedness of human and cosmic destiny.

Creation somehow "knows" its current state isn't final or permanent. The groaning described in verse 22 expresses not just pain but expectation, not just suffering but hope. Every natural disaster, every extinction, every moment of environmental degradation occurs within the context of assured future liberation.

This perspective revolutionized my understanding of natural suffering during my pastoral ministry. When believers questioned why God allowed earthquakes, hurricanes, or other natural disasters, I could point them to Romans 8:21. These events aren't meaningless tragedies but birth pangs of the new creation struggling to emerge, signs that the current order is passing away and something glorious approaches.

The eager anticipation also explains why humans consistently find themselves drawn to natural beauty and disturbed by environmental destruction. As image-bearers of God, we're designed to exercise dominion over creation and find fulfillment in its flourishing. Our environmental concerns reflect not just enlightened self-interest but deeper theological realities about our relationship to the created order and its destiny.

Romans 8:21 thus stands as one of Scripture's most hopeful promises about the future, assuring us that God's redemptive purposes encompass not just human souls but the entire cosmos. The corruption that currently characterizes creation isn't permanent but provisional, serving God's purposes until the time of ultimate liberation when the children of God are revealed in glory and creation itself obtains the freedom for which it was destined from the foundation of the world.

Chapter Twenty-Two

The Groaning of Creation

"For we know that the whole creation has been groaning together in the pains of childbirth until now." Romans 8:22

Romans 8:22 brings us to one of Scripture's most profound and mysterious statements about the current state of creation. This verse reveals the cosmic scope of sin's effects and provides the theological foundation for understanding why our world experiences such widespread suffering and disorder.

During my years as a Marine, I witnessed destruction in various forms: natural disasters, environmental damage, and the aftermath of human conflict. Later, as a pastor and seminary professor, I often fielded questions from believers struggling to reconcile their faith with the reality of natural suffering. Why do earthquakes kill innocent people? Why do diseases ravage both the righteous and the unrighteous? Romans 8:22 provides the biblical answer: all creation participates in the consequences of the fall and eagerly anticipates the coming redemption.

The Scope of Creation's Groaning

Paul uses the phrase "whole creation" (*pasa ktisis* in Greek) to indicate the comprehensive nature of this groaning. This isn't limited to animate creatures but encompasses the entire created order, from subatomic particles to distant galaxies, from single-celled organisms to complex ecosystems. Reformed theology has always maintained that sin's effects permeate every aspect of reality, and this verse confirms that cosmic scope.

The Greek word "groaning" (*systenazo*) appears only here in the New Testament and literally means "to groan together." Creation doesn't suffer in isolated pockets but experiences a unified, symphonic expression of distress. Every natural disaster, every extinction event, every moment of environmental degradation participates in this cosmic chorus of pain.

I remember standing on a California hillside after a devastating wildfire during my time in the Marine Corps. The blackened landscape stretched for miles, punctuated by the skeletal remains of once-majestic oak trees. Someone asked me why God allowed such destruction. Romans 8:22 provided the framework for my response: this wasn't divine punishment for specific sins but the inevitable result of living in a fallen world where even creation itself groans under the weight of corruption.

The Metaphor of Childbirth

Paul chooses the metaphor of childbirth pains (*odin* in Greek) deliberately. Childbirth involves genuine suffering, intense, sometimes overwhelming pain that seems unbearable. Yet this pain serves a purpose: bringing forth new life. The agony isn't meaningless but productive, leading to joy when the child is born.

This metaphor transforms how we understand natural suffering. The earthquakes, hurricanes, famines, and diseases that characterize our world aren't random occurrences or signs of divine abandonment. They're birth pangs, painful but purposeful contractions that signal something magnificent is coming. Creation groans not in despair but in expectation, not in hopelessness but in anticipation of the new birth that approaches.

Reformed theology emphasizes that God sovereignly ordains all things, including natural disasters, to serve His ultimate purposes. This doesn't make Him the author of evil, but it does mean that even creation's groaning operates under divine providence, serving the greater good of bringing about the new heavens and new earth.

During my seminary teaching, I often used the childbirth metaphor to help students understand theodicy, the problem of evil and suffering. Just as a woman in labor doesn't doubt the value of childbirth because of the pain involved, we shouldn't doubt God's goodness because of creation's current suffering. The groaning indicates not divine failure but divine promise; something wonderful is being born.

The Unity of Creation's Experience

The prefix "*syn*" in *systenazo* in Greek emphasizes that creation groans "together." This suggests a remarkable unity in the experience of corruption and suffering. The same physical laws that govern stellar collapse also govern cellular decay. The same entropy that causes mountains to erode also causes living organisms to age and die. The second law of thermodynamics affects everything from galaxies to garden flowers.

This unified groaning refutes any notion that natural suffering results from localized divine displeasure. Instead, it reveals that the entire created order operates under conditions that guarantee suffering, decay, and death. Sin introduced disorder into the very fabric of reality, affecting not just human moral behavior but the fundamental processes that govern physical existence.

Reformed theology's doctrine of total depravity extends beyond human nature to encompass all creation. Just as every aspect of human personality bears the marks of sin's corruption, so every level of created reality exhibits the effects of the fall. The food chain requires death, weather systems produce destructive storms, and geological processes cause earthquakes and volcanic eruptions.

The Temporal Dimension

Paul adds "until now" (*achri tou nyn* in Greek) to emphasize that creation's groaning characterizes the entire period between the fall and the final redemption. This isn't a recent development or temporary setback but the persistent condition of unredeemed creation. From the moment sin entered the world through Adam's disobedience until Christ returns to establish the new heavens and new earth, all creation continues groaning in anticipation.

This temporal marker provides comfort during particularly difficult periods when natural disasters seem especially frequent or severe. Creation's groaning doesn't intensify based on human moral behavior or approach some critical threshold that triggers divine intervention. It remains constant throughout history, a steady reminder that the current order is temporary and provisional.

During my military service, I witnessed the aftermath of natural disasters in various parts of the world. The consistency of human vulnerability to natural forces, regardless of culture, religion, or moral standing, illustrates Romans 8:22's teaching about creation's universal groaning. Rich and poor, righteous and unrighteous, all live under the same physical laws that guarantee suffering and eventual death.

Theological Implications

Romans 8:22 has profound implications for how believers understand their relationship to the natural world. First, it provides a biblical foundation for environmental concern without falling into nature worship. We care for creation not because it's divine but because it participates in the same redemptive hope we possess. Our environmental stewardship becomes a form of compassionate ministry to fellow sufferers.

Second, this verse explains why technological progress cannot eliminate natural suffering. We can build better earthquake-resistant buildings and develop more effective vaccines, but we cannot eliminate earthquakes or diseases themselves. The groaning operates at a fundamental level that only divine intervention can address.

Third, Romans 8:22 challenges any theology that promises believers exemption from natural suffering. Christians get cancer, die in earthquakes, and suffer from genetic disorders at the same rates as unbelievers because they inhabit the same groaning creation. Our redemption secures our eternal destiny but doesn't exempt us from participating in creation's current suffering.

The Groaning and Human Experience

Paul's reference to creation's groaning prepares us for verse 23, where he describes believers as also groaning inwardly while awaiting redemption. This parallel suggests a profound solidarity between redeemed humans and unredeemed creation. We're not separate from or superior to the natural world but fellow participants in the cosmic experience of suffering and hope.

This solidarity shaped my pastoral counseling approach when believers faced natural disasters or environmental-related health issues. Rather than offering simplistic explanations about God's specific purposes for their suffering, I helped them understand their experience as participation in creation's universal groaning, meaningful because it points toward the coming redemption, but not necessarily carrying individualized divine messages.

The groaning also explains why believers often feel a deep emotional connection to natural beauty and environmental destruction. As image-bearers of God, we're designed to exercise dominion over creation and find fulfillment in its flourishing. When we see environmental damage or experience natural disasters, we participate in creation's groaning at both physical and emotional levels.

Romans 8:22 thus stands as one of Scripture's most important statements about the relationship between redemption and the natural world. It assures us that creation's current suffering isn't permanent or meaningless but purposeful and temporary, birth pangs that herald the coming of God's new creation where righteousness dwells and corruption has no place. Until that day arrives, we join with all creation in groaning for the redemption that will transform not just human hearts but the entire cosmos itself.

Chapter Twenty-Three

The Waiting of the Redeemed

"And not only the creation, but we ourselves, who have the firstfruits of the Spirit, groan inwardly as we wait eagerly for adoption as sons, the redemption of our bodies." Romans 8:23

As we move from creation's universal groaning to Romans 8:23, Paul shifts his focus to believers themselves. This verse reveals a profound truth that shaped my understanding during my time of pastoral ministry: even those who possess salvation experience a deep longing for something more. Paul doesn't describe believers as exempt from groaning but as participants in it alongside all creation. Yet our groaning differs fundamentally from creation's because we possess "the firstfruits of the Spirit."

The Firstfruits of the Spirit

Paul's agricultural metaphor would have resonated powerfully with his original audience. In ancient Israel, farmers brought the first portion of their harvest to the temple as an offering to God. These firstfruits served as both thanksgiving for what God had already provided and confident expectation of the full harvest to come.

When Paul describes believers as having "the firstfruits of the Spirit," he means we possess a genuine but partial experience of our ultimate redemption. The Holy Spirit dwelling within us represents the authentic beginning of our transformation, not merely a promise of future blessing. We taste real spiritual life, experience genuine communion with God, and receive actual power for holy living.

During my time as a seminary professor, I often encountered students who struggled with this concept. They wondered why they still battled sin, faced doubts, or experienced spiritual dryness if they truly possessed the Spirit. Romans 8:23 provided the answer: we have the firstfruits, not the full harvest. Our current experience of salvation is real but incomplete.

This understanding proved invaluable in my pastoral counseling. When believers confessed their ongoing struggles with temptation or their sense that something was still missing in their spiritual lives, I could assure them that their dissatisfaction actually confirmed rather than contradicted their salvation. The Spirit within them created a holy discontent with anything less than perfect fellowship with God.

Internal Groaning

Paul specifies that believers "groan inwardly" (*en heautois stenazomen* in Greek). This internal groaning distinguishes our experience from creation's external manifestations of futility. While earthquakes and diseases represent creation's outward groaning, believers experience a deep, internal longing that often defies articulation.

This groaning manifests in various ways throughout the Christian life. Sometimes it appears as dissatisfaction with our current level of spiritual maturity. We read Scripture and recognize the gap between what we understand and how we live. We pray and sense the distance between our hearts and God's holiness. We serve others and notice how mixed our motives remain.

Other times, this groaning emerges as grief over sin's continued presence in our lives. Reformed theology's teaching about the believer's remaining corruption means we continue struggling with sinful desires and behaviors even after conversion. The Spirit within us creates conflict with these remaining sinful patterns, producing the internal groaning Paul describes.

I experienced this groaning acutely during my military service. Surrounded by moral compromise and often participating in activities that grieved my conscience, I felt a constant tension between my redeemed identity and my unredeemed environment. The Spirit within me longed for conditions where righteousness could flourish without resistance. This internal groaning also appears as longing for deeper communion with God. Even our richest experiences of worship, prayer, and fellowship with other believers leave us wanting more. We catch glimpses of God's glory that create hunger for the face-to-face fellowship we'll enjoy in the new creation.

Waiting for Adoption

Paul describes this groaning as "waiting for adoption as sons" (*huiothesian apekdechomenoi* in Greek). At first glance, this seems puzzling since he already identified believers as God's children in verses 14-16. The apparent contradiction resolves when we understand adoption as both a present reality and future completion.

In Roman law, adoption was a dramatic legal transaction that immediately transferred a person from one family to another with full rights and privileges. Paul uses this metaphor to describe both our current status as God's children and our future experience of that status in its fullness.

We presently possess adoption through our union with Christ. God legally declares us His children, grants us inheritance rights, and treats us as family members. The Spirit witnesses to our spirits that we are God's children, assuring us of our new identity and relationship.

However, our experience of adoption remains incomplete in our current state. We still inhabit bodies subject to death, live in a world dominated by sin's effects, and struggle with remaining corruption in our hearts. The full experience of our adoption awaits the resurrection when we receive glorified bodies and dwell in the new creation.

During my pastoral ministry, I noticed that many believers struggled with feeling like "real" Christians because their experience didn't match their expectations. They possessed genuine faith but still battled depression, faced financial difficulties, or dealt with chronic illness. Understanding adoption as both present reality and future completion helped them embrace their current identity while maintaining hope for future transformation.

The Redemption of Our Bodies

Paul specifically mentions "the redemption of our bodies" (*ten apolytrsin tou smatos hemn* in Greek) as the object of our waiting. This phrase captures the physical dimension of our salvation that distinguishes Christian hope from merely spiritual or ethereal expectations.

Greek philosophy generally viewed the body as a prison for the soul, something to escape rather than redeem. Some early Christian groups adopted this perspective, teaching that salvation meant liberation from physical existence. Paul explicitly rejects this view by describing bodily redemption as central to our hope.

The "redemption of our bodies" refers to the resurrection when believers receive glorified physical bodies suited for life in the new creation. These won't be completely different bodies but our current bodies transformed and perfected. Just as Christ's resurrection body retained continuity with His pre-resurrection body while possessing new qualities, our resurrection bodies will maintain our personal identity while being freed from corruption, weakness, and mortality.

This hope sustained me through various physical challenges during my military service and later years. When injury, illness, or aging reminded me of my body's limitations, I remembered that my current physical struggles represent part of creation's groaning, not God's final word about embodied existence.

The emphasis on bodily redemption also validates the importance of physical stewardship in Christian living. Since our bodies will be redeemed rather than discarded, how we treat them matters. We care for our physical health not as an ultimate goal but as proper stewardship of what God will eventually perfect.

The Nature of Christian Waiting

Paul's description of believers "waiting" (*apekdechomenoi* in Greek) reveals important characteristics of genuine Christian hope. This isn't passive resignation or wishful thinking but active, confident expectation based on God's promises and past faithfulness.

The verb Paul uses suggests eager anticipation, like a child waiting for Christmas morning or a soldier counting the days until deployment ends. Our waiting involves certainty about the outcome combined with patience regarding the timing. We know God will complete our redemption because He has already begun it through the Spirit's presence within us.

This waiting also requires perseverance through current difficulties. Understanding that our groaning serves a purpose, pointing toward future glory, helps us endure present suffering without despair or bitterness. We can acknowledge our struggles honestly while maintaining hope that they're temporary.

Reformed theology's doctrine of perseverance of the saints provides the foundation for this patient waiting. God doesn't merely offer salvation and leave its completion uncertain. He guarantees that those He begins to save, He will bring to final glorification. Our waiting rests on divine commitment, not human effort.

Practical Implications

Romans 8:23 shapes Christian living in several practical ways. First, it validates the reality of an ongoing struggle in the believer's life. When we feel tension between our redeemed identity and current experience, we can recognize this as evidence of the Spirit's work rather than proof of spiritual failure.

Second, this verse provides a proper perspective on suffering and difficulty. Our groaning participates in creation's larger pattern of longing for redemption. Individual trials take on cosmic significance as part of the birth pangs preceding God's new creation.

Third, Romans 8:23 guards against both despair and false triumphalism. We minimize neither our current struggles nor pretend they don't exist. We acknowledge them honestly while maintaining confident hope in their ultimate resolution.

Finally, this verse cultivates proper priorities for Christian living. Since we're waiting for bodily redemption and dwelling in the new creation, we hold current circumstances and achievements lightly while investing in what will endure. We serve God faithfully in our present context while maintaining an eternal perspective on our activities and relationships.

The internal groaning Paul describes thus becomes not a source of frustration but a mark of spiritual health. Those who possess the Spirit's firstfruits naturally long for the full harvest. Our dissatisfaction with anything less than perfect fellowship with God confirms rather than contradicts our salvation, pointing forward to the day when waiting will end and we'll experience the fullness of what God has prepared for those who love Him.

Chapter Twenty-Four

Hope that Saves

"For in this hope we were saved. Now hope that is seen is not hope. For who hopes for what he sees?" Romans 8:24

Romans 8:24 moves from describing our present groaning to explaining the nature of the hope that sustains us. Paul's words cut to the heart of what salvation actually means and how it functions in the believer's life.

When Paul writes, "in this hope we were saved," he uses the aorist tense in Greek, indicating a completed action in the past. This doesn't contradict his earlier teaching about ongoing salvation but highlights a crucial aspect of our redemption. We were saved by hope, not just saved and then given hope as an additional benefit. Hope itself formed part of the saving transaction.

This challenges modern evangelical thinking, which often treats salvation as a simple past event followed by Christian living. Paul presents salvation as fundamentally future-oriented from its very beginning. When God saved us, He saved us into a hope that reaches forward to complete redemption. Our salvation never existed apart from this forward-looking dimension.

During my years in pastoral ministry, I encountered many believers who struggled with assurance because they focused exclusively on their initial conversion experience. They wondered if their faith was real because they couldn't pinpoint the exact moment when everything changed. Paul's teaching here provides tremendous comfort for such believers. We were saved by hope, saved into a future we don't yet fully experience but confidently expect.

The Greek word for hope (*elpis*) carries stronger connotations than its English equivalent. Biblical hope isn't wishful thinking or uncertain longing but confident expectation based on reliable promises. When Paul says we were saved "in this hope," he means we were saved into a certain future secured by God's character and power.

Reformed theology's doctrine of eternal security finds strong support in this verse. If we were saved by hope in future glorification, then our salvation depends on God's ability to bring that future to pass, not our ability to maintain faith or obedience. The hope that saved us initially continues to sustain us precisely because it rests on divine commitment rather than human performance.

The Paradox of Unseen Hope

Paul's next statement reveals the essential nature of biblical hope: "Now hope that is seen is not hope. For who hopes for what he sees?" This paradox illuminates why faith remains necessary throughout the Christian life and why believers continue to struggle with doubt and uncertainty.

Hope, by definition, concerns the unseen. Once we see something, we no longer hope for it but possess it. This means Christian hope necessarily involves an element of uncertainty from our human perspective, even while resting on divine certainties. We don't see our future glorification, the resurrection of our bodies, or the new heavens and earth. We believe in them based on God's promises revealed in Scripture.

This creates what I call the "tension of faith" living between the "already" and "not yet" of God's kingdom. We've already been saved, justified, and adopted as God's children. Yet we don't yet experience the fullness of these realities. Our bodies still decay, our minds remain clouded by sin's effects, and we face trials that test our faith. Hope bridges the gap between what God has declared about us and what we currently experience.

Some Christians become frustrated with this tension, wanting more tangible evidence of their salvation. They seek dramatic spiritual experiences, miraculous healings, or other visible confirmations of God's work in their lives. While God sometimes provides such experiences, Paul teaches that their absence doesn't indicate weak faith. Mature faith actually learns to hope in what remains unseen.

During my military service, I learned the importance of trusting orders even when I couldn't see the full battle plan. A good soldier follows commands based on confidence in his commanding officers, not because he understands every strategic detail. Similarly, Christian hope operates on trust in God's character and promises rather than a complete understanding of His methods or timing.

The unseen nature of Christian hope also protects us from disappointment with temporary circumstances. If our hope focused on immediate improvements in our lives, relationships, or circumstances, we'd face constant discouragement. Since our hope reaches beyond present experience to guaranteed future realities, current difficulties can't ultimately defeat it.

Faith and Hope Distinguished

Paul's emphasis on unseen hope clarifies the relationship between faith and hope in Christian experience. While Scripture sometimes uses these terms interchangeably, they have distinct functions in the believer's life.

Faith primarily concerns trust in God's character and reliance on His promises. Faith believes what God has revealed about Himself, about sin, about salvation, and about the future. Faith accepts these truths even when they contradict human wisdom or experience.

Hope takes faith's content and projects it forward, creating confident expectation about the future. Hope says, "Because I believe God's promises about salvation, I confidently expect resurrection and eternal life." Hope transforms faith's truths into motivation for present living.

This distinction helps explain why believers can have strong faith while struggling with discouragement about the future, or conversely, maintain hope despite intellectual doubts about specific doctrines. Faith and hope support each other but operate somewhat independently in our experience.

The writer of Hebrews captures this relationship perfectly: "Now faith is the assurance of things hoped for, the conviction of things not seen" (Hebrews 11:1). Faith provides the foundation for hope by establishing confidence in God's promises. Hope then gives faith a forward-looking orientation that motivates perseverance and obedience.

During seminary, I studied under professors who had endured significant personal trials, loss of children, spouse's serious illness, financial hardship, or ministry disappointments. What struck me most was how they maintained hope despite circumstances that might have crushed optimistic people. Their hope wasn't based on positive thinking or denial of difficulty but on a deep faith in God's ultimate purposes and promises.

Hope as Present Reality

While hope concerns the future, it functions as a present reality that shapes current experience. Romans 8:24 doesn't present hope as merely future consolation but as a current possession that influences how we live now.

The hope that saved us continues to save us daily by providing a perspective on present circumstances, motivation for obedience, and comfort in suffering. Hope transforms our understanding of current trials by placing them in the context of future glory. Hope energizes our service to God by connecting present faithfulness with eternal rewards. Hope sustains us through disappointment by assuring us that our deepest longings will ultimately be satisfied.

This present dimension of hope distinguishes biblical Christianity from purely otherworldly religions that encourage escape from current reality. Christian hope doesn't withdraw us from engagement with the world but equips us for faithful living in difficult circumstances. We can invest ourselves fully in present responsibilities because hope assures us that nothing done in faith is ultimately meaningless.

Reformed theology's emphasis on God's sovereignty strengthens this present aspect of hope. Since God controls all circumstances and works everything according to His purposes, we can maintain hope even in seemingly hopeless situations. Our hope doesn't depend on favorable circumstances but on God's character and plan.

The corporate dimension of hope also deserves emphasis. Paul writes, "we were saved" and "we hope," indicating that Christian hope is shared by the entire community of believers. Individual believers don't hope in isolation but participate in the church's collective expectation of Christ's return and the consummation of God's kingdom.

This corporate hope provides mutual encouragement when individual faith wavers. The church's worship, particularly in the Lord's Supper, proclaims Christ's death "until he comes" (1 Corinthians 11:26), regularly refreshing our hope in His return. The fellowship of believers serves as a foretaste of the ultimate fellowship we'll enjoy in the new creation.

Hope and Perseverance

The connection between hope and perseverance appears throughout Paul's writings and finds clear expression in Romans 8:24-25. Since hope concerns the unseen, it requires patient waiting and steadfast endurance. This isn't passive resignation but active persistence in faith and obedience despite contrary circumstances.

Hope-based perseverance differs qualitatively from mere human determination or optimism. Human persistence eventually exhausts itself when faced with overwhelming odds or extended trials. Hope-based perseverance draws its strength from confidence in God's promises rather than human resources.

This divine foundation for perseverance explains why Christians can maintain hope in situations that would defeat purely human optimism. The cancer patient who continues trusting God despite physical decline, the missionary who persists in ministry despite apparent lack of results, the parent who keeps praying for a rebellious child despite years of disappointment, all demonstrate hope that transcends human understanding.

During my pastoral ministry, I observed that believers who understood hope's biblical nature generally handled trials better than those who viewed faith primarily as a means to improve current circumstances. When Christians expect faith to solve all their problems immediately, disappointment often follows. When they understand that faith saves them into hope for future glory, they can endure present difficulties with greater stability.

The community aspect of perseverance also proves crucial. Individual believers may experience times when hope feels weak or distant. The corporate worship, mutual encouragement, and shared testimony of the church help sustain individual hope during such periods. We persevere not only through our own hope but through participation in the hope of the entire body of Christ.

Hope that saves thus encompasses both our initial salvation and our ongoing experience as believers. It reaches back to our conversion, extends forward to our glorification, and operates powerfully in our present circumstances. This hope doesn't disappoint because it rests on God's proven faithfulness and unchanging character. As Paul will declare in the climax of Romans 8, nothing can separate us from the love of God in Christ Jesus our Lord, and that includes the ultimate fulfillment of the hope by which we were saved.

Chapter Twenty-Five

Patience in Expectation

"But if we hope for what we do not see, we wait for it with patience." Romans 8:25

Romans 8:25 follows naturally from Paul's declaration about hope in verse 24. This verse reveals a crucial dimension of the Christian life that many believers struggle to understand and practice. The patience Paul describes isn't mere resignation or passive waiting, but an active, confident expectation grounded in God's promises.

The Greek word translated "patience" here is *hypomone*, which carries the idea of steadfast endurance, remaining under pressure without giving way. This isn't the patience we exercise when waiting in a doctor's office or sitting in traffic. This is the patience of a soldier who holds his position despite enemy fire, the patience of a farmer who tends his crops through seasons of drought, the patience of a mother who never stops believing her prodigal child will return home.

During my years in the Marines, I learned the difference between merely waiting and waiting with purpose. A Marine on watch doesn't just pass time; he maintains alertness, readiness, and focus on his mission. Similarly, Christian patience isn't idle waiting but purposeful endurance sustained by confident hope in God's promises.

The connection between hoping and waiting proves inseparable in Paul's thought. We cannot genuinely hope for what we already possess. The very nature of hope requires that its object remain future and currently unseen. This creates the need for patience. Since we hope for what we do not yet see: our full redemption, the resurrection of our bodies, the renewal of creation, we must wait with endurance.

This waiting tests our faith more severely than perhaps any other aspect of Christian living. In our instant-gratification culture, patience has become almost a lost virtue. We want immediate answers to prayer, quick solutions to problems, and fast relief from suffering. But God's timeline rarely matches our preferences. His ways are higher than our ways, and His thoughts higher than our thoughts (Isaiah 55:9).

Reformed theology helps us understand why this patience proves necessary and how it serves God's purposes. Divine sovereignty means God orchestrates all events according to His eternal plan. The timing of Christ's return, the duration of our trials, the pace of our sanctification; all occur according to God's perfect wisdom, not our human impatience.

This theological foundation transforms our understanding of waiting. Instead of viewing delays as divine indifference or obstacles to overcome, we can receive them as opportunities for growth and expressions of God's perfect timing. The patience required by hope becomes a means of grace, conforming us more fully to the image of Christ.

The Nature of Christian Patience

Christian patience differs fundamentally from Stoic resignation or Buddhist detachment. Stoics sought to eliminate desire to avoid disappointment. Buddhists aim to transcend attachment to escape suffering. Christians maintain passionate engagement with God's promises while trusting His timing for their fulfillment.

This active quality of Christian patience appears throughout Scripture. Abraham waited twenty-five years for the fulfillment of God's promise regarding Isaac, but he didn't become passive during that time. He continued walking with God, interceding for Sodom, and growing in faith. David waited years between his anointing as king and his actual coronation, but he used that time serving Saul faithfully and developing the skills he would need as Israel's leader.

The patience Paul describes in Romans 8:25 operates from this same active engagement. We wait for our full redemption while actively pursuing holiness. We hope for the resurrection while faithfully stewarding our current bodies. We anticipate the renewal of creation while responsibly caring for the earth God has entrusted to us.

This patience also maintains a forward focus that sustains us through present difficulties. When I served as a pastor, I often counseled believers who struggled with discouragement because their circumstances hadn't improved despite faithful prayer and service. The key breakthrough usually came when they understood that their current situation, however difficult, was temporary, while their hope in Christ was eternal.

Paul's own life exemplified this patient endurance. Despite shipwrecks, beatings, imprisonments, and constant opposition, he maintained his hope in Christ's return and the completion of God's purposes. His patience wasn't grounded in optimistic temperament or philosophical resignation but in confident trust in God's character and promises.

The patience of hope also provides a perspective on the relative importance of present circumstances. When we truly grasp that "the sufferings of this present time are not worth comparing with the glory that is to be revealed to us" (Romans 8:18), we can endure current hardships with greater equanimity. This doesn't minimize real pain or struggle, but it places them in proper eternal perspective.

Patience as Spiritual Discipline

Patience functions both as a fruit of the Spirit (Galatians 5:22) and a spiritual discipline we must actively cultivate. Like all spiritual graces, patience grows through practice and the means of grace God has provided.

Scripture meditation proves essential for developing Christian patience. As we saturate our minds with God's promises and examples of His faithfulness throughout history, our capacity for patient endurance increases. The Psalms particularly help us learn patient waiting, as David repeatedly expresses both his struggles with waiting and his determination to trust God's timing.

Prayer also cultivates patience by maintaining our connection with God during times of waiting. Through prayer, we express our desires to God while simultaneously submitting to His will and timing. Prayer doesn't necessarily speed up God's answers, but it sustains our souls during the waiting process.

Corporate worship reinforces patient hope by connecting us with the broader community of believers who share our expectation of Christ's return. When individual faith wavers, the collective hope of the church provides stability and encouragement. The regular celebration of the Lord's Supper particularly strengthens our patient hope by proclaiming Christ's death "until he comes" (1 Corinthians 11:26).

Christian fellowship with mature believers also builds patience. Older saints who have walked with God through many seasons of waiting can provide wisdom, encouragement, and living examples of faithful endurance. Their testimonies of God's faithfulness in the past strengthen our confidence in His faithfulness for the future.

Service to others during our seasons of waiting prevents the self-focus that often accompanies impatience. When we invest ourselves in loving and serving others, we find purpose and meaning even during difficult waiting periods. This service also reminds us that God often uses our present circumstances to prepare us for future ministry opportunities.

The Connection Between Patience and Assurance

The patience Paul describes in Romans 8:25 flows from assurance of salvation rather than uncertainty about our standing with God. Believers who doubt their salvation often struggle with impatient anxiety about their spiritual condition. They want immediate confirmation of God's love and acceptance rather than learning to rest in the promises of Scripture.

Reformed theology's emphasis on the perseverance of the saints provides crucial support for patient endurance. Since God chose us in Christ before the foundation of the world and sealed us with the Holy Spirit, we can wait patiently for the completion of His work in us. Our salvation doesn't depend on our perfect patience, but our patience grows from confidence in our secure salvation.

This assurance enables us to view present trials as temporary afflictions rather than permanent conditions or signs of divine rejection. A believer experiencing prolonged illness, financial hardship, or relational conflict can maintain hope because these circumstances don't threaten their ultimate security in Christ.

The patience of hope also demonstrates the genuineness of our faith to ourselves and others. False converts often abandon their profession when immediate benefits don't materialize or when following Christ requires sacrifice. Genuine believers, sustained by the Spirit's work in their hearts, persevere through times of difficulty and delayed answers to prayer.

This patient endurance serves as evidence of spiritual maturity. New believers often expect rapid transformation and immediate answers to prayer. Mature believers understand that God typically works slowly, through ordinary means, over extended periods. They've learned to find satisfaction in small steps of growth rather than demanding dramatic breakthroughs.

The corporate dimension of patience also strengthens individual assurance. When we see other believers maintaining faithful hope through extended trials, our own confidence in God's promises increases. The church's patience throughout history provides a powerful testimony to the reliability of Christian hope.

Patience in Suffering and Sanctification

Romans 8:25 appears within Paul's broader discussion of suffering and glory, indicating that much of our patient waiting involves enduring present hardships while anticipating future relief. This patience in suffering requires careful theological understanding to avoid both presumption and despair.

Christian patience doesn't assume that all suffering will end in this life. Some believers experience healing from illness; others maintain faithful hope while their conditions worsen. Some find resolution to relational conflicts; others practice forgiveness while relationships remain broken. Our patience hopes ultimately for the resurrection and renewal of all things, not necessarily for the immediate improvement of current circumstances.

This realistic understanding of patience prevents the false teaching that sufficient faith will always produce immediate deliverance from trials. Such teaching destroys patience by suggesting that continued suffering indicates inadequate faith or hidden sin. Biblical patience recognizes that God sometimes calls His people to endure rather than escape their difficulties.

The patience required for sanctification proves equally challenging. New believers often expect rapid transformation into Christlikeness, becoming discouraged when old patterns of sin persist or when spiritual growth occurs slowly. Mature believers understand that sanctification typically proceeds gradually, requiring patient cooperation with the Spirit's work over many years.

This patience in sanctification acknowledges the reality of remaining sin while maintaining hope for progressive transformation. We don't excuse ongoing sin or become passive about spiritual growth, but we also don't demand perfection from ourselves or become paralyzed by failure. Patient hope enables us to confess sin, receive forgiveness, and continue pursuing holiness without losing confidence in God's grace.

The patience Paul describes ultimately finds its foundation and example in Christ Himself. Jesus waited thirty years before beginning His public ministry, endured rejection and opposition throughout His earthly life, and submitted to the Father's timing even unto death on the cross. His patient obedience provides both the model and the motivation for our own endurance as we await His return and the completion of all God's promises.

Chapter Twenty-Six

The Helper in Our Weakness

"Likewise the Spirit helps us in our weakness. For we do not know what to pray for as we ought, but the Spirit himself intercedes for us with groanings too deep for words." Romans 8:26

When I first encountered Romans 8:26 as a young believer, I thought I understood what Paul meant about the Spirit helping us in our weakness. I figured it was about getting divine assistance when I felt spiritually tired or when prayer seemed difficult. But after decades of pastoral ministry and careful study of Scripture, I've come to see that this verse reveals something far more profound about our condition and God's gracious provision. This single verse contains layers of theological truth that have sustained me through some of the darkest valleys of ministry and personal struggle.

The Reality of Our Weakness

Paul begins with "likewise," connecting this verse to the previous discussion about creation's groaning and our own inner groaning as we await redemption. Just as creation labors under the curse and believers groan inwardly for the redemption of our bodies, we also experience profound weakness in our spiritual lives. This isn't the weakness that comes from temporary fatigue or emotional stress, though those certainly qualify. Paul addresses something more fundamental to our fallen condition.

The Greek word for weakness here is *astheneia*, which carries the idea of being without strength, feeble, or powerless. It's the same word used to describe physical illness, but Paul applies it to our spiritual condition. Even as regenerated believers indwelt by the Holy Spirit, we remain profoundly weak in crucial ways. This weakness isn't sin, though it can lead to sin if we don't recognize our need for divine help.

I remember a particularly difficult period in my pastoral ministry when a young father in our congregation died suddenly, leaving behind a wife and three small children. As I sat with the grieving widow, trying to offer comfort and guidance, I felt the weight of my own inadequacy. What words could possibly address such devastating loss? How could I pray in a way that would bring genuine help rather than empty religious platitudes? In that moment, I experienced the weakness Paul describes, not knowing how to pray as I ought.

This weakness manifests in several ways. First, we lack a complete understanding of God's will in specific situations. We see only fragments of His eternal purposes and often misinterpret present circumstances. Second, our knowledge of what to request in prayer remains limited by our finite perspective. We might pray for things that would ultimately harm us or fail to pray for blessings God wants to give. Third, even when we know generally what to pray for, we struggle to pray with the intensity, persistence, and faith that circumstances require.

Reformed theology helps us understand that this weakness stems from the ongoing effects of the fall. Though we've been regenerated and justified, we won't experience complete restoration until glorification. Our minds remain partially darkened, our affections remain partially disordered, and our wills remain partially bound. We're saints who are still being sanctified, children of God who are still learning to think and act like our heavenly Father.

The Spirit's Help

Into this weakness steps the Holy Spirit with divine assistance. The word "helps" translates the Greek *synantilambanetai*, which literally means "to take hold of together with" or "to lend a hand together." It's a compound word that pictures someone coming alongside to share a burden that's too heavy for one person to carry alone. The Spirit doesn't take over our responsibility to pray, but He joins us in the work, providing strength where we lack it.

This help comes to us as believers who are already indwelt by the Spirit. Paul isn't describing the Spirit's work in bringing us to faith or sealing us for salvation; those works are complete. Rather, he addresses the Spirit's ongoing ministry in our daily Christian experience. The same Spirit who regenerated us, who testifies with our spirit that we are God's children, and who will raise our mortal bodies also assists us in our weakness.

The Spirit's help operates in ways both mysterious and practical. Sometimes I've experienced this as a sudden clarity about how to pray for someone or what Scripture passage to share in a counseling situation. Other times, the help feels less specific but equally real; a sense of God's presence during prayer, an assurance that He hears even when words fail, or strength to continue interceding when natural energy would have given up.

During my time as a seminary professor, I often taught Romans 8:26 to students preparing for ministry. I emphasized that this verse doesn't promise we'll always know exactly what to pray for or that prayer will become easy. Instead, it assures us that our ignorance and weakness don't disqualify our prayers or make them ineffective. The Spirit's help means our fumbling attempts at prayer reach the Father's ears as perfectly formed intercession.

Our Ignorance in Prayer

Paul specifically identifies our ignorance as a key aspect of our weakness: "For we do not know what to pray for as we ought." This statement might surprise believers who think spiritual maturity means always knowing how to pray correctly. But Paul includes himself among those who don't know what to pray for. If an apostle who received direct revelation from God admits this limitation, how much more should we acknowledge our own ignorance?

This ignorance manifests in several ways. We don't always know God's specific will for particular situations. Should we pray for healing or for grace to endure illness? Should we ask for financial provision or for contentment in material need? Should we intercede for a prodigal child's immediate return or for the deep work of repentance that might take years? We face these questions regularly without clear biblical directives for every specific case.

Our ignorance also extends to the manner of prayer. How long should we persist with certain requests? What levels of intensity appropriately match different concerns? When should we shift from petition to thanksgiving or from personal requests to worship? Even mature believers struggle with these practical aspects of prayer.

Perhaps most challenging, we don't always know our own hearts well enough to pray honestly. We might think we want one thing when we actually need something entirely different. We might pray for patience while unconsciously wanting to avoid the trials that develop patience. We might ask for spiritual growth while resisting the discipline that produces it.

I've experienced this ignorance countless times in pastoral ministry. Families would request prayer for financial blessing when what they really needed was wisdom about spending habits. Church members would ask for prayer about finding a spouse when their greater need involved learning contentment in singleness. Young men would seek prayer about "God's will" for their lives when their real struggle involved simple obedience to clear biblical commands.

The phrase "as we ought" indicates there are right and wrong ways to pray, appropriate and inappropriate requests. Jesus taught us to pray, "your will be done," suggesting that our prayers should align with God's purposes rather than merely expressing our immediate desires. But discerning God's will requires wisdom we don't naturally possess and understanding that comes only through the Spirit's illumination.

The Spirit's Intercession

Here we encounter one of the most remarkable truths in Scripture: "but the Spirit himself intercedes for us with groanings too deep for words." The Holy Spirit, the third person of the Trinity, personally intercedes on behalf of believers. This intercession doesn't supplement or correct our prayers; it transforms them into perfect communication with the Father.

The word "intercedes" (*hyperentynchanei*) means to meet with someone on behalf of another, to petition or make requests. It's the same word used later in Romans 8:34 to describe Christ's intercession for us at the Father's right hand. Both the Son and the Spirit intercede for believers, ensuring that our needs reach the Father's attention through perfect mediation.

The "groanings too deep for words" doesn't refer to speaking in tongues or to audible sounds the Spirit makes. Rather, they describe intercession that transcends human language altogether. The Spirit knows our needs, understands the Father's will, and communicates perfectly between the two without requiring words that human minds could comprehend.

These groanings connect to the broader theme of groaning that runs through Romans 8. Creation groans under the curse (verse 22), believers groan inwardly as we await redemption (verse 23), and now the Spirit groans in intercession (verse 26). All three groanings express longing for the complete restoration that will come when Christ returns and makes all things new.

During particularly difficult seasons of ministry, this truth about the Spirit's intercession provided immense comfort. When church conflicts seemed intractable, when personal struggles felt overwhelming, when words failed completely, I could rest in the knowledge that the Spirit was interceding with perfect understanding of both my needs and the Father's will. My stammering prayers were being translated into perfect communication within the Trinity itself.

The Implications for Christian Life

Understanding the Spirit's help in our weakness transforms how we approach prayer and spiritual disciplines. First, it humbles us by acknowledging our ongoing need for divine assistance. Mature believers don't graduate beyond this weakness; we simply become more aware of it and more dependent on the Spirit's help.

Second, it encourages us to pray even when we don't know exactly what to request. We don't need to figure everything out before approaching God's throne. The Spirit takes our honest but imperfect prayers and presents them to the Father in perfect form.

Third, it assures us that God hears and responds to our prayers even when they feel inadequate. The effectiveness of prayer doesn't depend on our eloquence, theological precision, or emotional intensity. It depends on the Spirit's perfect intercession on our behalf.

This truth also teaches us to trust God's responses to our prayers, even when they differ from our specific requests. If the Spirit is interceding according to God's will, then the answers we receive, including "no" and "wait" reflect perfect wisdom and love. Our limited understanding might not immediately grasp why certain prayers are answered as they are, but we can trust that the Spirit's intercession secures what's best for us.

The Spirit's help in our weakness reminds us that Christian life is fundamentally supernatural. We're not merely trying harder to be good people or following a moral philosophy. We're participants in the life of the Trinity itself, with the Spirit dwelling within us, interceding for us, and enabling spiritual growth that would be impossible through human effort alone.

Chapter Twenty-Seven

The Searcher of Hearts

"**And he who searches hearts knows what is the mind of the Spirit, because the Spirit intercedes for the saints according to the will of God." Romans 8:27**

The Spirit's intercession leads Paul to an even more profound truth in Romans 8:27. This verse reveals the perfect coordination within the Trinity as the Father, who searches all hearts, understands exactly what the Spirit communicates on our behalf. The phrase "he who searches hearts" refers to God the Father, drawing from the rich Old Testament tradition that describes God's complete knowledge of human thoughts and intentions. Jeremiah 17:10 declares, "I the Lord search the heart and test the mind, to give every man according to his ways, according to the fruit of his deeds." First Chronicles 28:9 reminds us that "the Lord searches all hearts and understands every plan and thought." This isn't casual observation; it's penetrating, comprehensive knowledge that reaches into the deepest recesses of human nature.

During my time as a pastor, I watched people struggle with the reality that God knows their hearts completely. Some found this threatening, imagining an angry deity cataloguing their failures. Others discovered it liberating, realizing they could stop pretending and present their authentic selves to God. The truth is both sobering and comforting: God's knowledge of our hearts means we can't hide our sin, but it also means we can't hide our sincere love for Him, even when that love feels weak or confused.

Perfect Communication Within the Trinity

The Father's perfect knowledge of the Spirit's mind ensures that the Spirit's intercession is perfectly understood and perfectly received. When the verse says God "knows what is the mind of the Spirit," it doesn't suggest the Father learns something previously unknown. Rather, it emphasizes the complete harmony and communication within the Trinity. The Spirit's groanings that are "too deep for words" for human understanding are perfectly clear to the Father.

This divine communication operates on a level far beyond human comprehension. When we intercede for others, we often misunderstand their true needs or pray for things that might actually harm them. Our knowledge is partial, our motives mixed, our understanding clouded by sin and limitation. The Spirit faces none of these obstacles. His intercession flows from perfect knowledge of our actual needs and perfect understanding of the Father's will.

Reformed theology has always emphasized the unity of purpose within the Trinity. The Father, Son, and Holy Spirit work together in perfect harmony for the salvation and sanctification of believers. We see this coordination throughout the work of redemption: the Father sends the Son; the Son accomplishes redemption; and the Spirit applies that redemption to individual believers. Here in Romans 8:27, we observe this same divine cooperation in the ongoing work of intercession.

I remember counseling a young mother whose child suffered from a serious illness. She prayed constantly for healing, but her prayers felt mechanical, desperate, filled more with fear than faith. She worried that her anxiety made her prayers ineffective, that God wouldn't hear her because she couldn't pray with perfect trust. I reminded her of this verse; that the Spirit was taking her heart's cry, her love for her child, her desperate hope, and translating all of it into perfect intercession that the Father understood completely. Her weakness in prayer didn't disqualify her; it created the very space where the Spirit's strength could operate.

According to the Will of God

The crucial phrase "according to the will of God" defines the nature and scope of the Spirit's intercession. The Spirit doesn't intercede according to our immediate desires, our emotional impulses, or even our carefully reasoned requests. He intercedes according to God's perfect will, which always aims at our ultimate good and God's ultimate glory.

This creates a remarkable dynamic in prayer. When we pray, we often focus on circumstances we want changed, health restored, relationships mended, financial problems solved, opportunities opened. These aren't wrong desires, but they represent our limited perspective on what we need. The Spirit sees the bigger picture. He understands how current struggles might produce future character, how apparent setbacks might redirect us toward better paths, how unanswered prayers might protect us from harm we can't foresee.

Reformed doctrine teaches that God's will is both sovereign and good. Everything that happens falls within God's permissive or directive will, and God works all things together for the good of those who love Him. The Spirit's intercession operates within this framework, ensuring that our prayers align with God's comprehensive plan for our lives and His kingdom.

During my time teaching at the seminary, I watched students wrestle with the tension between human responsibility in prayer and divine sovereignty in outcomes. Some concluded they shouldn't pray specifically since God would do whatever He planned anyway. Others swung toward demanding that God answer their prayers exactly as requested, as if prayer were a mechanism for controlling divine action. The truth of the Spirit's intercession cuts through both errors. We pray earnestly and specifically because prayer matters, but we trust the Spirit to translate our prayers into alignment with God's perfect will.

The Heart as the Center of Human Nature

The reference to God searching hearts points to the biblical understanding of the heart as the center of human personality, emotion, will, and spiritual life. In Hebrew thought, the heart wasn't merely the seat of emotions but the control center of the entire person. Proverbs 4:23 instructs us to "guard your heart with all vigilance, for from it flow the springs of life."

God's knowledge of our hearts means He understands our true motivations, our deepest fears, our genuine longings, and our actual spiritual condition. He sees past the masks we wear, the spiritual language we use, and the religious activities we perform. He knows when our prayers flow from genuine faith and when they spring from selfish ambition. He discerns between authentic spiritual hunger and mere emotional manipulation.

This comprehensive knowledge should humble us. We can't impress God with eloquent prayers or manipulate Him with emotional appeals. He sees through every pretense and knows exactly who we are. But this same knowledge should also comfort us. When we feel spiritually dry, when our prayers seem to bounce off the ceiling, when we struggle to find words for our deepest needs, God sees the authentic spiritual life within us that we might not even recognize ourselves.

One of the most profound counseling sessions I ever conducted involved a man who had struggled with addiction for years. He told me he felt unworthy to pray, that his repeated failures made him a hypocrite before God. As we studied this passage together, he began to understand that God saw his genuine desire for freedom, his authentic love for his family, his real hatred of his sin, all the heart-level realities that his behavior had obscured. The Spirit could take those deep heart cries and present them to the Father as perfect intercession, even when his conscious prayers felt empty and false.

Practical Implications for Prayer

Understanding that God searches hearts and that the Spirit intercedes according to His will transforms our approach to prayer in several practical ways. First, it encourages honesty in prayer. Since God knows our hearts anyway, we might as well speak truthfully about our struggles, doubts, fears, and failures. Pretending to be more spiritual than we are doesn't fool God and only hinders our spiritual growth.

Second, it relieves the pressure to pray perfectly. We don't need to find exactly the right words, strike precisely the right tone, or maintain flawless theological accuracy in our prayers.

The Spirit takes our imperfect communication and makes it perfect before the Father. This doesn't excuse carelessness in prayer, but it frees us from the paralysis that comes from trying to craft bulletproof petitions.

Third, it teaches us to trust God's response to our prayers. When God answers differently than we requested, we can trust that the Spirit's intercession secured what was truly best. Our limited perspective might not immediately understand why certain prayers receive "no" answers, but we can rest in the knowledge that perfect wisdom guided those decisions.

Fourth, it encourages persistence in prayer even during seasons of spiritual dryness. When prayer feels mechanical or our hearts seem cold, we can continue approaching God's throne, trusting that the Spirit is working beneath the surface of our conscious experience. The Spirit's intercession doesn't depend on our emotional state or spiritual fervor; it flows from His perfect love and understanding.

Finally, it deepens our appreciation for the supernatural nature of Christian life. Prayer isn't merely a human activity directed toward a distant deity. It's participation in the ongoing work of the Trinity, with the Spirit enabling communication between believers and the Father that transcends human limitation. This reality should fill us with wonder and gratitude as we recognize the privilege of being included in such divine interaction.

The truth that God searches hearts and perfectly understands the Spirit's intercession on our behalf provides one of the strongest foundations for confidence in prayer that Scripture offers. We need not fear that our weaknesses will disqualify our prayers or that our limitations will prevent God from understanding our needs. The Spirit bridges every gap, translates every groan, and ensures that our hearts' true cries reach the Father's ears in perfect form.

Chapter Twenty-Eight

The Assurance of Divine Purpose

"And we know that for those who love God all things work together for good, for those who are called according to his purpose." Romans 8:28

Romans 8:28 stands as one of Scripture's most quoted yet most misunderstood promises. I've heard it recited at hospital bedsides, whispered at gravesides, and offered as quick comfort in the face of tragedy. The words roll off the tongue with such familiarity that their profound theological weight often goes unnoticed.

During my time as a pastor, I watched this verse get weaponized as a simplistic band-aid for complex suffering.

Someone would lose a child, and well-meaning believers would immediately invoke Romans 8:28 as if it explained everything, solved everything, made everything acceptable. The grieving parent was expected to smile through tears and affirm that, yes, God was working this horror for good. That misapplication of Scripture caused more damage than I could fully measure.

The problem wasn't with the verse itself but with how we stripped it from its context and reduced it to a spiritual platitude. Romans 8:28 doesn't promise that all things are good or that we'll understand how tragedy serves divine purposes. It makes a far more specific, theologically rich claim about God's sovereign work in the lives of those He has called. Understanding this verse properly requires us to examine its components carefully, see how it fits within Paul's larger argument, and apply it with both boldness and appropriate restraint.

The Certainty of Knowledge

Paul begins with an assertion of certainty: "And we know." Not "we hope" or "we believe" or "we've been told." The Greek word *oidamen* carries the sense of settled, certain knowledge based on reliable evidence. Paul wasn't speculating or offering his personal opinion. He was stating an established reality that believers could count on with complete confidence.

This certainty doesn't come from empirical observation. When we look at circumstances with natural eyes, we often see chaos, injustice, and apparent randomness. Good people suffer while wicked ones prosper. Prayers go unanswered while disasters strike believers and unbelievers alike. If we relied only on what we could see and measure, we would never arrive at the confidence Paul expresses here.

The certainty comes instead from revelation and the Spirit's witness. God has disclosed His purposes and character in

Scripture, and the Holy Spirit confirms these truths within believers. We know that all things work together for good because God has said so, and the Spirit enables us to grasp and trust this reality even when circumstances seem to contradict it.

I remember one of my best friends "my brother" lying in a field hospital after taking shrapnel, waiting for evacuation while medics worked on Marines with worse injuries. Nothing about that situation felt good. His pain was overwhelming, the fear was real, and the uncertainty about whether he'd keep his leg dominated my thoughts. Yet beneath the chaos, a settled conviction remained: God had not lost control, my friend's suffering had not surprised Him, and His purposes were advancing even in circumstances I couldn't begin to understand. That wasn't wishful thinking or emotional denial. It was the Spirit-enabled knowledge Paul describes here.

This certainty matters because suffering always attacks our confidence in God's goodness and control. When life falls apart, our natural response is to question whether God really cares, whether He's truly sovereign, whether His promises remain valid. Romans 8:28 provides an anchor of revealed truth that holds firm when feelings and circumstances conspire to drag us into doubt.

The Scope: All Things

Paul's statement is comprehensive: "all things work together for good." Not some things, not most things, but all things. Every circumstance, every experience, every event, without exception, serves God's good purposes in the lives of His people. This scope is staggering in its implications.

The word "all" includes the tragedies that break our hearts, the betrayals that wound our souls, the diseases that ravage our bodies, the failures that shame us, and the losses that leave us empty. It encompasses not just the major crises but also the daily frustrations, the chronic disappointments, the seemingly random hardships that accumulate over a lifetime. Every single element of human experience falls within the scope of this promise.

This doesn't mean that all things are themselves good. Paul never suggests that sin is good, that injustice is good, that suffering is good in itself. The goodness isn't found in the individual components but in how God orchestrates them toward a beneficial end. The same providence that permits cancer also sustains faith through it. The same sovereignty that allows betrayal also produces character through it. The same wisdom that doesn't prevent loss also ensures that loss serves eternal purposes.

The phrase "work together" translates the Greek *synergei*, from which we get our word "synergy." It describes elements combining to produce an effect greater than any single component could achieve alone. God doesn't use just pleasant experiences to accomplish His purposes or restrict His instruments to morally neutral events. He weaves together the entire tapestry of human experience: joy and sorrow, success and failure, health and sickness, gain and loss, into a pattern that serves His good ends.

I've watched this synergy unfold in my own life over decades. The Marine Corps discipline that seemed brutal at the time shaped pastoral faithfulness later. The theological battles that divided churches in painful ways deepened my understanding of Scripture and prepared me to teach seminary students. Losing my oldest son at too young of an age. The loss of friends to death and distance created a capacity for compassion I couldn't have developed otherwise. None of those individual experiences felt good in the moment. Many of them I would have avoided if given the choice. But looking back across decades, I can trace how God wove them together into something that served purposes far beyond my comfort or immediate happiness.

The Beneficiaries: Those Who Love God

Paul's promise doesn't extend to humanity in general. It applies specifically to "those who love God," which he immediately defines as "those who are called according to his purpose." This limitation is crucial for proper application of the verse.

Universal application of Romans 8:28 creates both theological confusion and pastoral damage. When we tell unbelievers that all things work together for their good, we make a promise Scripture doesn't make. God's common grace restrains evil and provides many blessings to all humanity, but that's different from asserting that every circumstance serves their ultimate benefit. For those outside Christ, many experiences serve divine purposes of judgment, revelation of sin's consequences, or demonstration of humanity's need for redemption; purposes that ultimately lead to condemnation unless they turn to Christ.

The phrase "those who love God" describes believers, but even this description is carefully qualified. Paul defines it as "those who are called according to his purpose." Our love for God is itself a response to His prior call. We love because He first loved us. Our affection for God isn't the grounds of His working all things for our good; it's evidence that His call has taken effect in our lives.

This points to the Reformed understanding of effectual calling. God doesn't merely invite all people generally to respond to the gospel. He specifically and powerfully calls His elect, working in their hearts to produce genuine faith and love. Those who love God are those whom God has called to Himself through the Spirit's regenerating work. The promise of

Romans 8:28 rests on this foundation of divine election and calling, not on human emotion or religious performance.

The Outcome: For Good

The "good" Paul promises requires definition. It's not primarily health, wealth, comfort, or happiness, though God may grant any of these as He wills. The good is conformity to Christ's image, which Paul makes explicit in verse 29. God works all things to make believers like Jesus in character, priorities, affections, and perspective.

This good is comprehensive, touching every dimension of human existence. It includes spiritual maturity, moral transformation, experiential knowledge of God, refined faith, deeper joy, genuine holiness, and eternal glory. These benefits far exceed temporary comfort but also prove far more elusive to immediate perception. We can measure physical healing or financial provision quickly, but conformity to Christ unfolds across a lifetime and reaches completion only in glory.

Chapter Twenty-Nine

The Pattern of Predestined Conformity

"For those whom he foreknew he also predestined to be conformed to the image of his Son, in order that he might be the firstborn among many brothers." Romans 8:29

Romans 8:29 begins with a word that has generated centuries of theological debate: "For those whom he foreknew he also predestined to be conformed to the image of his Son." The term "foreknew" translates the Greek *proegnō*, and its proper understanding shapes our entire grasp of divine election.

Arminian theology interprets foreknowledge as God's advance awareness of who would believe. In this view, God looked down the corridors of time, saw who would freely choose to accept Christ, and elected them based on that foreseen faith. This interpretation makes human decision the determining factor in election and reduces God's foreknowledge to sophisticated prediction.

Reformed theology rejects this reading on both exegetical and theological grounds. In Scripture, knowledge, particularly God's knowledge, carries relational and covenantal significance beyond mere awareness of facts. When the Bible says God "knew" Israel among all the families of the earth (Amos 3:2), it doesn't mean He was aware they existed while remaining ignorant of other nations. The knowledge referenced is an intimate, purposeful, covenant-establishing relationship.

Similarly, when Jesus says, "I never knew you" to those who claimed His name (Matthew 7:23), He doesn't mean He lacked information about their existence. He means He never established a saving relationship with them. Throughout Scripture, God's knowing involves choosing, loving, and setting apart for Himself.

The verb tense matters here. Paul uses the aorist tense, pointing to a definite action in the past. God foreknew; He established a relationship with certain individuals before time began, before they existed, before they believed, before they did anything good or bad. This foreknowledge is God's sovereign choice to set His covenant love on particular persons.

I've watched students wrestle with this doctrine in my seminary classes. The resistance often stems from misunderstanding what's at stake. We think election threatens human responsibility or makes God arbitrary. But Paul anchors our assurance in God's initiative, not our decision. If salvation depends on God foreseeing our faith, then our faith becomes the foundation of salvation rather than God's grace. The comfort of Romans 8 dissolves if our faith, not God's choice, is the ultimate determining factor.

Predestination: The Purpose of Divine Choice

The text moves immediately from foreknowledge to predestination: "he also predestined." The Greek *proōrisen* means to determine beforehand, to decide in advance. This isn't God reacting to circumstances or adjusting His plans based on human choices. Before creation, before the fall, before our birth, God marked out our destiny.

The Westminster Confession defines predestination as "God's eternal decree, whereby He did, from before the foundation of the world, unchangeably ordain whatsoever comes to pass, and especially did choose a definite number of persons unto everlasting life." This doesn't make God the author of sin; the Confession is careful to distinguish between God's decree and human responsibility, but it does mean nothing occurs outside His sovereign purpose.

Paul's confidence in Romans 8 flows from this doctrine. If my salvation depended on my maintaining faith, my perseverance in love, my continued obedience, I'd have no basis for assurance. I know my fickleness, my weakness, my capacity for spiritual failure. But if God predestined me, if He determined my destiny before I drew breath, then my salvation rests on His unchanging purpose rather than my fluctuating faithfulness.

Critics charge that predestination makes humans into puppets or robots, stripping away genuine choice and moral responsibility. But this criticism misunderstands both divine sovereignty and human agency. God's decree doesn't eliminate human will; it establishes the context within which human will operates. We genuinely choose, but our choices unfold within the framework of God's sovereign plan.

I've made thousands of decisions across my lifetime: to enlist in the Marines, to pursue seminary education, to accept teaching positions, to marry, to stay faithful through hardship. None of those choices felt coerced. I deliberated, weighed options, and experienced genuine decision-making. Yet, looking back, I can trace God's hand guiding each step, opening certain doors, closing others, working in my heart to desire what He had planned. His sovereignty and my responsibility operated simultaneously without contradiction.

The Goal: Conformity to Christ's Image

Paul specifies the purpose of predestination: "to be conformed to the image of his Son." This phrase reveals what God has been working toward from eternity past and will continue working toward until Christ's return. The goal of election isn't merely to populate heaven or to rescue people from hell, though both are true. The goal is to reproduce Christ's character, nature, and glory in His people.

The word "conformed" translates *symmorphous*, meaning to share the same form or pattern. God intends His children to bear the family resemblance, to reflect the character of the firstborn Son. This conformity touches every dimension of our being: our thoughts, affections, desires, priorities, responses to suffering, relationships with others, and fundamental orientation toward God.

This conformity begins at regeneration when the Spirit imparts new life and continues through progressive sanctification as the Spirit works in us to will and to act according to God's good purpose. It reaches completion at glorification when we see Christ face to face and are fully transformed into His likeness.

The image of Christ to which we're conformed isn't primarily His earthly appearance or His miraculous powers. It's His moral character, His love for the Father, His submission to divine will, His compassion for others, His hatred of sin, His trust in sovereign providence, His willingness to suffer for righteousness. Paul describes this character throughout his letters: love, joy, peace, patience, kindness, goodness, faithfulness, gentleness, self-control.

I've observed this transformation in my own life over decades, though the progress often feels glacial. The angry young Marine who solved problems through force and intimidation bears little resemblance to the man I am now, though the change occurred so gradually I rarely noticed it happening. The impatient seminary student who valued intellectual precision over pastoral compassion learned, through painful experience, that truth without love is a clanging cymbal. The pastor, who once needed to be right in every theological debate, discovered that unity in Christ transcends many secondary doctrinal differences.

None of these changes originated from my effort alone. I cooperated certainly; I studied Scripture, pursued discipline, practiced spiritual habits, sought accountability. But the fundamental transformation came from the Spirit's work, conforming me to Christ's image according to the Father's predestined purpose. Every trial that refined my character, every hardship that deepened my faith, every loss that shifted my priorities served this goal.

The Firstborn Among Many Brothers

Paul adds a crucial phrase: "in order that he might be the firstborn among many brothers." This explains why God chose to save many rather than only Christ. The purpose wasn't just to redeem individuals but to create a family with Christ as the head and pattern.

The term "firstborn" carries significant theological weight. In ancient Near Eastern culture, the firstborn son held preeminence in the family, receiving the inheritance and the father's blessing. Applied to Christ, it doesn't mean He was created first. John's Gospel establishes that the Word was with God in the beginning and was God Himself. Rather, it speaks to Christ's supremacy and headship over the new humanity.

Christ is the prototype, the pattern, the firstborn of the new creation. His resurrection inaugurated the age to come. His transformation from humiliation to glory maps the journey every believer will complete. His victory over sin and death guarantees the victory of all who belong to Him. He blazed the trail from death to life, from earth to heaven, from suffering to glory, and we follow in His footsteps.

The phrase "many brothers" reveals God's intention to populate heaven with a vast family bearing Christ's likeness. We aren't meant to be isolated believers pursuing individual salvation. We're being knit together into a corporate body, a family, a community united by shared nature and common destiny. Christ isn't ashamed to call us brothers (Hebrews 2:11), and this familial relationship shapes both our identity and our relationships with fellow believers.

This brotherhood transcends all human distinctions. In Christ, there is neither Jew nor Gentile, slave nor free, male nor female. The family of God includes people from every tribe, tongue, and nation. What unites us, shared conformity to Christ's image, far exceeds what divides us. The Marine Corps taught me the power of shared identity to overcome differences. Men from vastly different backgrounds, with conflicting political views and divergent personalities, became brothers through common training and a shared mission. How much more does conformity to Christ create genuine brotherhood among believers?

The Certainty of Completion

The chain of salvation Paul outlines in verses 29-30 provides absolute assurance. Everyone God foreknew, He predestined. Everyone He predestined, He called. Everyone He called, He justified. Everyone He justified, He will glorify. No link breaks in this chain. No one falls through the cracks between election and glorification.

This certainty doesn't depend on our maintaining faith through our own strength. It rests on God's unchanging purpose and irresistible grace. The same God who initiated salvation will complete it. The same Spirit who began the good work will carry it through to completion.

I've watched believers struggle with assurance, wondering if they've truly believed, if their faith is genuine, if they'll persevere to the end. These doubts often intensify during times of spiritual dryness or moral failure. But Romans 8:29 shifts our focus from our faithfulness to God's. The question isn't whether I can maintain my commitment to God but whether God will maintain His commitment to me. And Paul's answer is unequivocal: what God starts, He finishes.

This doctrine of perseverance doesn't promote carelessness about sin or a casual approach to obedience. Rather, it provides the secure foundation from which genuine holiness grows. When I know God won't abandon me despite my failures, I'm freed to confess sin honestly rather than hiding it. When I trust that the Spirit will complete the work He started, I can pursue sanctification without fear that temporary setbacks disqualify me from salvation.

Chapter Thirty

The Chain of Salvation's Glory

"And those whom he predestined he also called, and those whom he called he also justified, and those whom he justified he also glorified." Romans 8:30

Romans 8:30 presents one of Scripture's most remarkable statements. Five actions, all executed by God, forming an unbreakable chain from eternity past to eternity future. What strikes me most about this verse is Paul's use of the past tense throughout, even for glorification, which hasn't yet occurred. He wrote with such confidence in God's sovereign purpose that he described our future glory as an accomplished fact.

I've meditated on this verse countless times over the decades, both in foxholes and classrooms, both in moments of spiritual victory and times of profound doubt. It stands as one of the most comforting passages in all of Scripture, yet also one of the most controversial. The chain Paul describes leaves no room for human contribution to initiate or maintain salvation. God predestines, God calls, God justifies, God glorifies. From beginning to end, salvation is the Lord's work.

The five links: foreknowledge, predestination, calling, justification, and glorification, form a seamless progression. Paul already covered foreknowledge and predestination in verse 29, establishing that God's choice preceded any human response. Now he moves to the temporal outworking of that eternal purpose through calling and justification, then leaps forward to the guaranteed result: glorification.

The Effectual Call

"Those whom he predestined he also called." This calling differs radically from the general invitation of the gospel that goes out to all people. Jesus said, many are called, but few are chosen, distinguishing between the outward call that can be rejected and the inward call that cannot. Reformed theology terms this the effectual call or irresistible grace, not because people can't resist initially, but because God's call ultimately overcomes all resistance and brings the elect to faith.

I've preached the gospel to countless people over the years. Some listened politely and walked away unchanged. Others grew angry at the message. Still others appeared interested but never committed. Yet some heard the same words and responded with genuine repentance and faith. What made the difference? Not my eloquence, not their superior intellect or morality, but God's sovereign call working in their hearts.

The effectual call works through the gospel message but adds the Spirit's illumination and regeneration. The same truth that bounces off hardened hearts penetrates chosen hearts. The Spirit opens blind eyes to see Christ's beauty, unplugs deaf ears to hear His voice, softens stone hearts to respond to His love. The called person doesn't just receive information; they experience transformation. They don't just understand facts about Christ; they encounter Christ Himself.

This calling is irresistible not because it overpowers human will but because it changes human will. God doesn't drag unwilling people into His kingdom; He makes willing people out of rebels. The Spirit grants new birth, creating a new nature that desires what it once hated. The called sinner suddenly finds Christ infinitely desirable, sin infinitely ugly, and grace infinitely precious. They come to Christ freely and gladly, yet they come only because the Father drew them.

I remember my own conversion, how the truths I'd heard a hundred times suddenly blazed with new meaning. The gospel I'd known intellectually since childhood became personal and urgent. I saw my sin not as minor mistakes but as cosmic treason against a holy God. I recognized Christ not as a historical figure or moral teacher but as my only hope for reconciliation with God. I responded with faith and repentance, convinced my choice was utterly free, yet now I understand that my freedom to choose Christ came only after God's call liberated me from slavery to sin.

The Declaration of Righteousness

"Those whom he called he also justified." Justification represents the legal verdict God pronounces over everyone who responds to His call with faith. It's a forensic term, drawn from the courtroom, describing not an internal change but an external declaration. God declares the believing sinner righteous based on Christ's righteousness credited to their account.

This doctrine formed the cornerstone of the Reformation. Martin Luther discovered that righteousness comes not through human works but through faith in Christ's finished work. He found peace when he understood that the righteousness God requires, God provides. We don't become righteous and therefore get declared righteous; rather, God declares us righteous and then begins making us righteous through sanctification.

The ground of justification is Christ's perfect obedience, both active and passive. His active obedience, thirty-three years of flawless conformity to God's law, provides the positive righteousness we need. His passive obedience, enduring the cross and bearing God's wrath, removes the penalty our sins deserved. Through faith, we're united to Christ so that His righteousness becomes ours and our sin becomes His. God punished Christ for our sins, then credits Christ's righteousness to us. It's the great exchange, purchased at Calvary and applied by the Spirit.

Justification happens once, at the moment of conversion, and never needs repeating. Unlike sanctification, which progresses gradually, justification is instantaneous and complete. God doesn't declare us partially righteous with plans to increase the verdict later. He declares us fully righteous in Christ, as righteous as we'll ever be, based on Christ's perfect work rather than our imperfect progress.

This truth sustained me through every spiritual battle. During times when my sanctification seemed stalled, when the same sins kept tripping me, when my prayers felt hollow and Scripture felt dry, I clung to the unchanging reality of my justification. My standing with God didn't fluctuate based on my spiritual temperature. I remained as justified on my worst days as on my best days because justification rests on Christ's righteousness, not mine.

Paul's progression here is crucial: those whom God called, He justified. Not those who called themselves, not those who tried hard enough, but those whom God called. The connection is absolute. Everyone God effectually calls, He justifies. The call produces faith, and faith receives justification. No one hears God's call and remains unforgiven. No one responds to the gospel and gets rejected by God.

Already Glorified

"Those whom he justified he also glorified." This statement should take our breath away. Paul used the past tense for something that hasn't happened yet. From our perspective, glorification remains future, awaiting Christ's return or our death. Yet Paul described it as accomplished, as certain as justification and calling.

This grammatical choice reveals Paul's confidence in God's unchanging purpose. What God intends, He achieves. What God promises, He delivers. Since God has already decided to glorify everyone He justified, their glorification is as guaranteed as if it already occurred. The future is so certain it can be spoken of as past.

Glorification represents the final stage of salvation, when God removes all remaining traces of sin and transforms us into Christ's perfect likeness. Our bodies will be raised imperishable, powerful, glorious, and spiritual. Our minds will be freed from deception and doubt. Our wills will be liberated from sinful inclinations. Our emotions will be purified of selfish desire. We'll finally become what God always intended: image bearers reflecting His glory without distortion.

The connection between justification and glorification is absolute. Everyone God justifies, He glorifies. No exceptions, no failures, no lost cases. This destroys any notion that salvation can be lost. If everyone justified gets glorified, then justified believers cannot forfeit their salvation. The chain doesn't break between justification and glorification any more than it breaks between predestination and calling.

I've wrestled with believers who feared they'd committed the unpardonable sin or fallen beyond redemption. Their struggles with ongoing sin, their doubts about God's goodness, their seasons of spiritual coldness convinced them they'd lost salvation. But Romans 8:30 offers rock-solid assurance: if God justified you, He will glorify you. Your glorification isn't contingent on your performance but on God's purpose.

The Unbroken Chain

The beauty of this verse lies in its seamless progression. Everyone God foreknew, He predestined. Everyone He predestined, He called. Everyone He called, He justified. Everyone He justified, He glorified. No dropouts, no failures, no ones who almost made it. The chain extends unbroken from God's eternal counsel to our eternal glory.

This doesn't mean believers never struggle with doubt or sin. It doesn't mean the Christian life is easy or that faith never wavers. But it does mean that God's purpose cannot be thwarted. He who began a good work will complete it. The Spirit who indwells believers will not abandon them. The Father, who chose them before the foundation of the world, will bring them safely home.

Critics argue that this doctrine promotes complacency. If salvation is guaranteed, why pursue holiness? Why resist temptation? Why persevere through trials? But this objection misunderstands both the doctrine and human nature. Assurance doesn't breed carelessness; it provides the security necessary for genuine transformation. Children don't obey parents better when constantly threatened with abandonment. They thrive when secure in their parents' unchanging love.

Moreover, God doesn't just decree the end; He ordains the means. He predestined not just our glorification but our sanctification. He called us not just to salvation but to holiness. Those whom God justified, He also sanctifies. The same unbreakable chain that guarantees our final glorification guarantees the progressive transformation that prepares us for it.

Personal Reflection

I've lived long enough to witness God's faithfulness across decades. I've seen Him sustain believers through crushing grief, devastating illness, financial ruin, and spiritual darkness. I've watched Him restore backslidden saints, renew cold hearts, and revive dying faith. I've never seen Him abandon anyone who belonged to Him.

This chain of salvation transformed my ministry. Early in my pastoral work, I felt a crushing responsibility for my congregation's spiritual state. I believed their perseverance depended on my preaching skill, my counseling wisdom, my leadership ability. The weight was unbearable. But Romans 8:30 lifted that burden. My role is to faithfully proclaim truth and shepherd God's flock, but their salvation rests on God's sovereign purpose, not my competence in ministry.

The military taught me that the mission's success depends on each link in the chain. One broken link compromises everything. But in God's chain of salvation, no link can break because God Himself forges each one. He predestines according to His eternal purpose. He calls according to His irresistible grace. He justifies according to His perfect righteousness. He glorifies according to His unchanging promise.

This verse silences every accusation the enemy throws at believers. Satan whispers that we're not really saved, that our sins disqualify us, that we'll never make it to heaven. But Romans 8:30 declares that everyone God justified, He also glorified. The verdict is already rendered. The outcome is already determined. Our glorification is as certain as God's character.

When I stand before God's throne, it won't be my righteousness, my perseverance, or my faithfulness that gains entrance. It will be the unbreakable chain of God's sovereign purpose, executed through Christ's perfect work and applied by the Spirit's effectual call. From election to glorification, salvation is the Lord's accomplishment, secured by His power and guaranteed by His promise.

Chapter Thirty-One

God is Our Invincible Ally

> "What then shall we say to these things?
> If God is for us, who can be against us?"
> **Romans 8:31**

Paul just laid out the unbreakable chain of salvation. Now he asks the question that should dominate every believer's consciousness: What do we say in response to these truths? His answer reshapes everything we thought we knew about spiritual warfare, opposition, and ultimate security.

The "these things" Paul references encompasses everything he's written from verse 28 onward, perhaps from the beginning of chapter eight, or even from the start of Romans. God works all things together for good. He predestined, called, justified, and glorified His people. These realities demand a response, and Paul provides it in a question that has sustained believers through twenty centuries of persecution, suffering, and spiritual attack.

The Logic of Divine Alliance

"If God is for us, who can be against us?" The question isn't rhetorical flourish or wishful thinking. It's ironclad logic built on the foundation Paul just established. If the sovereign Creator who holds all power, who predestined us before time began, who called us with irresistible grace, who justified us by Christ's righteousness, and who promises to glorify us without fail, if this God stands on our side, then what opposition matters?

I've faced enemies in combat and adversaries in ministry, but neither compares to having God as an ally. During my Marine years, we assessed threats based on capability and intent. An enemy with intent but no capability posed little danger. An enemy with capability but no intent required monitoring. But an enemy with both demanded immediate action. Paul flips this assessment on its head. Our spiritual enemies possess both intent and significant capabilities, but they face an ally whose power renders their capabilities meaningless.

The conditional "if" doesn't express doubt about whether God is for us. In Greek, this construction assumes the truth of the condition. Paul could have written, "Since God is for us," but "if" invites believers to test the premise against their own experience and the scriptural evidence Paul just provided. Examine your calling. Consider your justification. Recall God's promises. The evidence confirms that God indeed stands for His people.

What "For Us" Means

God being "for us" transcends mere favoritism or preference. It means God actively works toward our ultimate good, our conformity to Christ's image, and our final glorification. He doesn't just passively approve of us or mildly prefer our welfare. He commits His infinite resources, His unchanging purpose, and His sovereign power to guarantee our salvation and transformation.

This truth wrecked my early misconceptions about God's disposition toward believers. I grew up viewing God as perpetually disappointed, barely tolerating my failures, ready to abandon me if I stepped too far out of line. But Romans 8:31 demolishes that caricature. The God who predestined me before I drew breath, who called me while I was His enemy, who justified me despite my ongoing sin, this God is definitively, actively, unchangeably for me.

"For us" also carries legal connotations. In a courtroom, having someone "for you" means they advocate your case, defend your interests, and work toward your acquittal. God doesn't just observe our trial from the gallery. He serves as judge, advocate, and the one who paid our penalty. Every aspect of the judicial process works toward our vindication because God Himself ensures it.

The Impossibility of Effective Opposition

"Who can be against us?" The answer: plenty of beings are against us, but none can be against us effectively. Satan opposes us. The world system fights us. Our own flesh wars against the Spirit. False teachers attack the truth. Persecution targets the faithful. But opposition and effective opposition are different categories entirely.

I watched believers in communist countries face imprisonment, torture, and death for their faith. Their enemies possessed terrifying power. Secret police could arrest them without a warrant. Courts could convict them without evidence. Guards could kill them without consequence. Yet, those believers displayed a peace and confidence that baffled their captors. They understood Romans 8:31. Yes, enemies could destroy their bodies, ruin their reputations, and devastate their families. But they couldn't touch what mattered most; their relationship with God and their guaranteed glorification.

The question "who can be against us?" expects the answer "no one effectively." Paul doesn't deny the reality of opposition. He's declaring its ultimate futility. Our enemies may wound us, but they cannot destroy us. They may delay our progress, but they cannot derail God's purpose. They may cause temporary suffering, but they cannot prevent eternal glory.

The Nature of Divine Support

When God is "for us," what does His support entail? Everything. He provides wisdom for decisions, strength for battles, grace for failures, comfort for sorrows, and power for transformation. He doesn't support us; he's like a distant patron who occasionally sends aid. He indwells us by His Spirit, constantly working within us to will and to work for His good pleasure.

This support operates on multiple levels. Spiritually, God provides everything necessary for life and godliness. He grants repentance, sustains faith, produces fruit, and guarantees perseverance. Emotionally, He offers comfort that transcends understanding, peace amid chaos, and joy despite circumstances. Physically, He works all things, including sickness, loss, and suffering, toward our ultimate good and His greater glory.

I've experienced this support in ways that defy natural explanation. During my darkest pastoral seasons, when congregational conflict threatened to crush my spirit, when my teaching faced vicious attack, when personal failures left me questioning my calling, God's sustaining presence never wavered. He didn't remove the trials. He didn't shield me from consequences. But He provided strength I didn't possess, wisdom beyond my education, and endurance that had no natural source.

Historical Opposition and Divine Vindication

Church history testifies to the truth of Romans 8:31. Roman emperors threw believers to the lions. Medieval authorities burned reformers at the stake. Communist regimes imprisoned pastors in gulags. Islamic extremists martyred missionaries. Yet the church not only survived but thrived. The blood of martyrs became the seed that produced exponential growth. Persecution refined rather than destroyed God's people.

Polycarp faced execution in the second century. Officials offered him freedom if he'd curse Christ. His response echoed Romans 8:31: "Eighty-six years I have served Him, and He has done me no wrong. How can I blaspheme my King who saved me?" Polycarp understood that regardless of what Rome did to his body, God's support guaranteed his ultimate victory.

The Reformation's opponents wielded immense power; political, ecclesiastical, and military. They excommunicated reformers, confiscated property, executed leaders, and waged wars. But truth prevailed because God stood behind it. The gates of hell cannot prevail against the church because the church's ally is invincible.

Personal Enemies and Divine Protection

This verse applies not just to cosmic spiritual warfare but to daily opposition. When colleagues undermine your work, when neighbors mock your faith, when family members reject you for following Christ, God is for you. When disease attacks your body, when financial disaster threatens your security, when depression clouds your mind, God remains actively committed to your good.

I've counseled believers facing devastating opposition. Cancer patients uncertain about survival. Betrayed spouses dealing with infidelity. Parents grieving wayward children. Employees fired for refusing to compromise convictions. In each case, Romans 8:31 provided an anchor. The circumstances didn't change immediately. The opposition remained real and painful. But the assurance that God stood with them transformed their response.

One Marine I served with faced court-martial for refusing an order that violated his conscience. His career, reputation, and freedom hung in the balance. He could have compromised, rationalized obedience, or hidden behind orders. Instead, he quoted Romans 8:31 and accepted whatever consequences came. The court ultimately vindicated him, but even if they hadn't, God's support guaranteed what mattered most, his integrity before God and his eternal reward.

The Foundation of Christian Courage

Knowing God is for us produces courage that confounds observers. Peter and John faced the Sanhedrin with a boldness that astonished their accusers. Stephen faced stoning with a vision of glory. Paul endured shipwrecks, beatings, imprisonment, and eventual execution with unwavering confidence. Their courage didn't stem from personality or training. It flowed from the certainty that God stood with them.

This courage doesn't mean foolhardiness or presumption. It doesn't justify reckless behavior or unnecessary risks. But it does mean that when God's call leads through danger, His people can advance without fear. When obedience requires sacrifice, believers can give without reservation. When truth demands a costly stand, the faithful can speak without wavering.

I've needed this courage repeatedly throughout my life. Combat required physical courage, advancing under fire, making decisions that risked lives, facing enemies who wanted me dead. Ministry required moral courage, confronting sin in powerful members, teaching unpopular truths, maintaining standards despite pressure to compromise. Aging requires yet another kind of courage, facing mortality, accepting limitations, trusting God through decline. In every case, Romans 8:31 provided the foundation. If God is for me, what do I have to fear?

The Unanswerable Question

Paul's question demands an answer: Who can effectively oppose those whom God supports? Satan? He's a defeated enemy, disarmed at the cross. The world? It's passing away along with its desires. Sin? Christ condemned it in His flesh. Death? It holds no terror for those guaranteed resurrection. Human authorities? They serve God's purposes whether they acknowledge Him or not.

The question isn't answered because it can't be answered. No power in creation can ultimately harm those God determines to save and glorify. Opposition may succeed temporarily, believers suffer, churches face persecution, individual Christians die, but the final outcome remains certain. God's purpose will prevail. His people will be glorified. His enemies will be vanquished.

This doesn't mean believers live charmed lives free from hardship. Paul himself faced constant opposition; beaten, imprisoned, shipwrecked, slandered, rejected. Yet he knew no opposition could separate him from God's love or thwart God's purpose. The worst his enemies could do amounted to nothing compared to what God promised to accomplish.

Romans 8:31 stands as the believer's declaration of independence from fear. Not independence from God; we're utterly dependent on Him, but independence from the power of circumstances, enemies, or opposition to dictate our response or determine our destiny. God is for us. That changes everything.

Chapter Thirty-Two

The Supreme Proof of God's Love

"He who did not spare his own Son but gave him up for us all, how will he not also with him graciously give us all things?" Romans 8:32

Romans 8:32 presents what I consider the most compelling logical argument in Scripture. Paul constructed an argument from the greater to the lesser. If God performed the costliest act imaginable, surrendering His Son, then every lesser gift flows naturally from that supreme sacrifice.

I learned logic in seminary, studied formal reasoning, and mastered the structure of valid arguments. But no syllogism I encountered matched the devastating force of Paul's reasoning here. The premise: God gave His Son. The conclusion is: God will give everything else. Between those two statements lies a chasm no counterargument can cross.

During my years of teaching theology, students occasionally challenged divine providence. "How can we trust God with our circumstances when He seems distant from our suffering?" Romans 8:32 answered that question every time. The God who sacrificed His Son hasn't suddenly become stingy or indifferent. The cross proves His commitment to our ultimate good in a way nothing else could.

He Did Not Spare

The phrase "did not spare" carries devastating weight in Greek. Paul chose a word loaded with Old Testament resonance, deliberately echoing Abraham's near-sacrifice of Isaac. When God stopped Abraham's hand, the angel declared, "You have not withheld your son, your only son." But God did what He prevented Abraham from doing, He withheld nothing, spared nothing, held back nothing when our redemption hung in the balance.

I've stood at military funerals, watched fathers receive folded flags, heard mothers sob over sons who died serving their country. The grief cuts deep because parents should never outlive their children. Every instinct rebels against it. Yet God chose that path. He delivered His Son to torture, mockery, and execution when one word could have stopped it all.

The cross wasn't an unfortunate accident God couldn't prevent. It wasn't a tragedy that caught Him off guard. Acts 2:23 states Christ was "delivered up according to the definite plan and foreknowledge of God." Before creation, before sin entered the world, before Adam drew breath, God determined to sacrifice His Son. That decision cost more than we can fathom.

Reformed theology emphasizes God's sovereignty in salvation. He initiates, He accomplishes, He completes. Romans 8:32 reveals the price of that sovereignty. God didn't wait for humans to make the first move. He didn't offer salvation contingently, hoping we'd accept. He gave His Son while we were still enemies, still rebels, still dead in sin. The initiative, the cost, the sacrifice, all God's.

His Own Son

Paul emphasized "his own Son," not merely a prophet, not just a messenger, not simply a created being elevated to special status. God surrendered the Second Person of the Trinity, co-equal, co-eternal, sharing the divine essence. The Father gave up the Son with whom He enjoyed eternal fellowship, perfect communion, infinite love.

Theologians debate the Trinity's inner life, speculate about the relationships within the Godhead, and propose theories about eternal generation and procession. But this much we know with certainty: the Father loves the Son with a love that transcends anything we experience. When God declared at Christ's baptism, "This is my beloved Son, with whom I am well pleased," He revealed a relationship of infinite depth and joy.

That makes the sacrifice even more staggering. God didn't give up something peripheral. He surrendered the one He loved most, the one who brought Him greatest joy, the one whose fellowship defined eternity. Parents who've lost children glimpse a fraction of that anguish. But even the most devoted earthly father can't match the Father's love for the Son.

I've counseled parents through devastating losses. I've watched them wrestle with God, demand answers, rage against the unfairness. And I've pointed them to Romans 8:32. God understands that pain. He chose it voluntarily. He entered into it deliberately. The cross reveals a Father willing to sacrifice everything for His children's redemption.

Gave Him Up for Us All

The Greek word translated "gave him up" carries the sense of handing over, delivering, surrendering. It's the same word used when Judas betrayed Christ, when Pilate delivered Him to be crucified, when the soldiers handed Him over to executioners. God actively delivered His Son to suffering and death.

This wasn't passive permission. God didn't merely allow events to unfold. He orchestrated them, appointed them, determined them from eternity. Isaiah 53:10 states, "It was the will of the LORD to crush him." The Father wounded the Son. The righteous Judge condemned the innocent substitute. The holy God poured out wrath on the beloved Son.

Reformed theology's doctrine of penal substitutionary atonement finds its clearest expression here. Christ didn't die merely as an example or to demonstrate love or to inspire devotion. He died as a substitute, bearing the punishment we deserved, satisfying divine justice on our behalf. God gave Him up to condemnation so we could receive justification. He delivered Him to wrath so we could inherit mercy.

The phrase "for us all" requires careful examination. In context, Paul addressed believers: those called according to God's purpose, those predestined, those justified and glorified. The "us all" refers to all the elect, all whom God determined to save, all who would ultimately believe. Christ's death possesses infinite value, but its application extends specifically to those the Father gave the Son.

I've debated Arminian colleagues about the atonement's extent. They argue Christ died equally for everyone without exception. But Romans 8:32's logic collapses under universal atonement. If God gave Christ for absolutely everyone, why doesn't everyone receive all things? Why do many perish? The "us all" must refer to the elect, those for whom Christ's death guarantees every other blessing.

How Will He Not Also Give Us All Things?

Paul's question expects an obvious answer: of course God will give us everything else! If He performed the costliest act, every lesser gift follows inevitably. The logic proves unassailable. The God who spared nothing to accomplish our redemption won't withhold anything needed to complete it.

"All things" encompasses every blessing required for our ultimate glorification. Not necessarily everything we want, not every comfort we desire, not every circumstance we'd choose. But everything necessary for conforming us to Christ's image, sustaining us through suffering, completing our sanctification, and bringing us safely to glory.

During my Marine career, I saw brothers die in combat. I watched young men, strong, faithful, devoted to Christ, cut down by bullets or explosions. I questioned God's provision. Where were "all things" when my friend bled out in my arms? Where were the promised blessings when that mortar round destroyed a fireteam?

Romans 8:32 didn't erase those questions immediately. But over time, I understood that "all things" includes strength to endure, grace to persevere, hope that transcends death, and the certainty of resurrection. God didn't promise to spare us from suffering. He promised to provide everything needed within it and beyond it. My friend received the ultimate blessing, immediate entrance into glory, freedom from sin, completion of the race. God gave him all things, just not the ones I wanted to see at that moment.

Graciously Give

Paul added "graciously" to emphasize the nature of God's giving. These blessings don't come as payment for the Son's sacrifice, as if we're owed them because Christ died. They come as grace, unmerited, undeserved, flowing from God's generous character rather than our worthiness.

The Greek word here appears throughout Paul's writings, always carrying connotations of free favor, lavish generosity, gracious bestowal. God doesn't dispense blessings grudgingly, measure them carefully, or ration them stingily. He pours them out abundantly, gives them freely, bestows them joyfully.

I've watched Christians approach God like beggars hoping for scraps, uncertain whether He'll provide, anxious about whether they've earned His favor. Romans 8:32 demolishes that mindset. The God who gave His Son delights in giving everything else. We don't grovel for blessings; we receive them confidently based on the cross.

This doesn't mean presumption or demanding God fulfill our wishes. It means approaching the throne of grace with confidence, knowing the Father who sacrificed His Son to redeem us will certainly supply everything required to complete that redemption. Prayer becomes less about convincing a reluctant God and more about aligning ourselves with His generous purposes.

What "All Things" Includes

The "all things" God promises encompasses several categories. First, spiritual blessings, continued sanctification, increased holiness, growing Christlikeness, deeper communion with God. The Father who gave His Son won't abandon the sanctification process halfway through. He'll complete what He started.

Second, providential care, daily bread, necessary resources, sustaining grace, temporal provisions. Not unlimited wealth or constant comfort, but everything genuinely needed for our journey. God's definition of "needed" differs from ours, but His wisdom surpasses our understanding.

Third, relational restoration, reconciliation with God, adoption into His family, fellowship with other believers, eternal communion with the Trinity. The cross opened the way for relationship. God won't close the door He purchased at such cost.

Fourth, resurrection and glorification, transformed bodies, sinless nature, perfect holiness, eternal joy. The ultimate "all things" includes everything promised in glory. Death can't steal it, sin can't corrupt it, Satan can't destroy it.

Fifth, present help, strength for trials, comfort in grief, wisdom for decisions, courage for obedience. The Spirit who indwells us brings every resource needed for each moment. God doesn't withhold what we need when we need it.

I've tested this promise across decades. In combat, God provided courage when fear threatened to paralyze me. In ministry, He supplied wisdom when complex situations demanded discernment. In grief, He offered comfort when loss seemed unbearable. In doubt, He granted faith when questions multiplied. Not always immediately, not always how I expected, but always sufficiently.

The Security This Provides

Romans 8:32 establishes unshakable security for believers. If our salvation depended on our performance, we'd have reason to fear. We fail constantly, sin repeatedly, fall short continually. But our salvation rests on God's gift of His Son, not our achievement. And the God who gave that supreme gift guarantees every subsequent blessing.

This security doesn't produce laziness or license. It generates gratitude, devotion, and worship. How can we respond to such sacrificial love with indifference? The cross compels obedience, not from fear of losing salvation, but from overwhelming love for the One who gave everything.

I've counseled believers paralyzed by the fear of losing their salvation. "What if I commit an unforgivable sin? What if I fall away? What if God gives up on me?" Romans 8:32 answers every objection. The God who sacrificed His Son to save you won't abandon the project partway through. He'll complete what He started. He'll supply everything needed. He'll bring you safely home.

This verse has anchored my faith through storms of doubt, valleys of suffering, and seasons of spiritual dryness. When circumstances suggested God had forgotten me, Romans 8:32 declared otherwise. When trials made me question His goodness, the cross proved His commitment. When Satan whispered accusations, this truth silenced every charge. God gave His Son. He'll give everything else. That settles it.

Chapter Thirty-Three

No Accusation Can Stand

"Who shall bring any charge against God's elect? It is God who justifies." Romans 8:33

Romans 8:33 asks a rhetorical question that demands reflection. Paul structured this verse as a legal challenge, with language drawn from courtroom proceedings. The word "charge" translates from the Greek *enkaleō*, meaning to formally accuse, to bring legal action against someone, to present evidence of wrongdoing in a judicial setting. Paul imagined a courtroom scene with believers standing trial and challengers ready to prosecute.

But the question itself contains the answer. Who could possibly succeed in bringing charges that stick? The very nature of the question, "who shall?" anticipates the response: no one. Not because believers have no sins to accuse them of, but because of who declares them righteous.

I've watched this truth transform lives paralyzed by guilt. A veteran who couldn't forgive himself for actions in combat. A woman devastated by an abortion decades past. A man crushed under the weight of adultery that destroyed his family. Each carried accusations against themselves more severe than anything others leveled against them. Romans 8:33 spoke into their despair: God declares you righteous. Who dares contradict that verdict?

The Identity of the Accusers

Paul's question invites us to identify potential accusers. Several candidates present themselves. First, Satan himself, whose very name means "accuser" or "adversary." Revelation 12:10 calls him "the accuser of our brothers...who accuses them day and night before our God." He specializes in bringing charges, highlighting failures, cataloging sins, presenting evidence of unworthiness.

I've experienced his accusations throughout my Christian walk. In combat, he whispered that my participation in war disqualified me from ministry. After retirement from the Marines, he suggested my violent past made me unfit to teach theology. In pastoral ministry, he pointed out every failure, every mishandled situation, every person I couldn't help. His accusations never ceased.

Second, our own conscience accuses us. Romans 2:15 describes the conscience as bearing witness, with thoughts sometimes accusing, sometimes defending. Our internal voice often proves harsher than external critics. We know our secret sins, hidden motives, internal struggles. Conscience recites our failures in detail, presenting irrefutable evidence of our guilt.

Third, other people bring accusations. Sometimes legitimately, calling out genuine sin that requires repentance. Sometimes falsely, from misunderstanding or malice. Sometimes from mixed motives, where truth gets twisted to serve agendas. The world watches believers constantly, eager to expose hypocrisy, quick to condemn failure.

Fourth, the law itself accuses. Paul explored this thoroughly in Romans 1-3, demonstrating how the law reveals sin, exposes guilt, and pronounces judgment. The law's holy standard condemns everyone who falls short. And everyone does fall short.

Against this array of accusers, Satan, conscience, people, the law, Paul posed his challenge. Who shall bring charges? The question doesn't deny the reality of our sin or the legitimacy of some accusations. It declares their ultimate futility in light of God's justification.

The Meaning of Election

Paul identified believers as "God's elect." This term carries profound theological weight, especially within the Reformed understanding of salvation. Election refers to God's sovereign choice before the foundation of the world to set His love upon specific individuals, predestining them for salvation through Christ.

Ephesians 1:4-5 elaborates: "He chose us in him before the foundation of the world, that we should be holy and blameless before him. In love he predestined us for adoption to himself as sons through Jesus Christ, according to the purpose of his will." Election wasn't an afterthought or response to foreseen faith. God chose deliberately, purposefully, lovingly.

This doctrine troubles many because it challenges human autonomy and raises questions about fairness. How can God choose some and pass over others? Doesn't this make Him arbitrary or unjust? These objections assume God owes salvation to everyone, that He operates under obligations to His creatures. But Scripture presents a different picture.

Romans 9 addresses election directly. God told Moses, "I will have mercy on whom I have mercy, and I will have compassion on whom I have compassion" (Romans 9:15). Paul concluded, "So then it depends not on human will or exertion, but on God, who has mercy" (Romans 9:16). Election flows from God's sovereign mercy, not human merit or effort.

I struggled with election during my early years as a Christian. It seemed to undermine evangelism. Why preach if God has already chose who gets saved? It appeared to remove human responsibility. If God predetermined everything, how could people be held accountable? These questions drove me deeper into Scripture, where I discovered election doesn't eliminate human responsibility but establishes the foundation for genuine assurance.

Election means my salvation never depended on my decision, my faith, my perseverance. Those things matter and are necessary, but they're not the ultimate cause. God chose me before I existed, before I could choose Him, before I did anything good or bad. That choice can't be undone by my failures because it wasn't made based on my performance.

The Significance of Justification

Paul's answer to the accusation question centers on justification: "It is God who justifies." This verb carries courtroom connotations, declaring someone legally righteous, pronouncing a verdict of "not guilty," establishing someone as right before the law.

Justification in Reformed theology represents a legal declaration rather than an internal transformation. God doesn't justify us by making us inherently righteous; that's sanctification, a separate though related process. He justifies by declaring us righteous based on Christ's righteousness credited to our account. This happens instantaneously at conversion and remains unchanging regardless of our subsequent performance.

The doctrine rests on imputation, Christ's righteousness transferred to believers, our sin transferred to Christ. Paul explained in 2 Corinthians 5:21: "For our sake he made him to be sin who knew no sin, so that in him we might become the righteousness of God." This exchange, this great trade, forms the foundation of justification.

I've preached this truth countless times, watched it penetrate hearts hardened by legalism or crushed by failure. Justification means God doesn't declare us righteous because we've achieved some level of holiness. He declares us righteous because Christ achieved perfect holiness on our behalf. Our standing before God depends entirely on Christ's record, not ours.

This produces profound security. If justification depended on our righteousness, we'd face constant uncertainty. Did I pray enough today? Did I sin too much this week? Am I holy enough to remain justified? The questions never end, and the answers always condemn. But justification based on Christ's righteousness stands firm regardless of our fluctuating performance.

Who Dares Contradict God?

The force of Paul's argument builds on who does the justifying. Not a human judge whose verdict might be overturned. Not an angel whose knowledge has limits. Not even our own conscience, however well-informed. God Himself justifies.

God's authority exceeds all other authorities infinitely. His knowledge encompasses all facts: past, present, future. His judgment never errs, never gets swayed by emotion or manipulation, never misses evidence. His verdicts stand eternally, subject to no appeals process, no higher court, no overruling power.

When God declares someone justified, that settles the matter absolutely. Satan can bring accusations, conscience can recite failures, people can level charges, the law can pronounce condemnation, none of it changes God's verdict. The Judge of all the earth has spoken. The case is closed.

I've counseled believers tormented by accusations they couldn't silence. A woman convinced her teenage rebellion disqualified her from God's love. A man certain his pornography addiction proved he wasn't truly saved. A pastor devastated by ministry failure who believed God had rejected him. In each case, I pointed them to Romans 8:33. God justifies. Who contradicts that verdict?

The practical impact of this truth transformed my own walk with God. For years after becoming a Christian, I lived under constant accusation. My Marine Corps service produced guilt. Had I taken lives God never intended me to take? My early failures in ministry fueled doubt. Had I misunderstood my calling? My ongoing struggles with sin generated fear; maybe I wasn't truly converted after all.

Romans 8:33 silenced those accusations one by one. Not by denying my failures or minimizing my sins, but by anchoring my standing before God in His justifying verdict rather than my performance. The accusations were often accurate; I had sinned; I had failed; I had fallen short. But God's justification trumped every charge.

The Finality of the Verdict

Paul's rhetorical question assumes a final answer: no one shall successfully bring charges against God's elect. The verb tense suggests an ongoing reality, not just that no one has brought charges that stuck, but that no one will, no one can, no one ever shall.

This finality flows from the nature of God's justification. He doesn't justify tentatively pending our future performance. He doesn't justify conditionally, subject to revocation if we fail. He justifies absolutely, based on Christ's finished work, secured by His sovereign purpose, guaranteed by His unchanging character.

Hebrews 7:25 reinforces this: "He is able to save to the uttermost those who draw near to God through him, since he always lives to make intercession for them." Christ's ongoing intercession maintains our justified status. Even when we sin, and we do, He advocates for us, applies His sacrifice to our account, ensures the Father's verdict remains unchanged.

I've tested this truth through decades of Christian life. Not intentionally, not by presuming on grace or treating sin casually. But through the inevitable failures that mark every believer's journey. I've sinned after conversion in ways I never imagined possible before conversion. I've faced temptations I thought I'd conquered. I've discovered depths of remaining sin that humbled and horrified me.

Yet through it all, God's justification stood firm. Not because my sins weren't serious; they were. Not because I deserved another chance; I didn't. But because justification never depended on my deserving it in the first place. God's verdict of righteousness based on Christ's work cannot be overturned by my work or my failure to work.

Living Under No Condemnation

Romans 8:33 connects directly to Romans 8:1: "There is therefore now no condemnation for those who are in Christ Jesus." No condemnation means no successful accusations. The charges may come, the evidence may be presented, the prosecution may make its case, but the verdict remains unchanged. Not guilty. Justified. Righteous in Christ.

This doesn't produce carelessness about sin. Understanding that accusations can't overturn God's justification should drive us to grateful obedience, not presumptuous license. The security of justification liberates us from performing for acceptance while motivating us to please the One who accepted us unconditionally.

I've watched two extremes in Christian circles. Some live under constant condemnation, never confident of their standing, always fearful of losing salvation, perpetually anxious about their spiritual status. Others treat grace casually, presuming on God's forgiveness, continuing in sin without remorse, displaying no evidence of regeneration.

Romans 8:33 addresses the first group directly: God justifies you. Stop listening to accusations that contradict His verdict. It also speaks indirectly to the second group: those whom God justifies, He also transforms. If someone remains comfortable in sin with no desire for holiness, they should examine whether they're truly among God's elect.

The proper response to "who shall bring any charge against God's elect? It is God who justifies" is neither terror nor presumption, but humble confidence. Confidence because God's verdict stands regardless of accusations. Humility, because that verdict depends entirely on Christ's righteousness, not ours.

This verse has become an anchor point in my theology and experience. When accusers come, and they always do, I return to this bedrock truth. God justifies. That ends the discussion.

Chapter Thirty-Four

Christ Our Perfect Advocate

"Who is to condemn? Christ Jesus is the one who died — more than that, who was raised — who is at the right hand of God, who indeed is interceding for us."
Romans 8:34

Paul's second rhetorical question follows the same pattern as the first: "Who is to condemn?" The expected answer is no one. This comes not from wishful thinking but from the multiple realities Paul immediately presents. Christ died, Christ rose, Christ reigns, Christ intercedes. Each truth builds an impenetrable wall against condemnation.

The question addresses our deepest fear. We know we deserve condemnation. Romans 3:23 established universal guilt: "All have sinned and fall short of the glory of God." Romans 6:23 stated the wage for that sin: death. We stand condemned by our own actions, our own thoughts, our own hearts. The law condemns us, conscience condemns us, Satan condemns us, and sometimes fellow believers condemn us.

Yet Paul asks boldly: who shall condemn? The question doesn't deny the reality of our sin or the justness of condemnation. It acknowledges both while pointing to the greater reality of Christ's work that removes condemnation completely.

I spent years at seminary wrestling with this truth. The more I studied theology, the more I understood the holiness of God and the depth of my sin. The more I grasped divine justice, the more I realized how thoroughly I deserved condemnation. My Marine training taught me about justice. Every action has consequences, every violation demands a penalty, every wrong requires correction. God's justice operates at infinitely higher standards than military justice.

So when Paul asks, "who is to condemn?" my initial response was, "everyone should condemn, because I deserve it." Only by working through the four realities Paul presents did I understand why no one successfully can condemn those Christ represents.

Christ Jesus Who Died

Paul's first answer points to Christ's death. The one person qualified to condemn us, the sinless Son of God, instead died for us. The Judge became the sacrifice. The righteous one took the penalty deserved by the unrighteous.

This substitutionary death lies at the heart of Reformed theology. Christ didn't die merely as an example or a martyr. He died as our substitute, bearing the condemnation we deserved, satisfying divine justice on our behalf. Isaiah 53:5 prophesied it: "He was pierced for our transgressions; he was crushed for our iniquities; upon him was the chastisement that brought us peace, and with his wounds we are healed."

Second Corinthians 5:21 explains the mechanics: "For our sake he made him to be sin who knew no sin, so that in him we might become the righteousness of God." The great exchange, our sin placed on Christ, His righteousness credited to us. The condemnation we deserved fell on Him. The justification we didn't deserve comes to us.

I've performed hundreds of counseling sessions during my pastoral career. The most common struggle I encountered was guilt, genuine, appropriate guilt over real sin. People came burdened by their failures, crushed by their mistakes, convinced they'd crossed some line beyond forgiveness.

My consistent response pointed them to Christ's death. Not to minimize their sin, it was every bit as serious as they feared. But to show them that Christ's death had already absorbed the condemnation their sin deserved. God doesn't condemn us for sins Christ already died for. That would be double jeopardy, punishing the same crime twice. Divine justice doesn't operate that way.

The death of Christ removes condemnation not by pretending sin didn't happen, but by ensuring the penalty was fully paid. When someone stands condemned by their own conscience, I ask: did Christ die for that sin? If so, and Scripture assures us He died for all the sins of His elect, then the condemnation was already borne. God will not condemn you for what He already condemned in Christ.

More Than That, Raised from the Dead

Paul doesn't stop with Christ's death. He adds "more than that" literally, "even more" Christ was raised from the dead.

The resurrection validates the death, proves its sufficiency, demonstrates its acceptance by the Father.

If Christ had remained dead, we'd have reason to fear condemnation might still apply. Perhaps His sacrifice wasn't sufficient. Perhaps the Father didn't accept it. Perhaps death still holds power over us. But the resurrection demolishes those fears.

Romans 4:25 connects resurrection to justification: "who was delivered up for our trespasses and raised for our justification." The resurrection declares our justification accomplished. Death couldn't hold Him because He conquered sin's power. The grave couldn't contain Him because He satisfied sin's penalty.

I preached countless Easter sermons during my pastoral years, but the resurrection's meaning deepened as I aged. Early in ministry, I focused on the historical evidence, the empty tomb, the eyewitness accounts, the transformation of the disciples. All important, all valid. But Romans 8:34 shifted my emphasis to the resurrection's implications for our standing before God.

Christ's resurrection means condemnation no longer threatens. If the Father accepted Christ's sacrifice, He raised Him. The resurrection is the Father's "amen" to the Son's "it is finished." When Christ died, He bore our condemnation. When Christ rose, He proved that condemnation was fully satisfied, completely exhausted, permanently removed.

First Corinthians 15 makes this connection explicit. Paul argues that if Christ wasn't raised, our faith is futile and we're still in our sins. But because Christ was raised, death's sting is removed, sin's victory is overturned, condemnation's power is broken. The resurrection guarantees that those united to Christ by faith share His victory over condemnation.

Who is at the Right Hand of God

Paul's third reality moves from past events to present position: Christ is at the right hand of God. This isn't a geographical location but positional authority. The right hand represents power, honor, and ruling authority. Christ reigns in the place of supreme authority in the universe.

Ephesians 1:20-22 expands this: God "seated him at his right hand in the heavenly places, far above all rule and authority and power and dominion, and above every name that is named, not only in this age but also in the one to come. And he put all things under his feet and gave him as head over all things to the church."

The One who died for us now reigns over all. No accuser can bring charges that Christ can't dismiss. No condemner possesses authority Christ doesn't override. He sits at the right hand of God, the position of absolute authority, representing those He redeemed.

Hebrews 1:3 describes this position: "After making purification for sins, he sat down at the right hand of the Majesty on high." The sitting indicates completed work. Old Testament priests never sat; their work was never finished. Christ sat because His atoning work was complete. His position at the right hand proves the Father's acceptance of that work.

During my Marine service, I learned about the chain of command. Orders from a higher authority override orders from a lower authority. When conflicting commands came, we followed the one from the highest-ranking officer. The same principle applies spiritually. When accusers bring charges, whether Satan, conscience, or other people, I look to the One at the highest position of authority. Christ at God's right hand outranks every accuser. His verdict of "no condemnation" trumps their charges of guilt.

This truth sustained me through multiple ministry challenges. Church conflicts produced accusations, sometimes justified, often not. My own failures generated internal condemnation. Satan whispered doubts about my salvation, my calling, my standing before God. In those moments, I clung to Christ's position. He reigns at God's right hand. He represents me there. His authority exceeds my accusers' power.

Who Indeed is Interceding for Us

Paul's fourth reality brings the argument home: Christ "indeed is interceding for us." Present tense. Ongoing action. Continuous advocacy. He not only died for us, rose for us, and reigns for us; He actively intercedes for us right now. Hebrews 7:25 expanded my understanding of this intercession: "Consequently, he is able to save to the uttermost those who draw near to God through him, since he always lives to make intercession for them." Always. Continuously. Without interruption. Christ's intercession never ceases.

What does this intercession involve? Not pleading with a reluctant Father to accept unwilling candidates. Christ isn't trying to convince the Father to show mercy. The Father sent the Son specifically to save His elect. Instead, Christ's intercession applies His finished work to our ongoing need.

First John 2:1 clarifies: "My little children, I am writing these things to you so that you may not sin. But if anyone does sin, we have an advocate with the Father, Jesus Christ the righteous." An advocate, a defense attorney, a representative, one who speaks on our behalf. When we sin, and John acknowledges we do, Christ advocates for us, applies His sacrifice to that specific sin, and ensures the Father's verdict of justification remains in force.

This intercession crushed my fear of condemnation more than any other truth. I understand Christ died two thousand years ago. I believe He rose and reigns. But those historical and positional realities sometimes felt distant from my daily struggles. Christ's ongoing intercession bridges that gap. Right now, this moment, as I battle temptation or confess sin or face accusation, Christ intercedes for me. He stands before the Father representing my case, applying His righteousness to my account, ensuring no condemnation sticks.

I watched this truth transform struggling believers repeatedly. A woman crushed by post-abortion guilt, Christ intercedes for her. A man haunted by pre-conversion immorality, Christ advocates for him. A teenager drowning in shame over ongoing sin, Christ represents her case before the Father.

The intercession isn't generic or impersonal. Romans 8:34 says He intercedes "for us," for specific individuals, for particular sins, for real accusations. He knows our names, our struggles, our failures. And He presents His finished work as sufficient for every charge.

The Cumulative Force

Paul presents these four realities cumulatively, each adding weight to the others. Christ died; which removes the penalty of condemnation. Christ rose; that validates the removal. Christ reigns; that establishes authority over all accusers. Christ intercedes; this applies His work to our ongoing need.

Together, they form an unbreakable defense against condemnation. Who shall condemn when Christ died in our place? Who shall condemn when Christ rose to prove that death's work succeeded? Who shall condemn when Christ reigns with all authority? Who shall condemn when Christ continuously intercedes on our behalf?

The rhetorical question demands the answer: no one. Not because we're innocent; we're not. Not because condemnation is undeserved; we deserve it. But because Christ's work comprehensively, finally, and effectively removed condemnation from those the Father elected, the Son redeemed, and the Spirit regenerated.

This doctrine doesn't produce carelessness. Understanding that Christ intercedes for us when we sin should produce gratitude, not presumption. It should motivate holiness, not encourage sin. Romans 6 already addressed that concern: "Are we to continue in sin that grace may abound? By no means!" The same grace that removes condemnation also transforms desires, changes hearts, produces new obedience.

But for those genuinely struggling with guilt, genuinely burdened by their failures, genuinely fearful of condemnation, Romans 8:34 offers rock-solid assurance. Christ Jesus died, rose, reigns, and intercedes. No condemnation can survive that fourfold defense.

Chapter Thirty-Five

The Unanswerable Question

"Who shall separate us from the love of Christ? Shall tribulation, or distress, or persecution, or famine, or nakedness, or danger, or sword?" Romans 8:35

Romans 8:35 shifts Paul's focus from condemnation to separation. Having established that no one can condemn God's elect, Paul now asks perhaps the most profound question in Scripture. The question itself reveals Paul's confidence. He lists seven potential separators, challenges them all, and invites any response. The silence that follows speaks volumes.

The Nature of the Question

Paul structured this as a rhetorical question expecting no answer because no legitimate answer exists. But the question itself matters. Paul didn't ask, "Can anything separate us from the love of Christ?" That would imply a possibility subject to verification. Instead, he asked, "Who shall separate us?" He personalized the question, challenging any entity to step forward and accomplish the separation. The challenge remains unanswered because no power, no force, no being possesses the ability to sever the bond between Christ and His people.

The love Paul references here is specifically "the love of Christ." Not our love for Christ, which fluctuates and fails. Not general divine benevolence toward creation. Paul speaks of Christ's particular, electing, redeeming, covenant love for those the Father gave Him. This love preceded our existence, motivated the incarnation, endured the cross, and continues through eternity. Understanding this love's source and nature explains why nothing can separate us from it.

Reformed theology distinguishes between God's general benevolence toward all creation and His particular, saving love for the elect. Christ's love in Romans 8:35 refers to the latter. He loves His sheep, His bride, those given to Him by the Father. John 10:11 states, "I am the good shepherd. The good shepherd lays down his life for the sheep." Not for everyone indiscriminately, but for His sheep specifically. This particular love cannot fail because it flows from God's eternal purpose, expressed in covenant commitment, secured by Christ's finished work.

I struggled with this distinction for years. My Arminian background taught me Christ loves everyone equally, that He died for everyone the same way, that the only difference between saved and lost is human decision. That framework made Romans 8:35 difficult. If Christ's love extends equally to all, and many perish, then something does separate people from His love, their choice. But Paul's question allows no such answer. He doesn't qualify it with, "Nothing shall separate us except our decision to walk away." He makes an absolute statement admitting no exceptions.

The Comprehensive List

Paul listed seven potential separators: tribulation, distress, persecution, famine, nakedness, danger, or sword. These aren't random. They represent categories of suffering believers face, arranged to cover the full spectrum of human hardship. Paul drew from personal experience; he endured each item on this list. Second Corinthians 11:23-28 catalogs his sufferings in detail. Paul knew what he was talking about. These weren't theoretical dangers but real threats he survived.

Tribulation translates the Greek "*thlipsis*," meaning pressure or crushing. It refers to the grinding weight of life in a fallen world, the accumulated stress of ongoing difficulty, the weariness that comes from prolonged hardship. Can this pressure separate us from Christ's love? Can the relentless grind of life crush our connection to Him?

Distress comes from the Greek "*stenochoria*," a compound word meaning narrow space or confinement. It describes situations with no escape, circumstances that corner and trap us, times when options disappear and walls close in. Can these boxed-in moments sever our bond with Christ?

Persecution specifies "*diogmos*," active hostility for righteousness' sake. Not general suffering common to all humanity, but suffering specifically because of Christian identity and testimony. Can opposition, hatred, or violence against us for Christ's sake separate us from His love?

Famine and nakedness address physical deprivation. Can hunger separate us? Can poverty? Can the loss of basic necessities drive a wedge between Christ and His people? These questions mattered in the first century when Christians often lost employment, property, and resources because of their faith. They matter today in regions where conversion costs everything.

Danger translates "*kindunos*," meaning peril or risk. It captures the uncertainty of threatening circumstances, the fear that accompanies vulnerability, and the awareness that harm could strike at any moment. Can living under constant threat separate us from Christ's love?

Sword represents violent death, martyrdom, the ultimate cost of discipleship. Can even death itself separate believers from Christ's love?

Paul's list moves from internal pressure to external confinement, from social persecution to physical deprivation, from ongoing danger to final death. Together, they encompass every form of suffering believers might face. And Paul challenges them all. Can any of these separate us from Christ's love? The implied answer thunders: No.

The Implied Answer

Paul didn't answer his own question yet. He let it hang, building tension, forcing readers to confront the challenge. But the answer had already emerged from the preceding verses. Who shall separate us from Christ's love? Not tribulation, because Christ intercedes for us. Not distress, because we're more than conquerors. Not persecution, because God chose us. Not famine or nakedness, because Christ died for us. Not danger, because Christ rose for us. Not the sword, because Christ reigns for us.

The question becomes unanswerable when we understand who Christ is and what He accomplished. If Christ is God incarnate, possessing all authority in heaven and earth, then no created thing can overrule His decision to love His people. If Christ's love motivated Him to endure the cross, then lesser sufferings cannot diminish that love. If Christ's love secured our justification before God, then human hardships cannot undo what divine love accomplished.

I remember counseling a missionary who had survived persecution overseas. He lost everything, property seized, savings confiscated, body scarred from beatings. He wrestled with doubt, not about God's existence, but about God's love for him personally. "If God loved me, would He let this happen?" he asked. I pointed him to Romans 8:35. Paul didn't deny that persecution happens to believers. He listed it as a real threat. But he challenged persecution's ability to separate believers from Christ's love. The missionary's sufferings proved his connection to Christ, not disconnection from Him. Persecution cannot separate because Christ's love doesn't promise absence of suffering but presence through suffering.

The Pastoral Application

Romans 8:35 addresses a specific pastoral concern: Can circumstances make God stop loving me? Can my suffering prove I've fallen from grace? Can hardship indicate God's rejection? False teaching in every age suggests yes. Prosperity gospel proponents claim suffering indicates sin or a lack of faith. Health and wealth preachers imply God's love manifests in comfortable circumstances. These lies make Romans 8:35 necessary.

Paul pre-emptively demolished such thinking. He anticipated believers would face tribulation, distress, persecution, famine, nakedness, danger, and sword. He didn't present these as possibilities for the unfaithful but as realities for God's elect. Suffering doesn't separate believers from Christ's love because Christ's love never promised exemption from suffering. It promised preservation through suffering.

This distinction transformed my pastoral ministry. Early in my ministry, I tried helping suffering believers by minimizing their pain or promising quick relief. "God will work this out soon," I'd say, or "This hardship will pass quickly." Sometimes those statements proved false. Hardships didn't pass quickly. Circumstances didn't improve. My well-intentioned words added guilt to suffering. Believers concluded their pain must indicate spiritual failure since their pastor promised better outcomes.

Romans 8:35 taught me better. I stopped promising an absence of suffering and started promising presence through suffering. I stopped claiming hardships prove distance from God and started explaining hardships cannot create distance from God. The shift mattered enormously. Believers needed assurance that their circumstances, however difficult, could not separate them from Christ's love.

The Theological Foundation

This assurance rests on solid theological ground. According to Reformed theology, God's eternal decree initiates salvation, Christ's particular redemption completes it, the Spirit's effectual calling implements it, and God's unfailing grace maintains it. Each link in this chain guarantees the next. If God elected us before the foundation of the world, temporal circumstances cannot reverse eternal decisions. If Christ died specifically for His sheep, His sacrifice secures them permanently. If the Spirit regenerated us, that new birth cannot unregenerate. If God justified us, who can condemn?

The doctrine of the perseverance of the saints flows from these truths. Not perseverance of our love for God, but the perseverance of God's love for us. We don't hold on to God; God holds on to us. Our grip might slip, but His never does. Romans 8:35 expresses this doctrine practically. It challenges anything to separate believers from Christ's love, confident nothing can.

Critics claim this doctrine produces carelessness. If believers cannot fall away, why pursue holiness? Why resist temptation? Why endure hardship faithfully? Paul already addressed this objection in Romans 6. The same grace that saves also transforms. True believers don't view assurance as a license for sin but as motivation for gratitude-driven obedience.

I've watched this theology produce exactly the opposite effect critics fear. Believers assured of Christ's unchanging love face suffering with courage, resist temptation with confidence, and pursue holiness with joy. They don't serve God to earn His love or keep His love but because they already possess His love permanently. That security produces authentic devotion, not careless presumption.

The Practical Comfort

Romans 8:35 offered me personal comfort repeatedly. During my Marine Corps years, I faced danger regularly. Combat situations raised real questions about mortality and divine protection. Would death separate me from Christ's love? Paul said no. The sword cannot sever what Christ's blood secured.

During difficult ministry seasons, I faced opposition, criticism, and occasional hostility. Churches split, leaders betrayed trust, and congregants attacked character. Did these troubles indicate God's displeasure? Had I somehow lost His favor?

Romans 8:35 answered clearly. Tribulation and distress cannot separate believers from Christ's love. Persecution for righteousness' sake proves connection to Christ, not disconnection.

During financial hardship, when seminary bills exceeded income and necessities strained budgets, I wondered if poverty indicated spiritual failure. Prosperity preachers suggested financial lack proves insufficient faith. Romans 8:35 demolished that lie. Famine and nakedness cannot separate us from Christ's love. Material circumstances don't measure spiritual standing.

The question Paul posed remains unanswerable because no legitimate answer exists. Nothing can separate God's elect from the love of Christ. Not because we're strong enough to hold on, but because Christ's love is powerful enough to hold us. Not because we deserve such security, but because Christ's work secured it. Not because circumstances don't threaten us, but because Christ's love transcends all circumstances.

This truth anchors faith when everything else shifts. Circumstances change, feelings fluctuate, doubts assault, and trials overwhelm. But Christ's love remains constant, unshakeable, eternal. That love chose us, redeemed us, called us, justified us, and will glorify us. Nothing, absolutely nothing, can separate us from it.

Chapter Thirty-Six

The Cost of Discipleship

"As it is written, "For your sake we are being killed all the day long; we are regarded as sheep to be slaughtered." Romans 8:36

Paul didn't leave verse 35's rhetorical question hanging in idealistic abstraction. He immediately grounded it in harsh reality by quoting Psalm 44:22. The shift from verse 35's triumphant question to verse 36's brutal acknowledgment startled me when I first studied this passage seriously. Paul just declared nothing can separate us from Christ's love, then immediately described believers as sheep marked for slaughter. The contrast seemed jarring. Doesn't inseparable love protect from slaughter? Doesn't divine favor shield from constant mortal danger?

Those questions revealed my shallow understanding of both discipleship and divine love. I expected God's love to manifest primarily through comfortable circumstances, material provision, and physical protection. Romans 8:36 demolished that expectation. Christ's love doesn't guarantee ease but sustains through difficulty. God's favor doesn't promise safety but provides purpose in suffering.

The Psalm Paul quoted came from Israel's corporate lament. The people faced persecution despite covenant faithfulness. They hadn't abandoned God or embraced idolatry, yet enemies threatened their existence. The psalmist cried out in confusion, asking why God allowed such suffering among His chosen people. Paul seized the ancient lament and applied it to Christian experience. Believers throughout history have faced a similar reality. Following Christ often leads not to earthly prosperity but to persecution, opposition, and death.

The Historical Witness

Church history confirmed Paul's warning. Within decades of writing Romans, Nero blamed Christians for Rome's fire and initiated brutal persecution. Believers died as human torches in imperial gardens, torn apart by wild animals in arenas, and crucified along Roman roads. "Regarded as sheep to be slaughtered" wasn't hyperbole. It was a literal description.

That persecution established a pattern that was repeated across centuries. Second and third century believers faced sporadic but intense imperial opposition. Fourth-century Donatists suffered under Constantine's enforcement of religious unity. Medieval Waldensians and Albigensians died by the thousands for challenging ecclesiastical corruption. Reformation martyrs burned at the stake for recovering biblical doctrine. Anabaptists drowned for insisting on believers' baptism. English Separatists fled persecution, sailed to hostile shores, and established colonies where many died from hardship.

Modern persecution continues this pattern. More Christians died for their faith in the twentieth century than in all previous centuries combined. Communist regimes killed millions. Islamic extremists target Christian minorities. Hindu nationalists attack churches. Secular governments imprison pastors. The slaughter Paul described never stopped.

I came to understand Romans 8:36 not as describing an unusual situation but as articulating normal Christian experience. Following Christ costs. Discipleship demands. Faith provokes opposition. The gospel threatens worldly powers, exposes sinful systems, and challenges cultural idols. Those powers, systems, and idols fight back. Believers bear the brunt of that conflict.

The Theological Significance

Reformed theology helped me grasp why God ordains such suffering. Several key doctrines intersect here.

First, the doctrine of total depravity explains hostility toward believers. Unregenerate humanity hates God and therefore hates God's people. Jesus warned His disciples that the world would hate them because it first hated Him. This hatred isn't personal animosity toward individual Christians but spiritual opposition to the gospel they represent. Fallen humanity suppresses truth in unrighteousness, and believers embody truth unregenerate people want silenced.

Second, the doctrine of divine sovereignty means persecution doesn't happen randomly or accidentally. God ordained it for purposes that serve His glory and our good. This doesn't make persecution less painful, but it does make it purposeful. We aren't random victims of cosmic chaos but participants in God's redemptive plan. Our suffering accomplishes divine objectives we may not fully understand this side of eternity.

Third, the doctrine of union with Christ explains why believers share Christ's sufferings. We died with Him, rose with Him, and live in Him. His experience becomes our pattern. He suffered rejection, opposition, betrayal, and execution. We shouldn't expect better treatment than our Master received. Union with Christ means conformity to Christ, including conformity to His sufferings.

Fourth, the doctrine of perseverance assures that suffering won't destroy faith. God preserves His elect through trials that would otherwise devastate them. The same power that raised Christ from death sustains believers through persecution unto death. We endure not through natural strength but through supernatural preservation.

The Personal Application

My Marine Corps training prepared me physically for hardship but not spiritually for opposition to faith. Boot camp taught me to endure pain, overcome obstacles, and persist under pressure. That training served me well in military contexts. But following Christ demanded different preparation.

I faced relatively minor opposition compared to martyrs throughout history. Academic ridicule in seminary when defending Reformed doctrine. Congregational resistance when preaching unpopular biblical truths. Denominational pressure when refusing to compromise doctrinal convictions. Professional consequences when prioritizing Scripture over cultural expectations. None of this compared to physical persecution, yet it still cost something.

The temptation during those seasons was to soften my message, compromise my convictions, or avoid controversial topics. I could have made ministry easier by preaching what people wanted to hear rather than what Scripture taught. I could have built larger congregations by offering therapeutic messages instead of theological depth. I could have avoided conflict by remaining silent on divisive issues.

Romans 8:36 convicted me that comfortable ministry probably indicates compromised ministry. If following Christ means being regarded as sheep for slaughter, then a ministry facing no opposition might not be truly Christian. Jesus said the world would hate His followers. Paul said believers face constant mortal danger. If everyone approves of my ministry, perhaps I'm not faithfully representing Christ.

This didn't mean seeking persecution or manufacturing conflict. Some Christians confuse faithful witness with obnoxious behavior. They provoke opposition through arrogance, insensitivity, or deliberately offensive presentation, then claim persecution when people respond negatively. That's not what Paul described.

True persecution comes from faithful gospel proclamation delivered with grace and truth. It results from uncompromising biblical conviction expressed with humility and love. It flows from living distinctively Christian lives in hostile cultures. We don't pursue suffering, but we accept it when faithful discipleship produces it.

The Counting of Cost

Jesus commanded potential disciples to count the cost before following Him. He compared discipleship to building projects and military campaigns that require a realistic assessment of required resources. Those who start without counting the cost often quit when difficulty arrives. Romans 8:36 forces honest cost assessment.

Following Christ may cost reputation. The world regards Christians as foolish, backwards, intolerant, and hateful. Academic circles dismiss faith as an intellectual weakness. Cultural elites mock biblical morality as primitive oppression. The media portray believers as dangerous extremists. Accepting this reputation requires dying to the natural desire for worldly approval.

Following Christ may cost relationships. Families divide over faith. Friendships end over doctrine. Marriages strain under unequal yoking. Jesus said He came to bring not peace but division, setting family members against each other. Those who love father, mother, spouse, or children more than Christ prove unworthy of Him.

Following Christ may cost career advancement. Believers who refuse to compromise biblical ethics face professional consequences. Doctors who won't perform abortions. Pharmacists who won't distribute abortifacients. Business owners who won't violate conscience for profit. Employees who won't lie, cheat, or steal to succeed. Faithfulness often limits worldly success.

Following Christ may cost freedom. Governments increasingly criminalize Christian conviction. Preachers face prosecution for hate speech when proclaiming biblical sexuality. Parents lose custody for refusing to affirm gender confusion. Business owners suffer legal persecution for declining to celebrate sin. Civil disobedience sometimes becomes necessary, bringing imprisonment.

Following Christ may cost life itself. Though Western believers currently face limited physical persecution, global Christianity bleeds. Brothers and sisters worldwide die for the faith we casually practice. Their martyrdom reminds us that following Christ means being regarded as sheep for slaughter. We live in a temporary calm before a potential storm.

The Daily Dying

Paul's phrase "all day long" indicated a constant, ongoing reality rather than an occasional crisis. Believers don't face martyrdom once but live under its shadow continuously. We are being killed, present tense, ongoing action. This describes daily dying to self, moment by moment crucifixion of sinful desires, constant mortification of remaining corruption.

This daily dying differs from physical martyrdom but shares its essence. We die to pride when accepting correction. We die to greed when giving sacrificially. We die to lust when fleeing temptation. We die to anger when forgiving offenses. We die to fear when trusting God's sovereignty. We die to comfort when embracing hardship for gospel advance.

Reformed theology taught me that sanctification requires this daily dying. The old self was crucified with Christ, yet remaining sin requires ongoing mortification. We put to death the deeds of the body through the Spirit. We count ourselves dead to sin and alive to God. We present our bodies as living sacrifices. All this language describes voluntary, daily dying.

I found this daily dying harder than I expected. Physical martyrdom, though terrifying, happens once. Daily dying continues endlessly. The flesh never stops demanding gratification. Sinful patterns never completely disappear this side of glory. Remaining corruption constantly reasserts itself. The battle against indwelling sin requires relentless, exhausting vigilance.

Yet this daily dying produces life. Jesus said, those who lose their lives for His sake find it. Grain that falls to earth and dies bears much fruit. Death leads to resurrection. Crucifixion precedes glorification. We die daily so we might live eternally.

The Shepherd's Care

The image of sheep destined for slaughter might seem hopelessly bleak except for one crucial detail. These sheep belong to the Good Shepherd. Christ laid down His life for the sheep. He calls them by name. He leads them to green pastures and still waters. He protects them from wolves. He carries weak lambs. He searches for lost sheep. He knows His own, and His own know Him.

Sheep for slaughter remain sheep under divine care. Our vulnerability doesn't indicate abandonment but demonstrates trust. Sheep can't defend themselves, can't navigate alone, can't survive independently. Their weakness forces dependence on the shepherd. Our position as sheep for slaughter similarly forces dependence on Christ.

This dependence became precious to me through years of ministry. I couldn't protect myself against opposition. I couldn't defend myself against accusation. I couldn't vindicate myself when slandered. I couldn't preserve myself through trials. My weakness drove me to Christ, who could do what I couldn't. His strength perfected itself in my weakness. His grace proved sufficient. His power sustained me.

The cost of discipleship remains high. Following Christ means being regarded as sheep for slaughter. But the Shepherd who leads us to slaughter also leads us through death to resurrection. The same Christ who calls us to die daily also promises eternal life. The love that permits our suffering also guarantees our glorification. Nothing, absolutely nothing, can separate us from that love.

Chapter Thirty-Seven

Super-Conquerors

"No, in all these things we are more than conquerors through him who loved us."
Romans 8:37

Romans 8:37 stands as one of Scripture's most triumphant declarations. Paul didn't write that we merely survive tribulation or endure persecution or outlast distress. He proclaimed something far greater. We are more than conquerors. The Greek word Paul used, *hypernikōmen*, appears nowhere else in the New Testament. He created a superlative by adding "*hyper*" to the verb "to conquer." Standard conquest wasn't sufficient to describe our position in Christ. We don't just win. We overwhelmingly win. We super-conquer.

This seemed absurd on first reading. How could people regarded as sheep for slaughter claim overwhelming victory? How could believers facing tribulation, distress, persecution, famine, nakedness, danger, and sword boast conquest? How could those killed all day long celebrate triumph? The paradox appeared insurmountable until I grasped the nature of spiritual warfare.

Military conquest meant defeating enemies, capturing territory, and establishing dominion. Conquerors subjugated opponents, seized resources, and imposed authority. They won through superior strength, a better strategy, or greater numbers. Their victory depended on overwhelming the opposition.

But spiritual conquest operates differently. Our enemies aren't flesh and blood. Our battle isn't against human opponents. Our warfare targets spiritual forces arrayed against God's kingdom. And in this cosmic conflict, apparent defeat often masks actual victory. The cross looked like catastrophic loss yet accomplished eternal triumph. Christ's death destroyed death itself. His apparent defeat became the ultimate conquest.

The Agent of Victory

Paul carefully identified the source of our super-conquering status. We are more than conquerors "through him who loved us." Victory doesn't spring from personal strength, natural ability, or human effort. We conquer through Christ alone. Apart from Him, we can do nothing. In Him we overwhelmingly conquer.

This truth contradicted everything my Marine training taught me. The Corps emphasized self-reliance, personal toughness, and individual capability. Marines conquered through discipline, training, and determination. We succeeded by being harder, stronger, and more committed than opponents. Victory came through superior performance.

But spiritual victory required opposite thinking. I couldn't conquer sin through willpower. I couldn't defeat Satan through determination. I couldn't overcome the world through effort. Every attempt at self-powered victory ended in defeat. Only when I acknowledged complete dependence on Christ did I experience genuine conquest.

Reformed theology helped me understand this principle. Total depravity meant I lacked spiritual ability to conquer anything. I was dead in trespasses and sins, enslaved to corruption, hostile to God. I couldn't contribute to my salvation, couldn't assist in my sanctification, couldn't achieve my glorification. Christ alone accomplished everything necessary for complete victory.

The beauty of this truth liberated me from crushing pressure. I didn't need to generate a victory. Christ already secured it. I didn't need to achieve conquest. Christ already accomplished it. I didn't need to earn triumph. Christ already won it. My role involved trusting His finished work, resting in His completed victory, depending on His accomplished conquest.

The Scope of Conquest

Paul specified exactly what we conquer. "In all these things" referred directly to the catalogue of tribulations he just listed. Tribulation, distress, persecution, famine, nakedness, danger, and sword. These specific trials become the arena of our super-conquering. We don't avoid them. We don't escape them. We conquer through them.

This distinction proved crucial in my pastoral ministry. Believers often assumed victory meant avoiding difficulty. They prayed for deliverance from trials, escape from persecution, and protection from suffering. They expected conquest to eliminate tribulation rather than triumph through it.

But Paul's teaching contradicted this expectation. We super-conquer in the midst of tribulation, not by avoiding it. We overwhelmingly triumph during persecution, not by escaping it. We achieve victory through suffering, not around it. The trials themselves become the battlefield where Christ displays His conquering power.

I watched this pattern unfold countless times. A cancer diagnosis became the arena where Christ demonstrated sufficiency. A financial crisis became the platform where God showed provision. A relationship breakdown became the opportunity where the Spirit produced reconciliation. A ministry failure became the context where Jesus displayed resurrection power. The very things threatening to destroy believers became the means of their greatest victory.

This made sense when I considered Christ's own conquest. He didn't avoid the cross. He endured it. He didn't escape suffering. He embraced it. He didn't evade death. He died. Yet through crucifixion, He crushed Satan. Through death, He destroyed death. Through apparent defeat, He accomplished ultimate victory. His pattern became ours.

The Nature of Super-Conquest

What makes us more than conquerors rather than merely conquerors? Regular conquest meant defeating enemies. Super-conquest meant something greater. I identified several dimensions of our overwhelming victory.

First, we conquer what natural conquerors cannot defeat. Human warriors subdue human opponents. They capture physical territory. They establish temporal kingdoms. But they cannot conquer death. They cannot defeat sin. They cannot overcome Satan. They cannot establish eternal dominion. Yet through Christ, we triumph over all these ultimate enemies. Death loses its sting. Sin loses its power. Satan faces ultimate defeat. We inherit an eternal kingdom. This victory exceeds anything earthly conquerors achieve.

Second, we conquer with weapons natural conquerors cannot wield. Earthly warfare employs physical armaments. Swords, spears, guns, bombs. Human strength, tactical skill, technological superiority. But our weapons aren't carnal. We wield truth, righteousness, faith, salvation, the Spirit, and God's Word. We fight with prayer, worship, obedience, and love. These spiritual weapons demolish strongholds physical weapons cannot touch.

Third, we conquer enemies that become our greatest treasures. Earthly conquerors destroy opponents or enslave them. But spiritual conquest transforms enemies into family. Those who opposed God become His beloved children. Those enslaved to sin become slaves of righteousness. Those destined for wrath become heirs of glory. Victory doesn't eliminate enemies but converts them into fellow conquerors.

Fourth, we conquer through apparent defeat. Natural warriors win through superior force. They conquer by overpowering opposition. But we triumph through weakness. We win through suffering. We conquer through death. This paradoxical victory exceeds comprehension yet demonstrates God's wisdom. His strength perfects itself in our weakness. His power displays itself through our frailty.

The Present Reality

Paul wrote in the present tense. We are more than conquerors, not we will be. This victory belongs to us now, not merely in future glory. Present suffering doesn't postpone conquest. Current tribulation doesn't delay triumph. We super-conquer right now, in the midst of ongoing trials.

This present-tense reality changed how I faced ministry challenges. I didn't need to wait until difficulties ended to claim victory. I didn't need to postpone triumph until circumstances improved. I could declare conquest while still experiencing tribulation. I could celebrate victory while enduring persecution. I could claim super-conquering status while feeling completely overwhelmed.

The seminary where I taught faced a financial crisis. Enrollment dropped. Donations declined. Budget cuts threatened faculty positions. Natural thinking saw only impending defeat. But faith recognized an opportunity for present conquest. God's provision, though mysterious, remained certain. His purpose, though unclear, continued advancing. His glory, though hidden, was being revealed. We were more than conquerors even while facing potential closure.

God sustained that institution through the crisis. But the conquest didn't consist primarily of financial survival. The real victory happened in hearts trusting God's sovereignty when circumstances screamed chaos. In minds resting in divine purpose when plans collapsed. In spirits clinging to promised glory when present darkness seemed absolute. We super-conquered not by avoiding crisis but by experiencing Christ's sufficiency through it.

The Source in Love

Paul grounded our super-conquering status in God's love. We overwhelmingly triumph "through him who loved us." Past tense. Completed action. Finished work. Christ's love for us, demonstrated at Calvary, secured permanent conquering status. Nothing we face can diminish that love. Nothing we endure can separate us from it. Nothing we suffer can overcome it.

This love makes all the difference between mere survival and super-conquest. Without divine love, tribulation would crush us. Persecution would destroy us. Suffering would defeat us. But loved by God, we transform every trial into triumph. Embraced by Christ, we turn every setback into victory. Sustained by the Spirit, we make every loss into gain.

Reformed theology taught me that God's love for His elect is eternal, unchanging, and invincible. He loved us before time began. He loved us while we were yet sinners. He loved us when we rebelled against Him. He loved us enough to send His Son. He loved us enough to justify us. He loved us enough to adopt us. He loved us enough to guarantee our glorification. This immutable love ensures our super-conquering status.

I saw this love transform defeat into victory throughout pastoral ministry. A woman whose husband abandoned her for another woman chose forgiveness instead of bitterness. She super-conquered through Christ's love. A man who lost his business to fraud refused to despair and started over. He super-conquered through divine provision. A teenager diagnosed with a terminal illness testified to God's goodness until her last breath. She super-conquered through promised resurrection. These weren't merely survival stories. They demonstrated overwhelming triumph through Him who loved them.

The present trials Paul catalogued remain real. Believers still face tribulation, distress, persecution, famine, nakedness, danger, and sword. We are still regarded as sheep for slaughter. Opposition hasn't decreased. Suffering hasn't diminished. The cost of discipleship remains high. But none of this changes our status. We are more than conquerors through Him who loved us. Always have been. Always will be. Nothing can alter this reality.

Chapter Thirty-Eight

The Comprehensive ListSuper-Conquerors

"For I am sure that neither death nor life, nor angels nor rulers, nor things present nor things to come, nor powers," Romans 8:38

Paul built his argument through Romans 8 like a careful craftsman constructing an unassailable fortress. Each verse added another layer of security. Each truth reinforced the previous one. Now he arrived at his climactic declaration. But instead of making abstract claims about divine love's permanence, he listed specific threats that cannot separate us from Christ. This comprehensive catalog addressed real fears that haunted believers then and continue haunting us now.

I learned early in my pastoral ministry that people struggle with abstract theology. Tell someone God loves them, and they nod politely. But their eyes betray doubt. Their questions reveal uncertainty. They wonder if God's love applies to their specific situation. Paul understood this human tendency. So he didn't leave assurance in the theoretical realm. He enumerated particular dangers and declared them powerless to sever our union with Christ.

"For I am sure," Paul began. Not "I think" or "I hope" or "I believe." The Greek word means absolute certainty, complete persuasion, unwavering conviction. Paul staked his apostolic authority on this declaration. His confidence didn't rest on personal optimism or religious enthusiasm. It grounded itself in the finished work of Christ, the eternal purpose of God, and the indwelling presence of the Holy Spirit. Everything he wrote in the preceding verses established the foundation for this unshakeable conviction.

My seminary training emphasized the importance of theological foundations. Reformed theology doesn't build on shifting emotional experiences or fluctuating feelings. It anchors itself in God's immutable character, His eternal decrees, and His accomplished redemption. Paul's conviction about inseparability from God's love rested on these bedrock truths. The Father who predestined also called. The One who called also justified. The One who justified will also glorify. This chain of divine action admits no breaks, permits no failures, allows no exceptions.

Death and Life

Paul began his list with the two most universal human experiences: death and life. Neither can separate us from God's love in Christ Jesus. This pairing deserves careful examination. Death represents the ultimate enemy, the final fear, the great unknown. Life encompasses all our present struggles, ongoing trials, daily battles. Between them, they cover our entire existence from birth to grave and beyond.

Death cannot separate us from Christ's love. This truth confronted my deepest fears during my wife's cancer diagnosis. Death loomed as an immediate possibility instead of a distant abstraction. Natural instinct wanted to rage against this enemy. But Reformed theology taught me something deeper. Death lost its separating power at Calvary. Christ died so that death could not sever our union with Him. He rose so death became a doorway instead of a destination. The grave no longer imprisons believers but graduates them to glory.

Paul's confidence about death's impotence reflected his understanding of Christ's resurrection. Romans 6 explained that we died with Christ and rose with Him. Our union with the Savior transcends mortality. Physical death ends biological life but cannot touch spiritual reality. The Christian who dies doesn't lose connection with Christ. Rather, that believer enters a fuller experience of the divine presence. Absent from the body means present with the Lord. Death separates us from earthly existence but draws us closer to heavenly reality.

My wife survived her cancer, but over the years other parishioners didn't. I stood beside hospital beds and watched saints take their final breaths. I preached funerals and committed bodies to the ground. Natural grief accompanied each loss. But beneath the sorrow ran a deeper current of certainty. Death hadn't conquered these believers. It hadn't separated them from Christ's love. It transported them from the faith's battlefield to the victory's celebration. From partial sight to complete vision. From hope's waiting to glory's realization.

Life cannot separate us either. This seemed almost more challenging than death. Life brings temptations that assault us daily. Doubts that plague our minds. Failures that mock our profession. Weaknesses that expose our frailty. The grind of daily existence wears down resolve. Years of struggle exhaust spiritual stamina. Long obedience in the same direction feels impossibly difficult. Yet life's challenges, however severe, cannot sever our connection to Christ.

Reformed theology taught me about the perseverance of the saints. God preserves those He justified. Christ keeps those the Father gave Him. The Spirit seals those purchased by Christ's blood. Our perseverance rests not on our grip of God but on His grip of us. Life throws everything possible against believers. Trials multiply. Difficulties compound. Opposition intensifies. But none of it breaks the bond forged by divine love. We remain united with Christ through every circumstance life presents.

Angels and Rulers

Paul next addressed supernatural forces. Neither angels nor rulers can separate us from God's love. This pairing opens into the spiritual realm. Created beings, however powerful, cannot override the Creator's purposes. Celestial authorities, however impressive, cannot veto divine decrees. The entire hierarchy of heaven and hell stands impotent before God's electing love.

Angels serve as God's messengers and ministers. Scripture presents them as mighty beings who execute divine commands. Yet Paul declared they cannot separate believers from Christ. This seems obvious until we remember how easily humans elevate spiritual experiences above solid doctrine. Some believers chase angelic encounters. Others claim special revelations from heavenly visitors. Paul warned the Colossians not to be disqualified by those delighting in angel worship. No angelic being, regardless of glory or power, can alter our standing in Christ.

Rulers translates a Greek term referring to spiritual authorities and powers. Paul used this language throughout his letters to describe demonic hierarchies. Ephesians 6 speaks of wrestling not against flesh and blood but against rulers, authorities, cosmic powers, and spiritual forces of evil. These malevolent beings oppose God's purposes and attack His people. Yet they cannot separate believers from Christ's love.

This truth became intensely practical during my years of pastoring. I encountered genuine spiritual warfare. Not the dramatized Hollywood version, but real demonic opposition to gospel advance. Believers faced unexplained oppression. Ministries encountered supernatural resistance. Prayer meetings revealed spiritual battles beneath the surface circumstances. Reformed theology kept me from two equal errors: denying spiritual warfare's reality or exaggerating demonic power.

Satan is real. Demons exist. Spiritual forces oppose God's kingdom. But they are created beings under divine sovereignty. They operate only within the boundaries God establishes. They cannot pluck believers from Christ's hand. They cannot cancel our adoption. They cannot reverse our justification. They cannot prevent our glorification. Every demonic attack must pass through God's permissive will. And He limits their activity to accomplish His purposes in His children.

The Reformation recovered biblical truth about God's absolute sovereignty. Nothing occurs outside His decree. No force operates independently of His control. Satan himself serves divine purposes, though unwittingly. Demons accomplish God's will while pursuing their rebellion. Spiritual rulers rage, but God laughs at their impotence. They cannot separate His elect from Christ's love. Not because they don't try, but because they lack the authority to override divine decrees.

Things Present and Things to Come

Paul moved from personal agents to temporal categories. Neither things present nor things to come can separate us from God's love. This comprehensive pairing covered all time. Everything happening now and everything that will happen later falls under these headings. Between them, they encompass our entire existence and future.

Things present include current trials. Present persecution. Ongoing illness. Financial stress. Relational conflict. Ministry failure. Personal sin. Unanswered prayer. Unfulfilled longings. Everything weighing on believers right now. These immediate pressures tempt us to doubt God's love. When suffering stretches endlessly, we question whether He truly cares. When prayers seem to bounce off heaven's ceiling, we wonder if He still hears. When darkness persists, we fear He has abandoned us.

Reformed theology anchored my faith when present circumstances screamed abandonment. I faced seasons when ministry produced no visible fruit. Years when prayer felt like talking to myself. Periods when God seemed absent despite desperate seeking. Things present threatened to convince me that divine love was conditional, temporary, or withdrawn. But Reformed truth insisted otherwise. Present circumstances don't determine spiritual reality. Current feelings don't override eternal facts. Temporary trials cannot nullify a permanent union.

God's love for His elect exists independently of circumstances. He loved us before we loved Him. He chose us before we chose Him. He justified us apart from our works. He adopted us based on Christ's merit, not our performance. This love doesn't fluctuate with our faithfulness. It doesn't increase when we obey or decrease when we fail. It remains constant because it rests on Christ's finished work, not our ongoing efforts.

Things to come include future uncertainties. Unknown trials. Anticipated suffering. Potential persecution. Expected loss. Coming judgment. Final death. Everything we fear might happen. These future possibilities haunt believers. We worry about losing faith under pressure. We fear denying Christ under persecution. We doubt our endurance through the coming trials. We question whether we'll finish well. Things to come loom as threats to our security in Christ.

But Paul declared them powerless to separate us from God's love. Future events, however severe, cannot override present reality. Coming trials, however difficult, cannot cancel completed justification. Anticipated suffering, however intense, cannot reverse eternal election. The future belongs to God as completely as the past. He knows every trial we'll face. He's already provided grace sufficient for each one. He guarantees our perseverance through every circumstance.

Chapter Thirty-Nine

No Separation

"nor height nor depth, nor anything else in all creation, will be able to separate us from the love of God in Christ Jesus our Lord." Romans 8:39

Paul's final verse shifted from temporal to spatial categories. Neither height nor depth can separate us from God's love in Christ Jesus. This vertical imagery carried rich meaning in the ancient world. Height and depth represented cosmic dimensions, spiritual realms, and astronomical forces that people believed controlled human destiny.

Height spoke of celestial powers. The heavens above. Angelic beings. Atmospheric rulers. Many first-century believers came from pagan backgrounds where they worshiped celestial deities. They feared heavenly forces. They consulted astrological charts. They believed cosmic powers determined their fate. Paul demolished these fears. No celestial force, no matter how powerful, can separate believers from God's love.

I encountered this worldview's modern equivalent throughout my ministry. Believers tormented by superstition. Christians consulting horoscopes. People who attribute authority to fate, luck, or cosmic forces. Even some Reformed churches harbored residual pagan thinking about spiritual powers. Seminary taught me that Scripture recognizes spiritual realities while denying them ultimate authority. Yes, celestial beings exist. Yes, spiritual hierarchies operate. But none possess power to override God's sovereign decree.

The height represents everything exalted, powerful, and seemingly unreachable. It includes whatever towers over us, threatens us, or appears beyond our control. Yet nothing in the heights can touch our standing in Christ. No power above can reach down and snatch us from God's hand. Our security doesn't depend on favorable cosmic conditions. Our salvation doesn't hinge on spiritual alignment. We're safe because God established our position, not because we navigated celestial powers successfully.

Depth spoke of underworld forces. The realm below. Demonic powers. The grave itself. Ancient cosmology pictured a three-tiered universe with heaven above, earth in the middle, and the underworld beneath. People feared what lurked in the depths. They dreaded death's power. They worried about forces rising from below to drag them down. Paul shattered these terrors. No power from the depths can separate us from Christ's love.

This truth sustained me through seasons of spiritual darkness. Depression that felt like descending into an abyss. Grief that threatened to swallow me whole. Temptation that seemed to drag me downward. Doubt that pulled me toward despair. The depths felt real, tangible, overwhelming. Reformed theology reminded me that feelings don't determine facts. Temporary darkness doesn't indicate permanent abandonment. Descending emotions don't mean a declining spiritual status.

God's love reaches into the deepest valleys. Christ descended into death itself and emerged victorious. No depth exists that His love cannot penetrate. No darkness is so thick that His light cannot pierce it. No grave is so deep that His resurrection power cannot reach it. We're safe in the depths because He already conquered them. Death couldn't hold Him. Hell couldn't contain Him. The grave couldn't keep Him. And these defeated powers cannot separate us from Him.

The Comprehensive Summary

Paul concluded with a sweeping statement that captured everything he might have missed. Nor anything else in all creation can separate us from the love of God in Christ Jesus our Lord. This final phrase functioned as a catch-all category. Whatever Paul didn't specifically mention fell under this heading. Nothing created possesses the power to separate believers from divine love.

The phrase "anything else in all creation" covered every possible threat. Physical dangers. Spiritual forces. Temporal circumstances. Cosmic powers. Human agents. Natural disasters. Personal failures. Everything that exists except God Himself belongs to creation. And creation cannot override the Creator's decrees. Nothing in the created order possesses the authority to cancel what God established.

This truth rested on God's absolute sovereignty over creation. He spoke everything into existence. He sustains everything by His power. He governs everything according to His purposes. Creation serves the Creator's will, not the reverse. Angels obey His commands. Demons operate within His boundaries. Nature follows His laws. History unfolds according to His plan. Nothing created can rebel successfully against His sovereign rule.

My Marine training taught me about the chain of command. Orders flow from superior to subordinate. Lower ranks submit to higher authority. The system works because everyone knows their place. The spiritual realm operates similarly, though infinitely more perfectly. God occupies the supreme position. Everything else exists beneath Him. All created beings, forces, and circumstances submit to His authority. They cannot countermand His decrees. They cannot reverse His decisions. They cannot separate those He united to Christ.

This understanding transformed how I faced trials. When relationships fractured, I recognized human will operates within divine sovereignty. When ministry failed, I understood circumstances serve God's purposes. When persecution arose, I knew my enemies possessed only the authority God granted. Nothing in all creation could touch my status in Christ without passing through my Father's permissive will.

The Source of Our Security

Paul's entire list pointed toward one central truth. Our security doesn't rest on our strength but on God's unchanging love. He didn't say we're strong enough to withstand these threats. He didn't claim we possess the power to overcome them. He didn't suggest we're capable of protecting ourselves. Instead, he anchored our confidence in God's love that nothing can diminish.

The phrase "the love of God in Christ Jesus our Lord" appeared twice in these verses. First in verse 37, and then again in verse 39. This repetition emphasized where our security originates. Not in our love for God, which fluctuates. Not in our commitment to Christ, which wavers. But in God's love for us, which never changes. This love existed before creation. It prompted our election. It guaranteed our calling. It secured our justification. It ensures our glorification.

Reformed theology insisted I distinguish between God's love and my feelings about that love. My emotions varied wildly. Some days I felt loved, cherished, secure. On other days I felt abandoned, alone, rejected. My circumstances influenced my feelings. My physical state affected my emotions. My spiritual condition colored my perceptions. But none of these changed the underlying reality. God's love for His elect remains constant regardless of our feelings about it.

This love flows through Christ Jesus our Lord. It's not a generic divine benevolence toward all humanity equally. It's a specific, particular, effectual love for those united to Christ. The Father loves the Son perfectly, completely, eternally. He loves those in the Son with that same divine affection. We're accepted in the Beloved. We're cherished as Christ is cherished. We receive the love the Father lavishes on His only begotten Son.

During my pastoral ministry, I watched believers struggle with assurance. They measured God's love by their performance. When they obeyed, they felt loved. When they failed, they doubted His affection. They treated divine love as conditional, earned, maintained by effort. This thinking produced anxiety, fear, and spiritual exhaustion. I pointed them to Paul's words. Nothing can separate us from God's love because that love doesn't depend on us. It depends on Christ.

The Foundation of Perseverance

This passage doesn't merely comfort struggling believers. It explains why genuine Christians persevere. We don't maintain our salvation through willpower. We don't preserve our standing through determination. God keeps us by His power through faith. The same love that chose us in eternity past carries us to glory in eternity future. Between those points, nothing can derail His purposes.

Reformed theology taught me that perseverance flows from preservation. God preserves what He purchased. He guards what He redeemed. He protects what He justified. Believers persevere because God preserves them. Our continued faith demonstrates His continued faithfulness. Our ongoing trust proves His ongoing grace. We don't generate perseverance through effort. We experience it through His power.

This truth sustained me through ministry seasons when perseverance seemed impossible. When I wanted to quit. When the cost felt too high. When the opposition grew too strong. When my strength failed completely. In those moments, Reformed doctrine reminded me that my perseverance didn't depend on my resources. God committed Himself to completing what He started. He promised to finish the work He began. He guaranteed to present me faultless before His throne.

Paul's list of threats essentially catalogued everything that might cause believers to fall away. Death could end our faith. Life could erode our commitment. Angels could deceive us. Demons could destroy us. Present trials could break us. Future terrors could overwhelm us. Heights could crush us. Depths could swallow us. Yet none of these possess power to separate us from God's love. Therefore, none can cause us to lose our salvation.

The Practical Application

These theological truths carry immense practical implications. They don't remove suffering. They don't eliminate trials. They don't prevent persecution. But they transform how we face these realities. We endure hardship differently when we know nothing can separate us from God's love. We face death differently when we're confident it cannot sever our union with Christ. We battle temptation differently when we trust God preserves those He justified.

This passage became my anchor during the darkest valleys. When my wife battled cancer, I clung to the promise that neither death nor life could separate us from God's love. When ministry opposition intensified, I remembered that neither angels nor demons possessed authority to override divine purposes. When financial pressure mounted, I recalled that neither things present nor things to come could cancel God's promises. When depression descended, I trusted that neither height nor depth could reach me in Christ.

The assurance Paul provided wasn't presumption. It wasn't a license to sin. It wasn't an excuse for complacency. It was confidence in God's faithfulness. The same God who elected us in eternity past will glorify us in eternity future. Between those points, He works all things for our good. He allows trials that sanctify us. He permits suffering that conforms us to Christ's image. He uses opposition to strengthen our faith. But He never abandons those He called.

Chapter Forty

Conclusion

The Journey Through Romans 8

As I reflect on our journey through Romans 8, I find myself overwhelmed with the theological riches we've uncovered in this magnificent chapter. What began as "no condemnation" concluded with "no separation," and between those twin pillars, Paul constructed an unassailable fortress of assurance for every believer. This chapter truly stands as the pinnacle of Paul's theological masterpiece, the crown jewel of his letter to the Romans, and perhaps the most comprehensive exposition of the gospel's implications in all of Scripture.

Throughout our exploration, we've traced Paul's argument from the believer's freedom from condemnation through the Spirit's empowering presence, our adoption as God's children, our certain hope amid suffering, the Spirit's help in our weakness, God's sovereign purpose in our salvation, and finally the absolute security of those whom God loves. Each truth builds upon the previous one, creating an ascending staircase of assurance that culminates in the triumphant declaration that nothing can separate us from God's love in Christ.

This journey has not been merely academic for me. As a Marine, a pastor, and a seminary professor, I've tested these truths in the crucible of real-life experience. I've seen Romans 8 sustain believers through cancer diagnoses, marital betrayal, financial ruin, persecution, and the darkest nights of the soul. I've watched these doctrines transform despair into hope, fear into courage, and defeat into victory. The truths we've explored aren't abstract theological concepts but living realities that anchor our souls in the storms of life.

The Central Themes of Romans 8

Throughout our study, several central themes have emerged that deserve final reflection. First, the absolute centrality of the Holy Spirit in the Christian life. Paul mentions the Spirit no fewer than 19 times in this chapter, more than in any other chapter in his writings. The Spirit liberates us from the law of sin and death, enables us to fulfill God's righteous requirements, leads us as God's children, witnesses to our adoption, helps us in our weakness, and intercedes for us according to God's will. Without the Spirit, the Christian life as Paul describes it would be impossible.

Second, the reality of our adoption as God's children. This familial relationship forms the heart of our Christian identity. We are not merely forgiven sinners or pardoned criminals; we are beloved children who cry, "Abba! Father!" This adoption isn't metaphorical but legal and real, giving us the full rights and privileges of God's sons and daughters. Our entire relationship with God flows from this fundamental reality.

Third, the certainty of future glory. Romans 8 vibrates with hope, not wishful thinking but confident expectation based on God's promises. Creation groans, believers groan, and even the Spirit groans, all pointing toward the certain hope of resurrection and renewal. The sufferings of the present time cannot compare with the glory that awaits those whom God has called according to His purpose.

Fourth, the unbreakable chain of salvation. Paul's "golden chain" in verses 29-30 establishes the absolute security of the believer. From foreknowledge to glorification, God completes what He begins. Nothing can break this chain because it depends not on human effort but on divine purpose. Those whom God justified, He will certainly glorify.

Finally, the inseparable love of God in Christ Jesus. Nothing in all creation can separate believers from this love. Not present trials, not future threats, not spiritual powers, not life, not death. This love forms the foundation of our security, the guarantee of our perseverance, and the source of our ultimate hope.

The Implications for Christian Living

The doctrines we've explored in Romans 8 transform how we live as believers. First, they liberate us from performance-based religion. Since there is no condemnation for those in Christ Jesus, we no longer serve God from fear but from gratitude. We don't obey to earn His favor but because we already have it. This freedom doesn't promote license but motivates genuine obedience flowing from love rather than fear.

Second, these truths provide stability amid suffering. When Paul asks, "Who shall separate us from the love of Christ?" he lists real threats believers face: tribulation, distress, persecution, famine, nakedness, danger, and sword. These aren't theoretical possibilities but actual experiences many Christians endure. Romans 8 doesn't promise exemption from suffering but transformation of suffering. Our trials serve God's purpose of conforming us to Christ's image.

Third, the doctrines of Romans 8 cultivate humility by emphasizing God's initiative in salvation. We contribute nothing to our election, justification, or glorification. God chose us before the foundation of the world, called us by His Spirit, justified us through Christ's righteousness, and guarantees our future glorification. This humbling reality eliminates all grounds for boasting and produces genuine gratitude for God's sovereign grace.

Fourth, these truths foster assurance without presumption. The security Paul describes doesn't promote carelessness about sin but confidence amid failure. When we stumble, we don't question our salvation but confess our sin, trusting the advocacy of Christ and the continuing work of the Spirit. True assurance doesn't lead to moral laxity but to grateful obedience.

Finally, Romans 8 inspires hope that transcends circumstances. Paul concludes that we are "more than conquerors" not despite our trials but through them. The victory Christ secured doesn't exempt us from battle but guarantees our ultimate triumph. This hope sustains us through the darkest valleys, assuring us that our present sufferings cannot compare with the glory that awaits us.

Romans 8 and Reformed Theology

Throughout our journey, we've approached Romans 8 through the lens of Reformed theology, and for good reason. This theological tradition, rooted in the Protestant Reformation and developed by figures like Calvin, Knox, and the Westminster divines, provides the most consistent framework for understanding Paul's teaching in this chapter.

Reformed theology emphasizes God's sovereignty in salvation, a theme that permeates Romans 8. Paul's language of predestination, calling, and the golden chain of redemption aligns perfectly with the Reformed understanding of unconditional election and effectual calling. God doesn't choose us based on foreseen faith or works but according to His own purpose and grace.

Similarly, the Reformed doctrine of definite atonement finds support in Paul's statement that God "did not spare his own Son but gave him up for us all" (8:32). This sacrifice guarantees that God will "with him graciously give us all things." Such certainty makes sense only if Christ's death actually secured salvation for those the Father gave Him, not merely made it possible for all people generally.

The perseverance of the saints, another hallmark of Reformed theology, receives perhaps its strongest biblical support in the closing verses of Romans 8. Paul's confidence that nothing can separate believers from God's love assumes that our security depends not on our faithfulness but on God's. He preserves those He justified and will certainly bring them to glorification.

Even the Reformed understanding of total depravity finds expression in Paul's teaching about "the mind set on the flesh" that "cannot please God" (8:7-8). Our natural condition renders us incapable of submission to God's law, making the Spirit's regenerating work absolutely necessary for salvation.

Far from being mere academic distinctions, these Reformed emphases provide the foundation for genuine assurance. If salvation depends ultimately on human decision, perseverance, or faithfulness, we can never be certain of our standing with God. But if it rests on God's sovereign purpose, Christ's perfect work, and the Spirit's unfailing power, we can face life's trials with unshakable confidence.

Answering Common Objections

Throughout my years of teaching Romans 8, I've encountered several common objections to the Reformed interpretation of this chapter. Some argue that the doctrine of predestination makes God arbitrary or unjust. But Paul anticipated this objection in Romans 9, where he affirms God's freedom to have mercy on whom He will have mercy. The question isn't why God doesn't choose everyone but why He chooses anyone, given universal human rebellion.

Others claim that the assurance Paul describes promotes moral laxity. If nothing can separate us from God's love, why strive for holiness? But this objection misunderstands both the nature of salvation and human psychology. God doesn't just save us from sin's penalty but from its power. The same Spirit who justifies also sanctifies. And security doesn't promote carelessness but grateful obedience. Children who are secure in their parents' love don't abuse that relationship but respond with love and gratitude.

Some suggest Paul's teaching applied only to the Roman Christians, not to all believers. But nothing in the context limits these promises to a specific historical situation. Paul grounds his assurance not in temporary circumstances but in Christ's finished work, the Spirit's ongoing ministry, and God's eternal purpose. These realities transcend time and culture.

Finally, some argue that Romans 8 must be balanced with warning passages elsewhere in Scripture. But proper interpretation doesn't pit Scripture against Scripture. The warnings serve as a means God uses to preserve His elect. They don't contradict the promises but work alongside them to accomplish God's purpose. The same God who guarantees believers' perseverance also warns against apostasy, and those warnings help ensure that true believers persevere.

Personal Application

As I conclude this journey through Romans 8, I want to offer some practical guidance for applying these truths to daily Christian living. First, cultivate a Spirit-oriented mindset. Paul contrasts the mind set on the flesh with the mind set on the Spirit. This isn't automatic but requires an intentional focus on spiritual realities through Scripture meditation, prayer, worship, and fellowship with other believers.

Second, embrace your identity as God's child. Let the Spirit's witness to your adoption shape how you approach God in prayer, how you view yourself, and how you face life's challenges. You're not a slave to fear but a beloved child of the Creator of the universe.

Third, view suffering through the lens of future glory. Your current trials, however painful, are not worth comparing with the glory God will reveal in you. They're not random accidents but purposeful preparation for eternal reward. This perspective doesn't eliminate pain but transforms how you experience it.

Fourth, rely on the Spirit's help in prayer. You don't need to formulate perfect prayers. When words fail, trust the Spirit to intercede according to God's will. This frees you from the pressure of performance and allows for honest, authentic communion with God.

Fifth, rest in God's sovereign purpose. He works all things together for the good of those who love Him and are called according to His purpose. This doesn't mean everything that happens is good in itself, but that God directs everything toward your ultimate conformity to Christ's image.

Finally, live confidently as more than a conqueror. Don't merely survive trials but triumph through them. The same love that took Christ to the cross sustains you through every hardship and guarantees your final victory. Nothing can separate you from that love.

Final Reflections

As I look back over our exploration of Romans 8, I'm struck again by the comprehensive nature of Paul's gospel presentation. He addresses our past condemnation, our present transformation, and our future glorification. He speaks of our relationship with God as Father, with Christ as elder brother, and with the Spirit as indwelling Helper. He acknowledges our current sufferings while assuring us of future glory. He confronts the reality of ongoing struggle while promising ultimate victory.

This comprehensive gospel answers the deepest human questions: Where do I stand with God? What purpose does suffering serve? How can I endure life's struggles? What hope exists beyond the present difficulties? The answers found in God's justifying grace, sanctifying Spirit, adopting love, and preserving power form the foundation for Christian living in every generation.

My prayer is that our journey through Romans 8 has strengthened your faith, deepened your understanding, and enriched your walk with Christ. May the truths we've explored become more than theological concepts but living realities that sustain you through every trial and empower you for faithful service. And may you live each day with the unshakable assurance that nothing can separate you from the love of God in Christ Jesus our Lord.

About the author

Bruce served in the United States Marine Corps, retiring with the rank of Gunnery Sergeant after deployments across the globe. His military service instilled in him a deep appreciation for discipline, sacrifice, and the bonds forged through shared hardship; themes that would profoundly shape his understanding of Christian discipleship and the believer's union with Christ.

Following his retirement from the Marine Corps, Bruce pursued theological education, earning a doctorate in theology with a focus on Biblical Studies. His academic journey deepened his conviction that sound doctrine must serve pastoral ministry, not exist in isolation from the real struggles believers face.

Bruce served as a pastor in a Reformed church, shepherding the congregation through seasons of joy and sorrow, growth and conflict, triumph and trial. Careful biblical exposition, compassionate counseling, and an unwavering commitment to the doctrines of grace that sustained him through his own darkest valleys marked his pastoral ministry.

Later in his ministry, Bruce transitioned to seminary education, where he taught Biblical Studies and Theology. His classroom became a bridge between rigorous academic study and practical pastoral application, as he mentored countless students preparing for ministry. Known for making complex theological concepts accessible without compromising their depth, Bruce helped shape a generation of pastors who carry his commitment to Reformed theology and pastoral wisdom into churches around the world.

Throughout his varied career, from the disciplined ranks of the Marines to the halls of academia, Bruce has maintained that the Christian life is fundamentally about union with Christ. This conviction, forged on battlefields and refined in classrooms, tested in hospital rooms and proven in pulpits, shapes every page of his writing.

Bruce and his beloved wife have walked together through the trials that test faith and prove God's faithfulness, including her courageous battle with cancer that deepened their understanding of what it means to be "more than conquerors through him who loved us."

When not writing or teaching, Bruce enjoys the simple pleasures of retirement while remaining active in his writing. He continues to believe that the doctrines of grace are not merely intellectual concepts to be debated but living truths that transform how we face each day, whether in the heat of battle, the quiet of a study, or the ordinary moments where faith becomes sight.

Romans 8: The Gospel's Crowning Glory represents the culmination of Bruce's lifelong journey with the passage that has sustained him through every season of life. It reflects his conviction that Paul's words offer not just theological instruction but supernatural transformation for all who embrace their truth.

www.ingramcontent.com/pod-product-compliance
Lightning Source LLC
Chambersburg PA
CBHW050853160426
43194CB00011B/2141